My Music, My Life

by
RAVI SHANKAR

With an Introduction by
YEHUDI MENUHIN

Simon and Schuster • New York

Published by Simon and Schuster
Rockefeller Center, 630 Fifth Avenue
New York, N.Y. 10020

First Printing

Library of Congress Catalog Card Number: 68-28918
Manufactured in the United States of America

PHOTO CREDITS

Photographs on the pages listed below appear
through the courtesy of the following services:
   Jay K. Hoffman Presentations, Inc.
      2, 16, 31, 36, 37, 38, 40, 41, 84, 90, 95, 105
   Perdan Films, Inc.
      12, 13, 57, 61, 62, 78, 95

Front cover: left, Dan Esgro; right, courtesy of San-
charini
Back cover: clockwise from upper right, David Gahr;
Eric Hayes; The New York Times; David Gahr;
David Gahr; Vic Gaskin, courtesy of World Pacific;
center, David Gahr

CONTENTS ᛉᛉᛉᛉᛉᛉᛉᛉᛉᛉᛉᛉᛉᛉᛉᛉᛉᛉᛉᛉᛉᛉᛉᛉᛉ

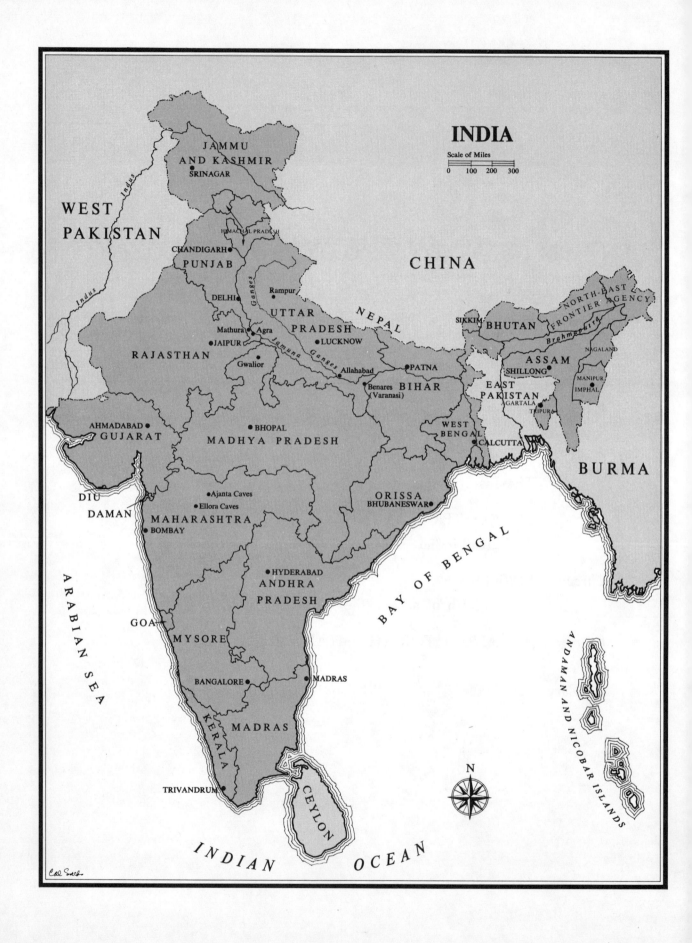

INDIA

Scale of Miles

0   100   200   300

WEST
PAKISTAN

CHINA

Indus

JAMMU
AND KASHMIR
• SRINAGAR

HIMACHAL PRADESH

CHANDIGARH •
PUNJAB

DELHI •

Rampur •

Ganges

UTTAR
PRADESH

NEPAL

SIKKIM

BHUTAN

NORTH-EAST
FRONTIER AGENCY

Brahmaputra

Mathura • Agra •
• JAIPUR

Jamuna

Ganges

• LUCKNOW

NAGALAND

ASSAM
SHILLONG •

RAJASTHAN

Gwalior •

Allahabad •

• PATNA

MANIPUR
IMPHAL •

Benares
(Varanasi)

BIHAR

EAST
PAKISTAN

AGARTALA •
TRIPURA •

AHMADABAD •
GUJARAT

• BHOPAL

MADHYA PRADESH

WEST
BENGAL
CALCUTTA •

BURMA

DIU
DAMAN

• Ajanta Caves

• Ellora Caves

MAHARASHTRA
• BOMBAY

ORISSA
BHUBANESWAR •

• HYDERABAD

ARABIAN SEA

ANDHRA
PRADESH

BAY OF BENGAL

GOA

MYSORE

BANGALORE •

• MADRAS

ANDAMAN AND NICOBAR ISLANDS

KERALA

MADRAS

TRIVANDRUM •

CEYLON

N

INDIAN   OCEAN

Col Smith

INTRODUCTION

To the Indian quality of serenity, the Indian musician brings an exalted personal expression of union with the infinite, as in infinite love. Few modern composers in the West have achieved this quality, though we revere it in the works of Bach, Mozart, Beethoven. Perhaps we should not admonish our contemporary composers for having lost this sense of serene exaltation, for indeed we have little enough of it in our civilization for them to draw upon; yet what quality is music, the organization of pure sounds, better suited to express? If the Indian musicians who now are so graciously beginning to bring their genius to us—musicians like Ravi Shankar—can help us to find this quality again, then we shall have much to thank them for.

The appeal that Ravi Shankar exercises over our youth—the magic aura his presence and his music evoke—is a tribute both to his great art and to the intuitive wisdom of the searching young.

In him they recognize a synthesis of the immediacy of expression, the spontaneity, truth and integrity of action suited to the moment, that is a form of honesty characteristic of both the innocent child and the great artist. In him they see the mastery and dedication of a discipline born of infinite experience and concentrated effort that are manifestations of not only the artist's own being but the generations preceding him.

Human history can be seen as though revealed to us by mirrors, mirrors at first small and dim, by which man could barely discern his aspect or his motives, mirrors that grew ever larger, revealing man to himself and as he appeared to others. With each increase in size and accuracy, the image seemed more awesome and frightening, until finally today mirrors are looming larger than man himself, and seem actually to dwarf him. That other inner mirror, our conscience, which expressed itself in religion and law, has become in many parts of the world monstrously enlarged to include informers and hangmen—betrayers—who almost outnumber their working, wretched victims. In *our* society, the outer mirror, the mirror reflecting ourselves to others or others to ourselves, has in the public-relations image also become monstrously enlarged, to the point that advisers and experts—manipulators—almost outnumber their clients.

This compulsive need to consult our mirrors—to find inner and outer approval (or, if not approval, at least justification), to be able to face at all times either a jury or a pack of journalists with ready statement—has now reached absurd proportions.

The artist who knows it all too well himself is now the "ambassador," a "high priest," an "innovator," the "cultural artifact"—he behaves like one, looks like one. In a debased sense he is shown as the end and the means, the alpha and omega, and is in danger of becoming a crystallized symbol covering an empty gesture, like Aubry's ghost disappearing on approach with a "most melodious twang." Yet, thanks be to God, at the moment of genuine creation there is an incandescence that dissolves all impurities, leaving only burnished gold.

It is a credit to our youth that they have recognized the pure gold in Ravi Shankar and in his art. In this noble and essential art the repetitive act, the approved "posture," has given way to an inspired and prolonged state of being—not bound by limits other than style and the inclination of the artists themselves.

It is again a tribute to our youth that many of them will forswear the easy and dangerous, the passive and destructive escape into the dream world of abandonment, in order to choose a discipline requiring years of perfection and refinement—a schooling as exacting as it is fulfilling.

When mastery will reward them, the mirrors will fall away and the elect will know that sensation of rightness which is independent of witness. They will achieve the creative purity and innocence in which "I am as I am" is "I do as I do."

Ravi Shankar has brought me a precious gift. Through him I have added a new dimension to my experience of music—one which belongs to all great music, including our own, but which, along with so much that should remain inspired and intuitive, is blueprinted out of our world.

But to the young people, who give their mind and heart to Ravi Shankar's art, he has made sense and brought order out of chaos, for he has restored the fundamental and supreme value of dedicated work, of self-control, of faith and of the value of living.

YEHUDI MENUHIN

PREFACE ᛜᛜᛜᛜᛜᛜᛜᛜᛜᛜᛜᛜᛜᛜᛜᛜᛜᛜᛜᛜᛜᛜᛜᛜᛜᛜᛜᛜᛜᛜᛜᛜᛜ

Since my childhood, I have traveled widely throughout both the East and West, and I have come to realize what a difference there is today in the response of listeners to the classical music of India. Over the past ten or twelve years, Indian musicians have been bringing their cultural traditions to the West, performing their music and trying to give a better understanding of this music to their audiences.

Many people have asked me if one must read, absorb, learn, and know about India's religions, philosophies, and spiritual atmosphere, or even come to India to visit and travel in order to understand our music, let alone play it. To this I would say yes, all this is necessary since our music is so closely connected to the complete unfolding of India's history and development. Should one want to become a performing artist of Indian music, this study is even more important. Without intense study of our traditions and culture, the music would appear false and synthetic.

Because the growth of music and dance, art forms I have dealt with all my life, is so tightly linked with the past, often I feel that I am closer to the past than to the present. When reflecting on India's growth today, her socio-economic problems and her expanding industrialism, I, along with many others, feel a deep concern and wonder where all this can lead.

India must grow, but we must also try to preserve the source of our past and those things that have made India different from any other country or civilization in the world.

Ever since I was a boy in my teens, living in Paris and touring with my brother Uday's troupe of dancers and musicians, I have felt a strong desire, almost like a missionary's zeal, to bring the beautiful, rich, and ancient heritage of our classical music to the West and to bring about a deeper comprehension and appreciation of it. With this aim in mind, I have prepared brief talks on our music—the melody forms and the rhythms we use and the instruments we play—that I give at most of my concerts before performing each *raga*. In addition, I was given the honor of teaching Indian music as a visiting professor at the University of California at Los Angeles and at City College of New York, and I have opened my own school of music in Bombay, with a branch in Los Angeles.

Now, with this book, I hope to reach an even wider audience and give a more thorough background and explanation of our music than I could through the talks at my concerts or an occasional lecture. Here I have tried to present a survey of the theory and history of Indian music, comprehensive enough to be meaningful to my readers, but not so complicated that the multitude of scholarly problems and disputes will cloud the reader's understanding of the general development of the music, for much of the history of our music is still unclear, and there are many factions of scholars and musicologists who have differing opinions on it. I myself do not pretend to be a scholar, and most of my knowledge of the traditions of our music I have received from my *guru* and other eminent musicians. Like most performing artists in India, I have a much clearer view of our past from about the fifteenth century to the present; for anything before this time, we must depend on scholarly texts and treatises that leave much open to debate. Unlike Western musicians who spend a number of years learning the entire history and background of their musical traditions and their own instruments, Indian musicians for the most part learn from their *gurus* as much practical, actually performed music as they can, and dwell relatively little on theoretical ideas and concepts of history. This has been the prevailing custom since the period in our history when the musicians, through language differences, lost contact with the old texts and were no longer able to read the Sanskrit of our ancient scriptures. Musicians, therefore, concentrated primarily on practical music and memorized the traditions handed down to them by their musical ancestors. Customarily, the *shishya*, or disciple, absorbed without question or criticism all that his *guru* taught, and so, analytical and objective judgment was never developed in the students. Because of this situation, today one often finds a certain tension between musicologists and performing artists in India, particularly in the North, where traditions are not as systematized and formalized as they are in the South.

Throughout this book, I have tried to present much of the historical fact that scholars are now generally agreed upon, but I have not wished to dwell on the diverse and complicated views that these men have set forth on many of the problems. As far as the spelling of Indian terms is concerned, I have chosen not to follow the usual rendering in the English language of Sanskrit words, with the system of dots and long marks. Instead, I have attempted to spell the words as they sound to the Western ear, so that Westerners will find them easier to pronounce.

My many years of traveling, my many concert tours and my strenuous efforts to awaken Westerners to the beauty and greatness of Indian music have made for me and my music many friends and admirers in all branches of Western music—from strictly classical to electronic, from jazz to folk, and even rock and pop, and for this I thank my stars and the blessings of my *guru*.

I would like to express my sincere gratitude to the people whose devoted assistance has contributed in a most important way to this book: my disciples Collin Walcott and Amiya Das Gupta for their invaluable work on the manual that constitutes the fourth section of the book; Professor Elise Barnett of the Department of Music at City College of New York for her scholarly counsel; Yehudi Menuhin for his affection and encouragement; and Harihar Rao, Dr. Penelope Estabrook, and Rajendra Shankar, who helped me in the book's initial stages.

Finally, and most of all, I would like to thank Carlie Hope Simon for all the time, effort, and talent she gave with such patience and warm devotion during the planning and writing of this book. I am not normally called upon to express myself at length through the written word, and so I particularly appreciate her dedication to the task.

RAVI SHANKAR

ONE

MY HERITAGE

The history, theory, and instruments
of Indian music

NARADA
LEARNS A LESSON

Guru, vinaya, sadhana—these three words form the heart of the musical tradition of India.

Guru, as many people now know, means master, spiritual teacher, or preceptor. We give a very important place to the *guru*, for we consider him to be the representation of the divine. There is a saying—

> *Pani piye chhanke*
> *Guru banaye janke*

—which means that one should drink water only after it has been filtered, and one should take a *guru* only after one feels sure of the decision. The choice of the *guru*, to us, is even more important than choosing

a husband or a wife. A potential disciple cannot make a hasty decision to take just any teacher as his *guru*, nor should he break the bond between *guru* and *shishya*, once the *ganda* or *nara* ceremony, the initiation, which symbolically binds the two together for life, has taken place.

Vinaya means humility; it is the complete surrendering of the self on the part of the *shishya* to the *guru*. The ideal disciple feels love, adoration, reverence, and even fear toward his *guru*, and he accepts equally praise or scoldings. Talent, sincerity, and the willingness to practice faithfully are essential qualities of the serious student. The *guru*, as the giver in this relationship, seems to be all-powerful. Often, he may be unreasonable, harsh, or haughty, though the ideal *guru* is none of these. Ideally, he should respond to the efforts of the disciple and love him almost as his own child. In India, a Hindu child, from his earliest

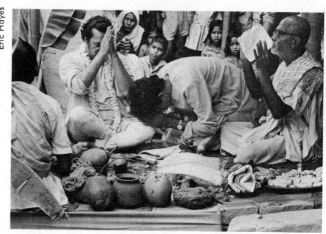

Eric Hayes

A new disciple greets me with a respectful pranam.
I respond with the namaskar and, as a priest looks on,
become his guru at the initiation ceremony.

years, is taught to feel humble toward anyone older than he or superior in any way. From the simplest gesture of the *namaskar*, or greeting (putting the hands palm to palm in front of the forehead and bowing), or the *pranam* (a respectful greeting consisting of touching the greeted person's feet, then one's own eyes and forehead with the hands held palm to palm) to the practice of *vinaya* or humility tempered with a feeling of love and worship, the Hindu devotee's vanity and pretension are worn away.

Sadly, this feeling of *vinaya* is lacking today in many young people, in the East and West alike. The Western student, especially, seems to have an excessively casual attitude toward his teachers and toward the process of learning. The teacher-student association is no longer patterned after the old father-son relationship, and the two are encouraged by prevailing attitudes to act as friends and to consider each other on an equal level. This system, of course, has its benefits, but it is far from ideal for studying Indian music and understanding our traditions. The Indian teacher finds this casualness disturbing, even in so small a thing as the position the student takes when he sits. Often the Western student will try to sit on the floor like an Indian, but since he is not accustomed to this (poor thing!), sooner or later he stretches out his legs and shows the soles of his feet to the *guru*. To us Indians, the feet are considered the most ignoble part

of the body, and this position is one of extreme irreverence.

Among our legends, there is a story that illustrates very well this quality of *vinaya*. Long ago, it is said, the great *rishi* (saint-sage) Narada was convinced that he had gained complete mastery of the art of music, both in theory and performance. The wise Vishnu decided to teach Narada a lesson and shatter his pride. So he brought him to the dwelling place of the gods, and as they entered one building, they saw many men and women with broken limbs, all weeping over their condition. Vishnu went up to them and asked what was the matter, and they told him they were the spirits of *ragas* and *raginis* created by Shiva. They said a certain *rishi* named Narada, who could neither perform nor understand music properly, had twisted and broken their limbs through his singing. And they said that, unless some great and skilled musician could sing them again correctly, they would never regain their unmarred wholeness. When he heard this, Narada was deeply ashamed and in all humility, knelt before Vishnu and begged forgiveness.

The third principal term associated with our music is *sadhana*, which means practice and discipline, eventually leading to self-realization. It means practicing with a fanatic zeal and ardent dedication to the *guru* and the music. If the student is talented, sincere, faithful to his *guru* and devoted in his practicing, and if

12

The shishya receives his first lesson after the ganda (red thread) has been tied on his right hand.

the *guru* is teaching with utmost dedication and not being miserly with his knowledge, there is a distinct pattern for learning Indian music. The student must begin by acquiring the most basic techniques of the voice or instrument. In vocal music, this skill is achieved by assiduously practicing first one note, trying to produce correct breathing, voice, and pitch control. Students both of vocal and of instrumental music then learn scales and *paltas* (also called *alankars*). *Paltas* are short melodic figures performed in sequential order within a scale and *tala* framework in different tempi. Then, the *sargams* must be learned—the various fixed compositions sung to the note-names. In some fixed compositions *talas* and tempi can be varied, and in others no *tala* is used at all. The student also learns various other fixed compositions called *bandishes*, which include songs in different styles sung to a meaningful text, slow or fast instrumental pieces (*gats*), or some melodic phrases in a variety of melodic motions and tempi (*tans*).

This elementary training, for a talented and persevering student, should last not less then five years, very much like the elementary training for any Western musical discipline. This means the student should practice every day for at least eight hours. In Western music, of course, the student has a visual advantage. That is, much of his learning can be taken from books, without the close supervision of a teacher. But with

Indian music, for the first five or six years, the student relies completely on the guidance of his *guru*. This is because the *guru* teaches everything to the *shishya* individually and directly, according to our ancient oral traditions, for very rarely do we use textbooks or manuals. Then, little by little, the student learns to improvise, and he works at it until he feels free and confident within a *raga*. From this point on, the aspiring musician must draw completely from within himself—from his own methodical musical training and his feelings and inspirations. As his musicianship grows, he acquires first a high degree of proficiency in the technical side of playing and then an ability to follow his imagination in whatever musical direction it leads. His technique must be highly enough developed to enable him to render instantaneously the mental pictures that flash before his mind's eye. It is such an exhilarating feeling to grasp a fresh idea and perform it spontaneously! Even after the student has become a fairly proficient performer and has created his own musical personality, he goes back to his *guru* from time to time for an evaluation of his development and to be inspired by new ideas. A true *guru* never stops growing musically and spiritually himself and can be a constant source of inspiration and guidance to the loving disciple.

So, starting from the very beginning, I would estimate that it requires at least twenty years of constant work and practice to reach maturity and a high standard of achievement in our classical music.

A BEAUTIFUL RELATIONSHIP IS FADING

The basis of our ancient system, known as *guru-shishya-parampara*—the continuity of tradition through master to disciple—seems to be disappearing today, obscured by the fast-moving mechanical and electronic age. At this stage in the history of Indian music, we should be extremely concerned with methods of teaching, and we must endeavor in every way to preserve our rich heritage through high standards in the teaching of its practical, theoretical, and historical aspects. Patterns of living have changed, and now we must sincerely try to find a new way for the essence of our ancient tradition to be maintained and passed on.

There was a time when classical musicians did not have to be so much concerned with the material side of life, for their artistry was widely proclaimed and the patronage of royalty and wealthy persons provided them with all the necessities of life. In turn, they were able to accept into their homes a number of disciples, so all their time could be devoted solely to music. The disciples could spend years staying with the *guru*, learning and serving him, immersed in the aura of music and absorbing to the fullest their *guru's* tradition and style, which they would later pass on. There have always been two distinct types of students: the "parrots," who passed on the exact tradition; and the creative geniuses, who absorbed the traditions and added to and enriched them. In the latter case, the basic purity and sanctity of the music remain, but ornamentation and new beauty are added. And that is why we say that, no matter how great a genius one is, without a very deep and proper training, one's contribution is meaningless and the effect of the music is lost or fleeting—the virtuosity of the playing shows no inner depth or tradition.

Times changed, patronage withered, and the *gurus* had to fend for themselves. Many were forced to move to larger cities, where they began to support themselves and their families by giving concerts. Their disciples were in a quandary. If they followed their *gurus* to the cities, they would not only have to find a place to stay in and practice in, but they would also have to provide their own food and clothing, which invariably cost more in the cities. A mere handful of disciples now receive government scholarships, and because most of them are not well-to-do, they are forced to find some kind of work to make ends meet —hardly an ideal situation; it is, in fact, a distraction that very often stands in the way of proper *sadhana*. Valuable time needed for concentrated study and practice is thus lost. Very often much damage is done when the disciple, to supplement his earnings, assumes the role of a teacher and starts giving lessons to

beginners without having first become competent himself. I do not believe that if someone cannot be a performer, he can always be a teacher. To be a good teacher, one has to be a good student; and even then, teaching is an art in itself. It requires not only a high standard of musicianship, but also a strong cultural and educational background and a familiarity with the methods of teaching. I do hope that the day will come when wealthy industrialists and businessmen in India will form foundations, the way their counterparts have in the United States and other parts of the world, to foster young and talented musicians who, because of economic stringency, are not able to continue their studies.

Apart from the time and energy lost nowadays in the attempt to combat the stress of mere existence, there are many new attractions that distract the student in the city. I remember the days I spent studying under my *guru* when the only relaxation and amusement we had was to take long walks, visit temples and shrines, and pay homage to deities, admire the sunset and beauties of Nature, or stop to watch an amusing *tamasha*, or impromptu roadside show. Otherwise, all our waking hours were spent in the lap of music, listening, learning, practicing, in an atmosphere charged by the very presence of the *guru*. There were occasions when, having lost all track of time, we were unaware of the outer world and were thrilled and absorbed by the gushing, sparkling stream of music that leaped out of the vast ocean of our *guru's* musical genius, as we sat, learning, at Baba's feet, sometimes for as many as seven or eight hours at a time. Living near the *guru* meant that we had to be ever alert and ready to receive whatever he felt inspired and disposed to teach us. Today, when I see the great rush to learn as many *ragas* as possible in a few months, I better appreciate the wisdom of Baba, who emphasized that it is always first necessary to learn the basic *ragas* well, then the other *ragas* would automatically unfold. We thus spent as many as four years working on a couple of *ragas*; a student these days would grumble if he were to spend four weeks on them! It is indeed a great pity that the beautiful relationship between the *guru* and *shishya* is fast disappearing. There was that rare joy and zeal on the part of the *guru* in giving

14

his time and energy to the teaching of the sacred traditions to his beloved disciples; and on the part of the *shishya* there was devotion to the *guru*, and dedication of his life to pleasing the *guru* with his *sadhana* and his service.

With all present-day conditions working against it, it seems impossible to retain the tradition of the *guru-shishya-parampara* in its original form. Nevertheless, I see no reason why it cannot be adapted in a modified form and retain some of the important aspects and basic approach. The main features of a fruitful *guru-shishya* relationship led to (1) purity of mind and body, humility, a sense of service, and a devotional and spiritual attitude; (2) a thorough grounding of the technique and science of music; (3) the gradual development of the disciple as he sits behind his *guru* at concerts and joins in when asked, but does not perform by himself until his *guru* finds him fit to do so; and (4) freedom from economic worries by the disciple, living and serving his *guru* as a member of his family.

These essential features, except perhaps the guarantee of economic freedom, could be retained in a modified form. Thus, the training regimen could be made thorough, not allowing the student to proceed to the next lesson before the earlier one has been perfected. There is always the danger of the student's being satisfied with the outer, superficial achievements, like learning the scales and a few compositions in one *raga* and then taking up another before exploring some of the endless variations on the first *raga*. It is only when the student becomes completely familiar with a few *ragas* and is at home to the extent of improvising, not mechanically, but aesthetically, that he should move on. This slow but meaningful progress that the *guru* regulated, and the seal of approval he gave before encouraging further steps, could well be retained.

In other words, there is no short cut to learning Indian music; but, in the case of a talented student, one can reduce many years of haphazard study to perhaps five years of planned, organized, and concentrated work. Unfortunately, too much stress is placed on technical studies and forms, with the result that most of the students who graduate from music schools and colleges today take the means to be the end and

miss the spirit and soul of our *ragas*. It takes many years of profound study of one's own inner self and of the *ragas* to be able to play Indian music with the immense emotional and spiritual effect that the music calls for.

SOUNDS, STRUCK AND UNSTRUCK

The traditions of Indian classical music are seemingly without beginning. Our musical history, which goes back approximately four thousand years, has been handed down orally from *guru* to *shishya* and recorded in Sanskrit verses that have later necessitated detailed commentaries and explanations. Historical fact is overshadowed by legend and mythology, and it is only recently that attempts have been undertaken to sort out history from myth.

We have been taught that the divine art of music was created by the Hindu holy trinity—Brahma the Creator, Vishnu the Preserver, and Shiva the Destroyer. It is Shiva, King of the Dancers, whose cosmic dance symbolizes the everlasting life-and-death rhythm of the universe and whose movements are the source of all movement. In turn, the art known as *sangeet*—the threefold art of vocal music, instrumental music, and the dance—was taught to mankind by the great *rishis*, or saint-sages. In ancient days, these *rishis* were both respected philosophers and men of religion. Living a pure life dedicated to wisdom, the *rishis* dwelled in out-of-the-way forests, where they were the centers of small communities known as *ashrams*—schools with residences for the disciples. There, we are told, the *rishis* delivered their teachings on medicine, science, music, astrology, astronomy, and other branches of learning which, along with the practice of yoga, were means to attain self-realization. Most of the time, this teaching was carried on orally, but some disciples recorded the *rishis'* words in verses on dried palm leaves, partly to help themselves memorize the lessons. These writings became almost sacred and were carefully copied down by one generation of disciples and passed on to the next, who in turn re-

Tony Roberts

copied them for future disciples. Even today, there are some families who possess scrolls which were handed down by their ancestors and date back many centuries.

Our tradition teaches us that sound is God—Nada Brahma. That is, musical sound and the musical experience are steps to the realization of the self. We view music as a kind of spiritual discipline that raises one's inner being to divine peacefulness and bliss. We are taught that one of the fundamental goals a Hindu works toward in his lifetime is a knowledge of the true meaning of the universe—its unchanging, eternal essence—and this is realized first by a complete knowledge of one's self and one's own nature. The highest aim of our music is to reveal the essence of the universe it reflects, and the *ragas* are among the means by which this essence can be apprehended. Thus, through music, one can reach God.

In the ancient scriptures we read that there are two types of sound—the one a vibration of ether, the upper or purer air near heaven, and the other a vibration of air, or the lower atmosphere closer to the earth. The vibration of ether is thought by some to be like the music of the spheres that Pythagoras described in the sixth century B.C. It is the sound of the universe, ever present and unchanging. This sound is called *anahata nad*, or "unstruck sound," because it is not produced by any physical impact. The other kind of sound is called *ahata nad*, or "struck sound," because it is always caused by physical impact. In this case, vibrations are set in motion at a given moment, a sound is created, and then it dies away as the vibrations cease.

The unstruck sound is most significant for yogis. It is the eternal sound they seek to hear from within, and it is possible for them to achieve this only after many years of meditation and discipline in yoga. Through *tapasya*, or meditation, the yogi tries to "wake up the *kundalini*," the divine creative force in man. Tantric philosophy, a medieval mystic system, describes it as a coiled serpent, symbolizing dynamism, that resides in the central part of the body. The yogis also try to awaken the *chakras*, or inner spinal centers of energy, and control them with the mind— what we call "piercing the *chakras*." When a yogi has

achieved this, he has complete control of his body and is able to accomplish supernatural acts like levitation or disappearing.

We are concerned here with the manifested sounds, of which there are two types: one that is musical, described as pleasing and soothing; and one that is not. Musical sounds reflect the orderly numerical patterns of the universe. Sounds can be produced not only by skillfully played musical instruments, but also by winds, rushing water, birds, the human voice, and other manifestations of nature.

MELODY IS THE BASIS OF OUR MUSIC

When listening to a music alien to one's own, one must keep an open mind. Many common meeting grounds may be discovered, but the comparative outlook should not result in adverse or uncritical evaluation of the art, whether it be of the East or the West. With open ears and an open mind, the receptive listener will be introduced to a whole new world of music, a new concept of sound, and thus to a widening horizon of art and people, of life itself.

Perhaps it would be wise, at the very beginning, to explain some of the basic differences between the classical music of the West and that of the East.

In the West, the musical system is based not only on a combination of melody and rhythm, but also on the highly developed elements that enrich the music— harmony (or the chordal, vertical structure of any given composition) and counterpoint (or the simultaneous sounding of two or more melodies). Indian music too is based on melody and rhythm, but has no comparable system of harmony and counterpoint. Rather, it is melody that has been developed and refined to a very high degree, with an infinite variety of subtleties that are completely unknown in Western music.

Another marked difference between the two is that whereas a Western composition may be based on many moods and tonal colors, often sharply contrasting, the Indian melody concentrates on only one principal mood or emotion throughout, dwelling on it, expanding, elaborating. Thus, the effect becomes intense and hypnotic and often magical.

Deep-rooted musical tradition in India dictates the position of the most prominent notes and their relationship both to each other and to the less important notes. That is, the fundamental form is a "given" quality on which the musician improvises and elaborates. In Western music, much emphasis is placed on the simultaneous motion of two or more melodies and the tension and relaxation of chord progressions. Melodies are often conceived within this harmonic assumption.

To the Westerner unfamiliar with Indian music, there are a number of external features that may initially jar the ear and make the music seem quite strange. For one thing, the Indian note system is divided into smaller units than the Western scale (in which the smallest pitch-interval between two notes is the semitone, or half tone, and each octave comprises twelve of these equidistant tones, in this "tempered" system). The Indian scale, like the Western diatonic scale, contains seven notes, and the octave may be further divided into the twelve semitones. But, when the Indian scale becomes the basis of a musical piece, the sensitive ear perceives that the octave is divided into even smaller units. According to the Indian system, then, there are within an octave twenty-two intervals that may be played and notated. These very small units are known as the *shrutis*, or microtones. In old and contemporary Indian music, the intervals between two consecutive scale steps are, however, always more than one *shruti*. (And theoretically, the Indian octave is made up of sixty-six still smaller units.) The use of the microtones, combined with the many kinds of grace notes and embellishments, and the constant sound of the drone notes, produce the characteristic quality of Indian music.

Another factor that Westerners find remarkable in our music is that we do not employ the technique of modulation, a change of key within a composition. That is, we do not usually change the fundamental note, the tonic (the tone on which any scale is based and from which it rises) within a composition. In fact, it is not unusual for an Indian performer to retain the same tonic, or key, throughout his musical life because of the range and qualities of his voice or the characteristics of the instrument he plays.

Music of any culture, East or West, is founded on relationships between sounds and is based on certain universal physical laws. But these proportions can be rendered in a great many ways, thus creating contrasting systems of music.

Generally speaking, Indian music belongs to the system of modal music. A mode, or scale type, is defined in terms of the relationships between the fundamental, unchanging note—the tonic—and successive notes of the scale. This relationship between the tonic and any other scale note determines whether a note is the interval of a second, a third, a fourth, a fifth, and so on. And in order for the musician or the listener to understand and hear this relationship, in any composition the tonic must constantly be sounded. It is for this reason that the *tamboura* (or *tanpura*), the background drone instrument, is so necessary in our classical music. It makes audible, and continuously registers, the tonic and the next important note, the dominant, in the minds of both the performer and the listener. The tonic thus forms the framework or foundation of any of our compositions.

All Indian classical music—*raga sangeet*—is based on vocal music, because the structural basis of our music is melody, which holds the prime place in our musical traditions. As already indicated, Indian music is built not on simultaneous melodies and chord patterns or vertical development as in the West, but rather on a development of one horizontal melody line. Every instrumental musician must undergo rigorous training of the voice, learning many fixed song compositions. This should give the artist a thorough insight into the *ragas* and make him more sensitive to music. The wind and bowed instruments are most closely associated with vocal music, for they imitate almost exactly the flow and expression of the human voice. At first, the plucked-string instruments also closely followed vocal patterns, but the physical nature and playing techniques of these instruments permitted each one to develop slowly its own personality and characteristics in playing styles. In particular, the sitar and the *sarod* evolved in a way to produce highly complex sounds. But even the sitar and the *sarod* copy the voice rather carefully in the first part of a composition, known as the *alap*, which is the slow, non-rhythmic "exposition" or elaboration of the *raga*. The second solo movement, or *jor*, which is rhythmic but has no cyclic rhythmic framework, is generally of a vocal nature as well and imitates singing patterns.

THE VEDIC FOUNT

The history of our country's music goes back to at least 2000 B.C. In recent excavations, archaeologists have discovered that the people of the very early Indus Valley, probably pre-Aryan, civilization were skilled in the playing of flutes, primitive drums, and stringed instruments known generically as *veenas* which were something like lutes. We know from abundant literary sources that Aryans living in India before the first millennium B.C. sang chants comprising a number of different tones as they performed religious ceremonies. The meeting point between history and legend is to be found in the Vedas, our religious scriptures in ancient Sanskrit verses. The Vedic literature contains many references to various kinds of stringed instruments and drums, to dances and particular songs, and also to the Vedic music itself. The chants of the Vedas, or *samans*, were set to melodies, in particular those of the *Sama Veda*, and were known collectively as *samagana*, which is believed to be the root of all our classical music.

The music of these hymns was characterized by a downward movement of notes, which numbered from two or three to seven. In the earliest Vedic music, these hymns were psalmodized just on one note, but soon evolved to a chant pivoting between two notes—the *udatta*, "raised," or higher note, and the *anudatta*, "unraised," or lower one. This singing became more extended when another tone was added to the *udatta* and the *anudatta*—the *svarita*, or "sounded" tone. These three notes formed the nucleus of what was to evolve as the full-octave scale. When a fourth note was added, the Indian tetrachord, considered as a

downward movement of notes, was formed. In the *Rikpratisakhya*, a musical treatise of the fourth century B.C., names are given to each of these notes. The Vedic hymns were later sung on five, six, or seven different notes. And so, long before Western classical music was formulated, the Indians had evolved the complete octave made up of seven notes, or *svaras*. This series of seven notes (1 2 3 4 5 6 7 1) is known collectively as the *saptaka*, or cluster of seven.

In different eras in our musical history, various notes were used as the starting point of the scale. But since medieval times, the system has been simplified by having the note SA as the tonic for all the scales. SA itself does not have a fixed pitch like middle C, for example, in the Western scale. It corresponds more accurately to what the Westerners call the movable DO. That is, when a Westerner sings the solfeggio syllables for a scale in any key—C major, E-flat, G, A minor—he will always sing DO RE MI FA SOL LA TI DO. And so, the Indian will sing, using the syllables SA RI GA MA PA DHA NI and SA, the abbreviations of the names of the notes. These are the seven tones of the *saptaka*, now used as the fundamental scale, and their full names are, in their ascending order from the tonic: *shadja, rishaba, gandhara, madhyama, panchama, dhaivata,* and *nishada*. One of our scholarly treatises explains that the tonic is the soul, RI is the head, GA the arms, MA the chest, PA the throat, DHA the hips, and NI the feet. Several ancient music scholars maintained that the intervals of the notes of the natural scale were determined by the sounds certain animals make. The cry of the peacock, some said, is like *shadja*, the octave, sounded from one tonic to the next. *Rishaba*, the major second, is sounded by the bull or, according to some scholars, by a certain bird. *Gandhara* is derived from the sound of the goat or sheep; and the heron or crane cries the fourth, *madhyama*. The song of the favorite bird, the cuckoo, or *kokila*, gives rise to *panchama*, the fifth; and the natural sixth comes from the raucous sound of the horse or, some say, the frog. And the elephant, we are told, sounds forth *nishada*. All these interesting derivations of the musical intervals were devised by the old scholars, who realized that the cries of many animals are made up of two notes. If the lower note the animal produces is regarded as the SA, then the different intervals can be determined from the different animal cries. Whether this theory is completely and scientifically true or not, it is nevertheless colorful and credible to a certain degree.

One of the Indian parent scales is considered to be the fundamental, unaltered, natural (*shuddha*) scale, made of "pure" notes. All the other notes used in the other scales are called *vikrits*, or variations, of these primary notes. A note may be altered by flatting or sharping it in various degrees. In the present Hindustani system of the North of India, the fundamental scale is *Bilaval*, which corresponds to the Western major scale. However, in the Karnatic system of the South of India, the first parent scale resembles the Western minor scale. The difference between the two may be connected with the fact that these scales are derived from different *gramas* (ancient scales), which have different intervals between the seven scale steps.

The *gramas*, of which there were three (*shadja, gandhara,* and *madhyama*), formed the basis of the old music. Actually they were fundamental scales using the notes SA, GA, and MA as their main notes, though not always as their tonics. The *gandhara grama*, based on GA, was said to have been used by celestial beings and had some magical properties. Why it fell out of use in ancient times is not adequately explained in the texts that are available to us today. For reasons too technical to explain here, the *madhyama grama* seems to have become unnecessary, according to some scholars, since its function could very easily have been taken over by the *shadja grama*. Now, all scales are indeed thought of as modifications or variations of the *shadja grama*. The many difficult problems the *gramas* present to modern musicologists are for the most part still unresolved, and there are any number of conflicting scholarly opinions about them.

During the middle period of development of our music—very broadly, from the sixth century B.C. to some time between the fifth and seventh centuries A.D. —the predominant musical foundation was the *jati*, which served the same function as the *raga* does now. That is, the *jati* was the basic melody type upon which compositions were constructed, a universal kind of proto-*raga* from which all later *ragas* devolved. Many people are of the opinion that the *jatis* were very much like the modal structures still found in Eastern Europe, the Middle East, and other Far Eastern countries.

STRUCTURAL ELEMENTS OF A RAGA

Many of the concepts behind our musical terms are difficult to explain to the Westerner, and so it is that the most significant feature of our music today is also the most complicated to explain and understand. That is the *raga*, the heart of our music.

There is a saying in Sanskrit—"*Ranjayati iti Ragah*"—which means, "That which colors the minds is a *raga*." As a blank canvas can be covered with colors and forms, so the receptive human mind can be "colored" or affected by the pleasing and soothing sound of a *raga*. The beauty of the *raga* leads the listener to a serene and peaceful frame of mind and brings him joy. In other words, the *raga* must create a forceful *effect* on the listener. Every note in our musical system not only is a tone, but also carries within it a certain expression or emotion. The total expression of the notes and theme of a *raga* create an intensely powerful musical entity. Because of the nature of the notes—considered both as musical tones and as representations of ideas—it could never be said that a musician "invents" a *raga*. Rather, a *raga* is discovered as a biologist might "discover" a new species or an explorer a new continent. The number of possible *ragas* is nearly infinite. Scholars have figured that given the seventy-two parent scales of Indian music, with all their permutations, each scale could give rise to hundreds of different patterns or combinations. That makes thousands of possible patterns in the seventy-two parent scales. But then, if other kinds of modes are taken into consideration, such as those which are formed from a combination of notes from two scales, the number of possible *ragas* becomes boundless. Actually, only several hundred *ragas* are in use.

In our literature the first mention of the *raga* as we know it today occurs in the *Brihaddeshi*, by Matanga, written some time between the fifth and seventh centuries A.D. at the beginning of a renaissance in Indian music. The term *raga* does, however, occur in much earlier works, used in conjunction with other musical forms. In the two great epics of the pre-Christian era, the *Ramayana* and the *Mahabharata*, there is mention of *ragas*, and a certain Narada, who wrote the *Shiksha* (usually referred to as the *Naradishiksha*) about the first century A.D., uses *raga* in compound musical terms, such as *gramaraga*. Later, we read of the *jatiragas* which are now taken to be direct ancestors of *marga*, or classical music, and *deshi*, which originally meant regional music, though some take it to mean nonclassical music. (Nonclassical music includes folk songs, light popular songs, and theatrical music, and it has about the same meaning as it does in the West.)

For the Westerner who is unfamiliar with the complexities of our music, it is perhaps better first to explain what a *raga* is *not*, before defining it in detail. The *raga* should not be mistaken for a scale or a mode or a key or a melody, although it has affinities with each of these. A *raga* is the melodic framework, established by tradition or born and inspired in the spirit of a master musician. One can theoretically perform any *raga* in any style of singing, or play it on any wind or stringed instrument, plucked or bowed. Only the drum is incapable of rendering a *raga* by itself; it must be used to accompany parts of a *raga* when sung or played by other instruments.

If the musician performs on a stringed instrument, it must be tuned to the correct intervals of the scale the particular *raga* uses. This is accomplished by adjusting the frets (which are movable on the sitar, for example) to the proper notes and tone units. There is a definite relationship between the scale on which the

raga is based and the tuning of the instrument, particularly the sympathetic resonating strings, which must also be tuned to the notes the *raga* uses.

Every *raga* must belong to a scale. This means that only those notes found in that particular scale pattern can be used in a given *raga*. Each *raga* evolves from one of the scales, which are also known as parent scales. Actually, we have two separate systems of scales in India, but they are derived from the same theories and traditions. In the South, where the Karnatic arrangement prevails, there are seventy-two primary scales, known as *melas*, or *melakartas* ("lords of melody"), which are produced by variations of the seven fundamental notes, or *svaras*. This system was finally classified in the seventeenth century by Pandit Venkatamakhi in his *Chaturdandi Prakashika*. According to the present Hindustani system of the North, there are ten primary scales called *thats*. Unlike the South, with its uninterrupted, continuous musical tradition, the North has no one system of classification of the scales or primary *ragas*. In fact, every eminent scholar has proposed a different arrangement! At the turn of this century, an attempt was made by V.N. Bhatkhande, the noted musicologist, to recodify the system. He proposed an order consisting of ten *thats*, or primary scales, and this order has gained fairly wide acceptance.* I myself, however, as well as a number of other musicians, do not feel that these ten scales adequately accommodate a great variety of *ragas*, for there are many *ragas* that use notes not contained in these ten *thats*. We therefore think it is more reasonable and scientific to follow the old *melakarta* system of the South, because it can sustain almost any *raga*, no matter how unusual its ascending and descending structures.

* See page 98 for the ten *thats* of the Hindustani system and their corresponding *ragas*.

Here are some of the basic *ragas*.

SHUDH SARANG

YAMAN KALYAN

DESH

DURGA

HINDOL

SHREE

MALKAUNS

BAHAR

The scale is theoretically divided into two groups of four notes, the upper and lower tetrachords. The lower group (SA RI GA MA) is known as the *pur-vanga*, or "first limb," and the upper is called the *uttaranga*, or "higher limb" (containing PA DHA NI and the next higher SA). This is in no way merely an arbitrary division, for the notes of the two tetrachords usually correspond closely with each other. A *raga* generally dwells predominantly in one or the other tetrachord, and this determines in part its expression or mood.

Every *raga* has a distinct ascending and descending structure, just as a Western scale is played from the lower tonic through the octave to the upper tonic and back down again. The ascending order is known as the *arohana*, and the descending is the *avarohana*.

The summary of the main recognizable phrases and features of a *raga*, that serve to identify it and distinguish it from all other *ragas*, is the *pakad*, sometimes called *svaroop*.

Chalan, which literally means "motion," is a somewhat more detailed concept than the *pakad* or *arohana* and *avarohana*. It introduces the main characteristics also connected with rhythm of the *raga*, such as holding a note longer, embellishing it with grace note, and so on, in the most concise and economical manner possible.

Every scale, whether it is called *that* or *mela*, consists of seven notes (1 2 3 4 5 6 7 and the upper 1, then descending, 7 6 5 4 3 2 1) but not every *raga* is made up of seven notes. The *ragas* may be classified into three *jatis* or classes (do not confuse this *jati* with the pre-*raga* melody type that is also called *jati*): *sampurna*, or heptatonic, which uses a complete scale of seven notes; *shadava*, which uses a group of six notes; and *audava*, which is pentatonic. And then the *ragas* may be further divided into six different "mixed" categories, selected from the three kinds of *jatis*. For example, a certain *raga* may be *sampurna* in the ascending order and *audava* in the descending—or *shadava* and *sampurna*. Some melodies may be made up of fewer than five notes, but these may not be classified as *ragas*. There are a few exceptions, however, for *Raga Malashree* has only three notes and *Raga Bhawani* uses just four. Besides the number of notes in the ascending and decending arrangements, the individual notes may be flatted or sharped. It is not uncommon, for instance, to have one or two notes flatted in the descent but natural in the ascent, or vice versa.

Apart from the SA, or tonic, which serves as the "home base," each *raga* has one predominant note, known as the *vadi* ("sonant"). This is the note that is used most in a *raga* and is emphasized the most strongly; in our traditional writings it is called the "King of Notes." The expression or nature of the *vadi* is one of the most important elements to set the mood for the entire *raga*.

We have already mentioned that the two tetrachords of a scale reflect or correspond to each other. Thus, there is a corresponding note to the *vadi* that is second in importance in the *raga* and is termed the *samvadi*, and it falls in the other tetrachord. The *sam-* *vadi*, always at the interval of a fourth or fifth from the *vadi*, strengthens the expression of the sonant. The other notes in a particular *raga*—apart from the *vadi* and *samvadi*—are called *anuvadi* or assonants. All the other notes *outside* a given scale are called *vivadi* ("enemies," or dissonant notes), and they may not be played in a *raga* to which they do not belong. Very rarely, however, a *vivadi* will be used in a *raga* for a special effect of dissonance.

A *raga* is an aesthetic projection of the artist's inner spirit; it is a representation of his most profound sentiments and sensibilities, set forth through tones and melodies. But the notes of a *raga*, by themselves, have no vitality or force. The musician must breathe life into each *raga* as he unfolds and expands it. A characteristic of the *raga*, impossible to describe but brought to it by the performing artist, is the *prana*—the life. Through the guidance of the *guru*, and by his own talent and genius, the musician learns how to make the bare notes vibrate, pulsate, come alive.

The primary device that creates the texture of a *raga*, that makes the notes themselves seem alive, is the system of ornamentation and embellishment. The *gamakas*, or grace notes—the many different ways of sounding, embellishing, and resolving notes—are the subtle shadings of a tone, delicate nuances and inflections *around* a note that please and inspire the listener. In our music, the transition from one tone to another is never made directly, as in most of Western music, but a subtle ornament, a kind of gliding, is added to soften and mellow the movement. The ornaments are not arbitrarily attached to a melody; rather, they seem to grow out of it. These embellishments are as essential to our music as harmony and counterpoint are to Western music. Just as there are no straight lines or strong contrasts in Indian art (as opposed, say, to classical Greek art), so Indian music is characterized by gentle curves, controlled grace, minute twining, winding whorls of detail. There is a boundless variety of these elaborate graces, such as *kampita* (a shake), *ahata* (sounding more than one note with one stroke), and *tiripa* (stressing one note of a phrase); and scholars have numbered and classified them in different ways. The actual sound—vocal or instrumental—of each ornamented note is difficult to describe, but the effect on the listener seems to be very great. The *andola*, or *andolita* (the "swing" effect), occurs when there is a delicate rocking between microtones. The *meend* is a short slide from one *svara* to another, almost like a delicate glissando. A series of another kind of *gamaka* produces a sobbing trill, which is heard very often in our music. In still another kind, a certain ascending succession of tones creates a sound like laughter.

RAGA:
THAT WHICH COLORS THE MIND

For a *raga* truly to "color the mind" of a listener, its effect must be created not only through the notes and the embellishments, but also through the presentation of a specific emotion or mood characteristic of each *raga*. Through the rich melodies of our music, every human emotion, every subtle mood in man and in nature, can be expressed.

Because each *raga* is associated with a particular passion or mood, each is also closely connected to a certain time of day or season of the year. The cycle of day and night, as well as the cycle of the seasons, is analogous to the cycle of life itself. Each segment of the day—such as the time before sunrise, noon, late afternoon, early evening, late night—is associated in our music with a definite sentiment. The explanation of the time associated with each *raga* may be found in the nature of the notes that comprise it, or in historical anecdotes concerning the *raga*, or, as some say, in the Hindu division of the day into lucky and less fortunate times. It is believed, for example, that *ragas* using *komal* RI (the flatted second) and *komal* DHA (flatted sixth) belong to the *sandhiprakasha* group—the times of sunrise and of sunset. These are some of the *ragas* belonging to the *Bhairava* and *Purvi thats*. *Ragas* with RI, GA, and DHA *shuddha* (natural) are early-morning or early-evening *ragas* and follow in performance time the *sandhiprakasha ragas*; some *ragas* from the *Bilaval*, *Kalyan*, and *Khamaj thats* fall into this category. Then, *ragas* using *komal* GA and *komal* NI usually represent late morning or late night. Associated with these times are *ragas Jaunpuri* and *Malkauns*. Other more technical musical factors, too complex to dwell on here, determine whether a *raga* is in the first part or the latter part of the day.

Theoretically, for a *raga* that describes the feeling of early evening to have its fullest effect, it should be played in the early evening. In the South of India, this tradition of the correct time for playing each *raga* has fallen out of general use in the last fifty years. This seems somewhat strange, for one hears so often that the Karnatic system of the South is the more orthodox and traditional, and that it adheres to the old ways far more rigidly than the Hindustani system of the North. It is understandable, though, that these Karnatic musicians changed their thinking about the time theory. Indeed, they are to be commended for having the foresight to realize how the modern concert hall would limit performances. In the South, concerts are usually, though not always, held some time between late afternoon and midnight. When these musicians boldly abandoned the time theory, they "saved" hundreds of beautiful early- and late-morning *ragas,* early-afternoon and late-night *ragas* that would have otherwise been lost to the listeners. Now, in the darkened, air-conditioned concert halls, a fine artist can develop a *raga* of any season or any time of day, and the receptive listener will feel the full effect and respond to the beauty of the music. In the North, adherence to the time theory also appears to be slackening, and though it may take some years, the Hindustani musicians are bound to follow the example of the artists of the South.

I try to follow the time theory as much as I can, and my personal view is that the theory should be upheld when possible, as in Northern India, where a performance may be given at any time of day—may, for example, last from late at night till early in the morning; or when concerts are held outdoors or in such places where the light and atmosphere of the outdoors can be seen and felt—in halls, for example, with long galleries of windows or skylights that one often finds in museums or schools. In these cases, one can look out and relate the *raga* to the time of day or night and to the sunshine or moonlight, thunder, rain, or clouds.

This illustration evoking the light, joyful mood of the raga Malwa Vasanta Ragini is based on a poem in the Ragmala. Lord Krishna (center), *dancing, holds mango shoots symbolic of growth and spring. The two women play a dholak and hand cymbals.*

Lord Krishna, as shown in a preliminary drawing for an eighteenth-century mural illustrating the Rasa Leela.

But what difference does it make inside such auditoriums as Royal Festival Hall in London, or Philharmonic Hall in New York, or Sanmukhananda Hall in Bombay? They look and feel the same at any hour of the day or night. And how much does adherence to the time theory matter in countries where the people do not associate the various times and seasons with specific *ragas*, as Indians do? Indeed, I have seen people in many countries appreciate and enjoy listening to morning and afternoon *ragas* as well as evening and night *ragas* at any time, and the same is true when listening to recorded music at home.

This view of mine may provoke some criticism, but my judges should look again at the Karnatic system, which they believe to be more orthodox and traditional, for that system itself has relaxed its strict

holding to the time theory over the past two generations.

There is a group of seasonal *ragas* that describe mostly spring or the rainy season. People in the West often seem amazed that there are *ragas* for the rainy season, because for them, the rain is such a bothersome and unromantic thing. In India, the rain or monsoon season has always been eagerly awaited after the scorching months of summer, when everything lies dried and withered. Then, the black clouds gather and cold breezes start up; the first drops of rain fall, and everything is cooled. And there is the smell of wet earth, and crickets sing, and frogs croak. The poets have written beautiful songs in praise of this season, describing nature and the first rains. Curiously, this is the time when girls feel most strongly

25

the absence of their lovers and when they are most romantic. Many beautiful *ragas* convey this feeling of longing.

In all our epic poetry and plays and stories of all sorts, we find that the spring season evoked the greatest inspiration. The spring festival known as *Vasanta Utsav* was always associated with greenery, flowers, birds—especially the cuckoo birds that we call *kokila*—dance, music, merriment, and love-making. After the lifelessness of winter come all the beautiful changes in nature, the rebirth and new life that so inspire artists and lovers. This season is also very much associated with Krishna and the *Holi* festival. There are thousands of songs and paintings that describe Lord Krishna as a youth joyously celebrating along with the *gopis* (milkmaids) in Vrindavan, singing and dancing the *Rasa Leela* and, during this festival, sprinkling powdered colors on everyone and spraying streams of red, blue, and pink colored water with little pumps.

THE NINE SENTIMENTS

Each *raga* has to have its own psychological temperament in relation to its tempo, or speed. Many of the heavy, serious *ragas* such as *Darbari Kanada* or *Asavari* should be sung or played in slow tempo. Others, such as *Adana* or *Jaunpuri*, which express a lighter mood, are best rendered in a medium or medium-fast tempo. This relationship of speed to the predominant expression of the music also exists in the West and is quite obvious, even to a nonmusician. A joyful *raga*, full of laughter, could not be executed in a very slow tempo any more than could a playful scherzo.

The performing arts in India—music, dance, drama, and even poetry (and to a lesser extent, painting and sculpture)—are based on the concept of *Nava Rasa*, or the "nine sentiments." Literally, *rasa* means "juice" or "extract," but here, we take it to mean "emotion" or "sentiment." Each artistic creation is supposed to be dominated by one of these nine sentiments, although it can also express related emotions in a less prominent way. The more closely the notes of a *raga*

conform to the expression of one single idea or emotion, the more overwhelming the effect of the *raga*. This is the magic of our music—its hypnotic, intense singleness of mood. It is now generally agreed that there are nine of these principal sentiments, although some scholars number them as eight or ten.

In the generally acknowledged order of these sentiments, the first is *shringara*, a romantic and erotic sentiment filled with longing for an absent lover. It contains both the physical and mental aspects of love and is sometimes known as *adi* (original) *rasa*, because it represents the universal creative force.

Hasya is the second *rasa*, comic, humorous, and laughter-provoking. It can be shown through syncopated rhythmic patterns or an interplay of melody and rhythm between singer and accompanist, or between sitarist and *tabla* player, causing amusement and laughter.

The third *rasa* is *karuna*, pathetic, tearful, sad, expressing extreme loneliness and longing for either god or lover. (Hindus tend to elevate mortal love into a divine love, so the lover can be an ordinary man or often a god, such as Krishna, or Shiva.)

Raudra is fury or excited anger. This *rasa* is often used in drama, but in music it can portray the fury of nature as in a thunderstorm. Musically, it can be shown through many fast, "trembling" ornaments, producing a scary, vibrating effect in the low notes.

Veera expresses the sentiment of heroism, bravery, majesty, and glory, grandeur, and a dignified kind of excitement. If it is overdone, it can turn into *raudra*.

Bhayanaka, the sixth *rasa*, is frightening or fearful. It is difficult to express in music through one instrument (though a symphony orchestra could do it easily) unless there is a song text to bring out its exact meaning.

Vibhatsa—disgustful or disgusting—is also difficult to show through music. This *rasa* and *bhayanaka* are used more for drama than music.

The eighth *rasa*, *adbhuta*, shows wonderment and amazement, exhilaration and even a little fear, as when one undergoes a strange new experience. It can be expressed by extreme speed or some technical marvels that, in certain kinds of singing or playing, provoke amazement.

The last *rasa* is *shanta rasa*—peace, tranquility, and relaxation.

Some people mention a tenth *rasa*, *bhakti*, which is devotional, spiritual, and almost religious in feeling; but actually, this *rasa* is a combination of *shanta*, *karuna*, and *adbhuta*.

In dance and drama, the *rasas* are expressed through the eyes, expression of the face, and movements of the hands and body or the words of the actors. The singer has the advantage of portraying the *rasa* through a song text; the instrumentalist, however, must convey the *rasa* to the minds of his listeners through the music alone. Thus, the effect of the music is more emotional than intellectual, and the listener is made to *feel* the meaning and the intention of the *raga*.

Certain *rasas*, of course, lend themselves more easily to one artistic medium than another. The two less appropriate *rasas*, as far as music alone is concerned, are *bhayanaka* (frightful) and *vibhatsa* (disgusting). These two are clearly more suited to stage representation, where the facial expression, gestures, and tone of voice within a theme or story can convey the intended feelings. Of the seven remaining *rasas*, there are three whose gentle and subtle qualities are especially well suited to our music, because of their spirituality—*shanta*, *karuna*, and *shringara*.

Rasas such as *veera*, *karuna*, *shanta*, and *adbhuta* are mostly associated with the old style of singing—*dhrupad* or *dhruvapada*. This style is dignified, majestic, austere, and spiritual in nature and calls for less ornamentation than the more recent styles. The *dhrupad* songs are solemn and religious, usually sung in a slow tempo. Because a *dhrupad* composition expands slowly and develops its theme in a very profound way, the musicians who followed the *dhrupad* tradition some centuries ago tended to keep to just one *rasa* throughout a *raga*, maintaining one single mood from beginning to end. The style of singing that developed after *dhrupad*, called *khyal*, has more freedom than *dhrupad* and is filled with delicate embellishments and romantic expressions. In this style of singing, the artist is concerned chiefly with displaying his own imagination, technical virtuosity, and speed. Occasionally, the text of a song may become just a melodic vehicle and of lesser importance. So we find that the *khyal* singer may use a number of related *rasas* in a composition and may eventually treat all *ragas* in the same fashion—as a device for a show of virtuosity. The most frequently used *rasas* in *khyal* singing, then, are *karuna*, *shringara*, and *adbhuta*. The style of singing that was developed quite recently, known as *thumri*, utilizes predominantly the extremely sensuous and romantic *shringara* and *karuna*. Since it may incorporate different *ragas* within one composition, it it may also portray flashes of different moods.

Today, the usual format of a *raga* performance by a well-trained, traditional musician is to begin in a very peaceful, slow manner, generally establishing the SA, or tonic. Then the musician plays the *vistar*, the elaboration or extension with long-drawn-out phrases, as he slowly unfolds the *raga*, expressing mainly the *shanta* and *karuna rasas*. As the tempo increases, the musician may bring out other *rasas*, and the spiritual feelings give way to more excitment, using *veera* or *adbhuta rasas*. In the old books written on music, we read that each *raga* should portray one specific *rasa*, depending on the "personality" of the notes of the *raga*. Now, however, performers of classical music do not always follow the old texts. Rather, we choose to take after the teachings of our *gurus*. And that is why I prefer to say that each *raga* has its *principal rasa*, for there may be other similar *rasas* associated with that same *raga*. For instance, I may play *Raga Malkauns*, whose principal mood is *veera*, but I could begin by expressing *shanta* and *karuna* in the *alap* and develop into *veera* and *adbhuta* or even *raudra* in playing the *jor* or *jhala*.

Similarly, I have often heard other musicians or scholars try to establish some preconceived ideas about the inherent emotional qualities of the notes. Some maintain that *komal* GA (the flatted third) is supposed to be *karuna*, or sad, and that it expresses pathos. Or that *shuddha* NI (natural seventh) is zealous, impulsive, pushy, and eager to move on to the next higher note, SA (the natural resolution of the seventh to the tonic). Or that MA (fourth) is full and heroic, strong and definite. And some say that next to the tonic itself, the PA (fifth) is the most peaceful and restful. On the other hand, the performing artist

The Metropolitan Museum of Art

can create the moods he himself chooses, depending on his over-all personality, his training, the style he adopts (*dhrupad*, *khyal*, and so on), the *gharana* (school or tradition) to which he belongs, and his control and mastery of the *raga*. Musicians who have been fortunate in receiving proper *taleem* (Urdu equivalent of the Sanskrit *shiksha*, or training) from a notable lineage of musical tradition (*gharana*) are taught by their *gurus* which basic moods are appropriate for certain principal *ragas*. That is, some of our *ragas* are so old and have such clear ideas connected with them that only one possible *rasa* can be used in association with them. *Raga Lalit*, for example, is an early-morning devotional *raga*, and *Bhairav* is associated with the ascetic Shiva. *Sarang* has a cooling effect on a hot summer afternoon. Other basic *ragas* that all musicians learn very thoroughly are *Vasanta*, which is descriptive of spring in full bloom; *Marva*, which shows renunciation; *Shree*, which also shows renunciation; *Malhar*, describing thunder, rain, and wind; and *Malkauns*, which shows dignity and heroism.

The mental images of some *ragas* are so well established that they have been rendered as paintings and miniatures through many centuries. Some of the best-known were executed between the seventeenth and nineteenth centuries at Rajasthan and Kangra.

There is no dearth of beautiful stories relating how great musicians and saint-musicians such as Baiju Bavare, Swami Haridas, or Mian Tan Sen performed miracles by singing certain *ragas*. It is said that some could light fires or the oil lamps by singing one *raga*, or bring rain, melt stones, cause flowers to blossom, and attract ferocious wild animals—even snakes and

(Upper left) *Raga Asawari may be evoked in this Rajput miniature of the late eighteenth or early nineteenth century. The dancing girl, dressed in provincial court costume, has her hands painted in the traditional manner. She has attracted two cobras, perhaps with the bell in her hand.*

(Lower left) *This seventeenth-century Rajput miniature evokes Malwa Sadh Malhara, related to Megh Malhar, which, when played correctly, is supposed to bring rain. Its mood of unsatisfied love-longing is shown by the ash-covered ascetic, the empty couch, and the peacocks who suffer from thirst waiting for the rainy season to come.*

tigers—to a peaceful, quiet circle in a forest around a singing musician. To us, in this modern, mechanical, materialistic age, all this seems like a collection of fables, but I sincerely believe that these stories are all true and that they were all feasible, especially when one considers that these great musicians were not just singers or performers, but also great yogis, whose minds had complete control of their bodies. They knew all the secrets of *Tantra, hatha yoga,* and different forms of occult power, and they were pure, ascetic, and saintly persons. That has been the wonderful tradition of our music—and even today, though such miracles may not be performed, one can see the immense impact on the listener and, as many put it, the "spiritual experience" the listener feels, especially the Western listener.

We may say, then, that a *raga* is a definite, scientific, subtle, aesthetic melodic form, made up of a series of notes within the octave, each one different from every other and distinguished by its own particular sequence of notes, number of tones, ascending and descending orders, most prominent notes, notes of different lengths, characteristic phrases, and principal mood. It is the melodic base in Indian classical music on which the musician improvises in any style, for any duration, and in any tempo, either as a solo or accompanied by drums, and it may have a composed base (song or instrumental *gat*).

TALA:
THE CLAP OF HANDS

As *raga* is the fundamental element of melody in Indian music, so *tala* is the essential element of time and rhythm. Tradition has it that the word *tala* has its origin in the syllables *ta* (from *tandava,* the cosmic dance of Shiva) and *la* (from *Lasya,* the feminine counterpart of *tandava;* a dance originally attributed to Parvati). And rhythm, we learn from our old texts, is given the name *tala* because it is the union of the First Principle, Shiva, and his consort, Parvati. Another interpretation of the word *tala* is that it refers to hand-clapping for keeping time. On another plane, one can

find the origins of Indian rhythms in the language, poetry, and literature of the country. Even until modern times, students learned their lessons by memorizing them in verse. The Sanskrit language and the numerous dialects derived from it classify syllables according to their temporal duration. The rules for versification are highly complex and very strict, and time length (as opposed to, say, accent in the West) is of prime importance in poetry.

Besides meaning rhythm in its broadest sense, *tala* also denotes an organized rhythmic cycle composed of various *matras,* or rhythmic units. Indian music has developed an extremely complex system of rhythm. One rhythmic cycle may be composed of from three to one hundred eight beats—or even more —though there are only about fifteen to twenty *talas* that are most often employed by musicians. Another thirty or forty *talas* are sometimes performed for a selected audience that has a deeper understanding of the music.

In each *tala* there are beats with different degrees of importance. The most strongly emphasized beat is the *sam.* The other important beats are called *tali,* and the unstressed beats (empty beats) are called *khali.* To keep time in our music, we indicate the beats by clapping our hands. The *sam* and *tali* are shown by hand-claps, *khali* by a wave of the hand. The other beats are counted on the fingers, starting with the little finger, ring finger, middle finger, and so on, according to the number of beats between the important ones.

There are three main speeds in our music—*vilambit* (slow), *madhya* (moderate), and *drut* (fast). These tempi may also be used in combinations, such as *madhya vilambit* (moderately slow) or *madhya drut* (moderately fast). There is also the term *ati drut,* which means very fast. So, the whole range of tempi goes from *ati vilambit* (very slow) to *vilambit,* then *madhya vilambit,* then *madhya, madhya drut, drut,* and *ati drut.* Any of the *talas,* in any tempo (*laya*), can be performed as solos in the hands of a master drummer.

Some of the most frequently used *talas* are:
Dadra—six beats, grouped 3–3. This is primarily played on the *tabla* or on other drums. It is used in

the light classical style known as *dadra,* which is characterized by simple melodies with syncopation which resemble compositions in the *thumri* style. This *tala* is also used for folk and popular tunes, *bhajans* (Hindu devotional songs), *qawali* (Muslim devotional songs), *ghazals* (vocal compositions in Urdu), and other types of light classical music.

Rupak—seven beats, grouped 3–2–2. This popular rhythm, generally played on the *tabla,* can be the accompaniment to either vocal or instrumental music in the *khyal* style.

Tivra or *teora*—seven beats, grouped 3–2–2. This is played for the most part on the old drum known as *pakhawaj* and employed to accompany a song composed in this *tala,* generally in a fast tempo.

Kaharva—eight beats, grouped 4–4. This is used for the same kind of light classical and popular music as the one in *dadra tala.*

Jhaptal—ten beats, grouped 2–3–2–3. This *tala* can be used, like *rupak tala,* to accompany *khyal* music. It is also played on the *pakhawaj* to accompany a *sadra* composition, a medium-fast *dhrupad* song.

Shooltal—ten beats, grouped 4–2–4. *Shooltal* is played on the *pakhawaj,* for *dhrupad* compositions, and also accompanied the old group of stringed instruments, such as the *been, rabab, sursringar,* and *surbahar.*

Chautal—twelve beats, grouped 4–4–2–2. Like *shooltal,* this rhythm is mostly used in *dhrupad* compositions and was played on a variety of early instruments.

Ektal—twelve beats, grouped 4–4–2–2. *Ektal* is played on the *tabla* exclusively for *khyal* compositions, and it can go in any tempo.

Dhamar—fourteen beats, grouped 5–5–4. This *tala* is played on the *pakhawaj* to accompany the old traditional songs which describe the *Holi* Festival that takes place in the spring.

Ada chautal—fourteen beats, grouped 2–4–4–4. This rhythm is heard primarily on the *tabla* with *khyal* compositions.

Jhumra—fourteen beats, grouped 3–4–3–4. *Jhumra* accompanies very slow *khyal* compositions and is rendered only on the *tabla.*

Chanchar—fourteen beats, grouped 3–4–3–4. This *tala* is played mostly on the *tabla* with the light *thumri* compositions, though it may also accompany stringed and wind instruments.

Teental—sixteen beats, grouped 4–4–4–4. *Teental* is the most popular *tala,* played on the *tabla* and used to accompany the voice in *khyal* songs. Though it is used with singing, *teental* is more often heard accompanying instrumentalists playing in any tempo.

Until thirty years ago or so, tradition restricted sitar and *sarod* players to the use of only *teental.* But then Ustad Allauddin Khan (my *guru*) introduced *gats* played in different *talas,* and since this innovation, Ali Akbar Khan and I have more or less established the style of playing *gats* in different *talas,* such as *rupak, jhaptal,* and *ada chautal.* I myself brought into vogue the style of playing the *gats* in such cycles as *matta tala* of nine beats, *chartal ki sawari* of eleven beats, *jai tal* of thirteen, *pancham sawari* of fifteen beats, *shikhar tal* of seventeen, and also some *talas* designated as having four and a half, five and a half, or six and a half beats, and so on. These *talas* with a "half beat" are not very traditional; actually, they are fast versions of *talas* with an odd number of beats. So, a *tala* of nine beats played fast becomes four and a half, and eleven beats would become five and a half. When I play such rhythmic cycles, I prefer not to give them altogether new, fancy names, but rather, to use the names of the odd-numbered *talas* from which they are reduced, and call them "half." Thus, *matta tala* of nine beats becomes *ardha* (half) *matta tala* of four and a half beats, and *ardha sawari* is five and a half, and *ardha jai* is six and a half beats.

→ The accompaniment of the *tabla* now has an extremely important role in Indian music, and instrumental music in particular. Even so, the status of the *tabla* accompanist until about thirty years ago was not especially high. Until recently, he was supposed to play only the *theka* (the basic sound syllables of a *tala* combined to form phrases of rhythm as executed on drums) and the sitar or *sarod* player performed his fixed pieces or improvisations on the same rhythmic framework of a certain *tala.* Rarely did the *tabla* player have a chance to do more than a few very short pieces of solo improvisation during an entire performance. Even now, there are still some musicians who prefer the more passive accompaniment of the *tabla* player. It was primarily because my *guru* Allauddin Khan liked and encouraged the more active participation of the *tabla* accompanist, and because Ali Akbar and I later promoted this, that the status of the *tabla* player as well as the proportion of *tabla* accompaniment in any piece have come to have so large a part in our music today.

The accompaniment of the *tabla* is known as *sangat*. One of the most popular types of accompaniment is the *jawabi sangat*, where the *tabla* player, in any tempo, imitates a rhythmic phrase executed by the instrumentalist. Another *tabla* accompaniment is the *sath* ("together") *sangat*, wherein the *tabla*

tries to follow very closely the rhythmic patterns of the main instrument, playing almost simultaneously the same phrases, and the two must end a phrase together on the *sam*. This is a very exhilarating and exciting moment for the listeners as well as the players, provided they have an excellent mutual understanding. When there is even more tension in the sitar-*tabla* or sarod-*tabla* dialogues, the *sangat* is known as *larant* ("fighting"). Many ardent music lovers sometimes feel that this particular style of *sangat* sounds much too harsh and unmusical. For some years now, there has developed a particular type of give-and-take, known as *jawab sawal* ("question-answer"), between the main instrumentalist and the drummer. Actually, this was started in a simpler form by my own *guru* as an explanation of a musical

Alla Rakha and I respond to the thrilling moment of reaching the last beat of a raga played at a concert given in Hong Kong during a recent tour of the Far East.

Eric Hayes

phrase by the teacher and a reply by the student, and I developed it later on when I had been inspired by the *tala vadya katcheri*, percussion ensembles made up of different drums in Karnatic music. In this *sangat*, first the musicians each play a very long phrase, usually four bars in whatever *tala* the piece is based on. They each play four bars, alternately, then two bars, then one, than a half bar back and forth, and then a quarter, and finally, they all join together for the climax. Ali Akbar and I continued with this idea and did some experiments with it in our duets. Now, this *jawab sawal* is very popular, and most instrumentalists and their *tabla* accompanists perform it. In fact, audiences have come to expect this brilliant, quick, exciting dialogue.

A WEALTH
OF STYLES

Of all the forms of singing and playing in Indian music, the highest place is given to the *alap*, or *rag alapana*, as it was originally called. A musician of good tradition usually begins a *raga* with the *alap*, which is a solo exposition. In the beginning of the *alap*, there is no rhythm, and it is very slow, serene, and spiritual, almost like an invocation. It expresses the *shanta* and *karuna rasas*. The entire *alap* describes the personality of the *raga*, pointing out its tonal centers, delineating its main expressive phrases. After gradually unfolding the whole range of the *raga*, the *alap* develops into what is known as the *num tum* (in singing) or the *jor* (in instrumental music), where the element of rhythm is added although no tight, cyclic rhythmic pattern frames the music. The *jor* can be performed from a slow to a medium to a fast tempo. As variations and developments of the basic *raga* are built up, the *raga* gains speed, and the melody patterns become more intricate. The *Beenkar* and *Rababiya gharanas* evolved a third section, or "movement," especially for instrumental music; it is broadly known as the *jhala*, and there are many different parts within it. The *jhala* is char-

acterized by increasing speed and excitement, ending with the climax.

India, with a history of classical music whose roots go back to antiquity, and with a geographical area that contains a multitude of different peoples, has an enormous wealth of melody and countless styles of singing. Many of these styles are designated first as singing styles, but it should be remembered that instrumental music is based on these same singing styles. Within the *raga sangeet*, or the domain of North Indian classical music, the most distinctive styles are the *dhrupad* and *khyal*.

It has often been said that *dhruvapada* (now called *dhrupad*) was invented in the fifteenth century by Raja Man Singh Tomar of Gwalior. We know now that although he did not actually create this style, it was he who developed it into an organized system and reshaped and popularized the existing *chhanda prabandha* type of singing. *Prabandha* means "bound up," or "knit together," and in music it refers to the orderly and organized classical songs, or *geetis*, that came into being before the Christian era and then developed through a number of musical periods. Until about the thirteenth century the *prabandha* form of music was the most popular, but from the fourteenth century to about the nineteenth, its prominence was replaced by the *dhruvapada*. A major difference between the two styles is that while the *chhanda prabandha* songs were in Sanskrit, the *dhruvapada* songs were in a dialect of Hindi.

The word *dhruva* means "definite," or "truth," and *pada* means "word." *Dhruvapada* are songs whose words are set in a fixed recurring pattern. At first, the song texts of the *dhruvapada* were grand and majestic praises of the gods and goddesses. Since this music was originally considered a means to elevate the soul and spirit to a higher plane and were sung in temples, the texts of early *dhrupad* compositions were all of a religious nature. Little by little, as musicians were taken into the royal courts and "protected" by the ruler, the texts of the songs changed from praises of God to elegant praises of the emperor or king, although they retained their feeling of awe, respect, and reverence. Some *dhruvapadas* were also sung in praise of nature. *Dhrupad* compositions are generally in a slow tempo and use little ornamentation, which makes them seem so grand and austere. Because *dhruvapada* provided a background for all subsequent musical development, this tradition is still studied and cultivated.

The major musical style that evolved after *dhruvapada* is *khyal*. The origins and derivations of *khyal* are still unclear, and many scholars have presented still unresolved views about them.

The word *khyal* may be Arabic-Persian in derivation, and has to do with imagination, fancy, or fanciful conception. *Khyal* music is, indeed, imaginative, elaborate, and romantic, unlike the profound, majestic, serious *dhruvapada* songs. *Khyal* compositions are highly ornamented and use all the *gamakas*, so that the texture is lacy and delicate, much like Muslim art and architecture.

Like *dhrupad*, the elements of *khyal* were in existence long before the style was popularized. Some scholars think that *khyal* singing was an offshoot of the *qawali*, Muslim devotional songs that were sung by the many Muslim Indians with Arabic-Persian heritage. Scholars also say that Amir Khusru, the great poet-musician of the thirteenth century, helped popularize the *khyal* style and may even have given it its name. In the fifteenth century, the Sharqui rulers, who were fine patrons of all the arts, promoted *khyal* singing, but then for the next few centuries, though it was in use, it did not have the prestige and importance of the *dhrupad* style in the royal courts. Under the rule of Sultan Mohammad Shah (1719–1748), Niyamat Khan, who acquired the title of Shah Sadarang (literally "ever colorful, ever gay") from the Sultan, had an enormous musical knowledge and brought *khyal* to its highest popularity and respect. From his time to the present, it has been of an attraction equal to *dhrupad*, and today it is the predominant style in our classical music.

Among the other types of singing is the *tappa*, originally a Muslim folk form sung by the camel-cart drivers from the Punjab and later developed to a classical level by the famous musician Mian Shori. His compositions in the Punjabi language are the best example of *tappa* songs and are still done by some singers from the Punjab and Benares. The songs are characterized by the extremely rich use of embellishment. They have a very definite rhythm and may be sung in different tempi, usually fast.

The *tarana* is a type of singing similar to the *sargams* or solfeggio exercises, but it uses nonsense syllables instead of regular words, and some say that there are also a few Persian words in these songs. Amir Khusru is said to have been the innovator of the *tarana* style of singing. There is a story that he had a singing contest with Nayaka Gopal, a very famous singer in the court of Sultan Allauddin Khilji. Gopal sang, and then Amir Khusru was to imitate and exactly reproduce the same songs. Gopal was amazed, then alarmed at Amir Khusru's abilities, and in desperation, he sang a very fast song in Sanskrit, fully aware that Amir Khusru did not know the language. But Amir Khusru, who was extremely sharp and intelligent, immediately mimicked the sound of the words, using nonsense syllables he made up as he went along, but keeping to the melodic and rhythmic structure that Nayaka Gopal had used. And from this clever trick of Amir Khusru, the *tarana* style of singing was born.

Another style that has come into vogue within the last hundred years is the *thumri*, a light, melodic, semiclassical composition. Some scholars are of the opinion that this style too has been in existence for many centuries, but it only acquired its importance at the court of Nawab Wazid Ali Shah of Lucknow in the last half of the nineteenth century. He was closely associated with the *kathak* style of dancing. The texts of the *thumri* songs are extremely romantic and erotic and often sad. Many of the songs describe feelings of desire and the longing of a girl for her lover, others are lamentations of loneliness because of the lover's infidelity. The central hero of the themes is Krishna, just as in the *dhamar* compositions, and he is the lover mentioned in most of the songs. *Thumri*'s relationship to *khyal* is similar to that of *dhamar* to *dhrupad*. There is a certain way of performing the *thumri* songs, very melodically, that differentiates this style from the *khyal*, and its lyricism and melodic romanticism can be expressed by the vocalist as well as the instrumentalist. Occasionally, one finds a kind of built-in modulation in *thumri* pieces, where the SA is shifted as the musician changes from one *raga* to another, for in this style, a number of different *ragas* may be used in one piece, along with bits of popular, regional, or folk tunes. The eminent *khyal* singers almost always sing a *thumri* at the end of their recitals. In fact, audiences expect it and clamor for it. A *thumri* is generally the *pièce de résistance* of *khyal* singers or instrumentalists. The best *thumri* singing comes from Benares and Lucknow, and is known as the *purab* style. These songs are characterized by much leisure and peace and pathos. Lately, the Punjab style has also become very popular because of its extremely sensuous approach and very delicate melodic embellishments.

OUR INSTRUMENTS

The instruments used in Indian music are divided into four categories: the stringed instruments, which may be bowed or plucked, the family of drums, the wind instruments, and various other small percussion instruments made of metal, wood, or porcelain. There is a surprisingly large number of instruments, each capable of expressing quite a broad range of tone and color, within the four divisions. The characteristics of the individual instruments—their shapes and sizes, their names, the way they are played—can be traced back to the oldest scriptures and treatises on music, and representations in sculpture and painting, for the instruments have not been appreciably modified over the centuries.

The category of stringed instruments is the largest and the most important, for strings are considered as the best accompaniment to singing, the prime element of Indian music. The stringed instruments vary considerably in size and shape and in the number of playing strings used. Some of them are equipped with sympathetic resonating strings, some are fretted, and some have one or two hollow gourds that act as resonators or sound boxes. There are some stringed instruments played with a bow, such as the *sarangi*, and others, such as the sitar, that call for a plectrum to be worn on the player's fingers.

VEENA

The stringed instrument par excellence, described in ancient texts and in use for perhaps over a thousand years, is the *veena* (also spelled *vina*). The *veena* is traditionally associated with Saraswati, the Goddess of Wisdom, and some of the very fine old *veenas* even have paintings on their bodies where Saraswati is represented. This instrument of the lute family is played in both the North and the South, though it is more popular with Karnatic musicians. The *veena* used in the South has a body resembling a Western lute, though larger, and the one used in the North is like a long stick flattened along one side, with a gourd on the underside at either end. Its tone is very sweet, and even though it does not have the projection of a Western fretted, plucked instrument, it is capable of far more subtle shadings and a fuller range of expression. Usually, the *veena* is fretted and has seven strings, but its size varies and it may have one or two resonating gourds. The artist plucks the strings with his fingers when playing, or he may wear a plectrum on two fingers of his right hand.

(Below) *Mayur veena. The peacock is associated with color and beauty.* Opposite page (upper left) *Beautiful old veena with resonating gourds. Note the bow.* (Upper right) *South Indian ivory inlaid veena with a belly somewhat like a Western lute.* (Center) *North Indian veena with a peacock at the end of the resonating tube.* (Lower left) *Kachchapi or tortoise veena. The shape is an excellent resonator.* (Lower right) *Makar veena resembling a crocodile.*
Courtesy of V. Shirali

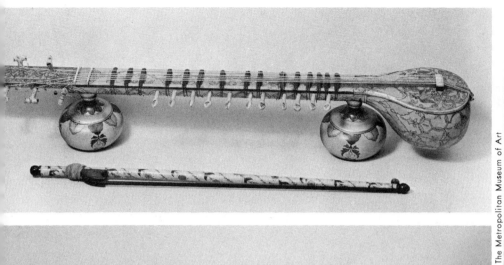

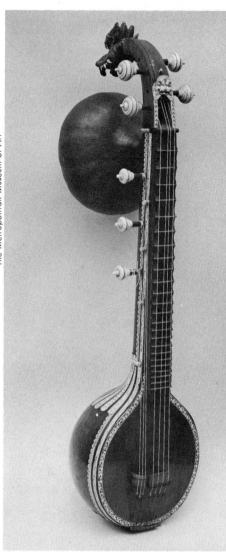

The Metropolitan Museum of Art

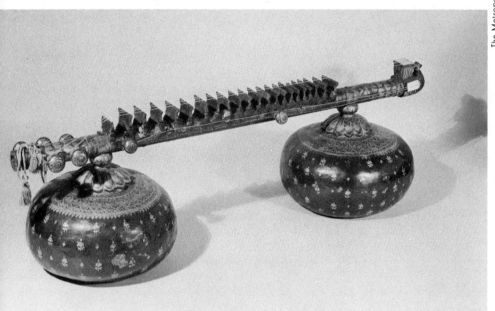

Courtesy of V. Shirali

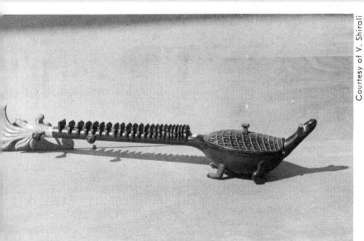

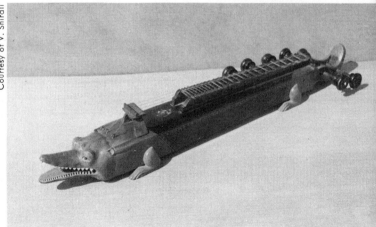

SITAR

In the styles and traditions of our music, as *khyal* gradually came into prominence and took the place of *dhrupad,* the sitar replaced the *veena* in the North and has remained one of the most popular stringed instruments of Hindustani musicians. (In the North, due to language differences and pronunciation habits, the *veena* has come to be called the *been.*) The sitar is similar to the *veena* in several respects, although it is not as complicated to play, technically. Its frets, tied on with gut or silk threads, are movable. Played with a plec-

trum worn on the right hand index finger, the sitar most often has seven strings that are actually touched by the fingers, and some models have a number of resonating strings as well that serve to give a richer sound. Some sitars have an extra hollow gourd at the end of the neck where the pegs are and some do not; there were even sitars with an additional gourd attached halfway down the back of the neck of the instrument. There are large sitars, middle-sized sitars, and small sitars that women play, each with a different tonal range and character.

(Left) *Seven-stringed sitar with carved designs.*
(Center) *An antique treasure, this three-stringed instrument decorated in red and gold.*

(Right) *My own "Stradivarius" sitar, fashioned for me by N. C. Mullick.*

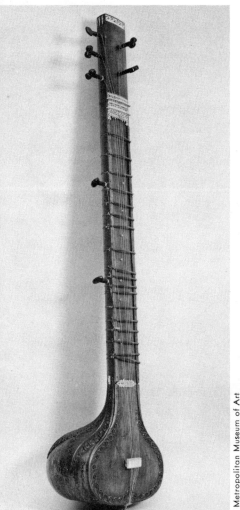

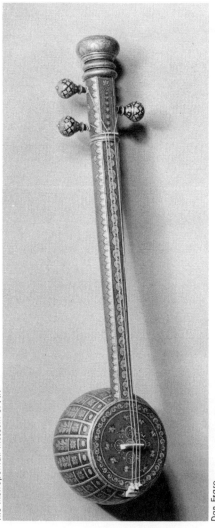

The Metropolitan Museum of Art

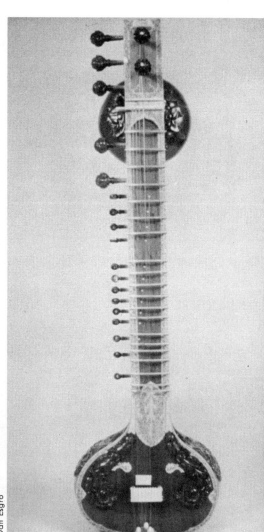

Don Esgro

SURBAHAR

A cousin of the sitar is the large, deep-toned *sur-bahar*. It has a flat resonating gourd attached to one end, and its extremely thick strings are tuned about five tones lower than the average sitar. This instrument is used exclusively to play the *alap*, *jor*, and *jhala* in the same way they used to be played on the *been*.

(Left) *Primitive tamboura with a neck of bamboo.*
(Center) *Extremely fine old tamboura with ivory inlays. Depicted on its face are the goddess Saraswati on a pea-*

TAMBOURA

The essential drone instrument is the *tamboura*, which is found in a wide range of sizes, many of them beautifully inlaid or richly decorated. The function of the *tamboura* is to sound the tonic repeatedly throughout a composition so that both the performer and the listener are always aware of the basic note of the *raga*. The *tamboura* therefore needs no frets; its open strings, numbering from four to six, are plucked continuously, one after the other, by the fingers without a plectrum.

cock, and the much-loved Ganesh, patron of new enterprises.
(Right) *Tamboura used today for accompanying vocal music.*

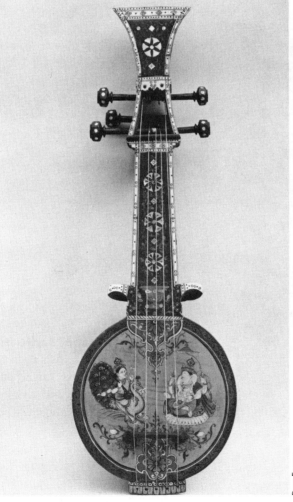

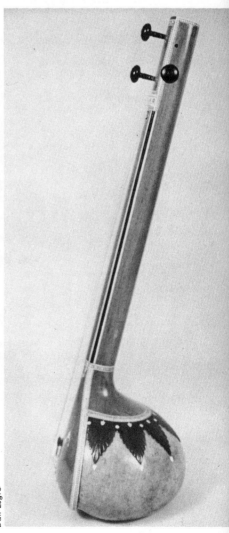

The Metropolitan Museum of Art

Don Esgro

SARANGI

Of the stringed instruments played with a bow, the *sarangi* is the most popular, and in the North it has the same importance as the violin which is used in the South. Most often, this heavy-bodied instrument is used to accompany *khyal* or *thumri* singing, but it can also be played for solo performances. The *sarangi* may have as many as forty sympathetic strings that vibrate under the playing strings. Usually the main three playing strings are made of gut, but if the instrument is tuned to a higher pitch, the first string may be of metal. As the performer holds the *sarangi*, its thick-waisted body and broad neck are in a vertical position. Several other bowed stringed instruments not as popular as the *sarangi* are the *dilruba*, *esraj*, and *sarinda*.

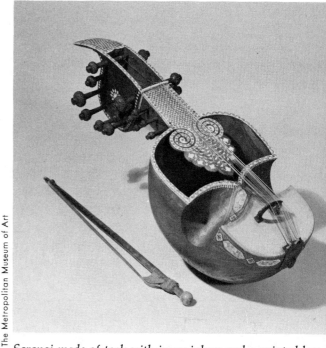

The Metropolitan Museum of Art

Sarangi made of teak with ivory inlays and a painted border around the parchment at the base. Note the delicate bow.

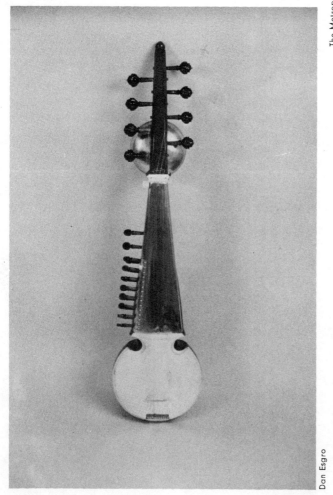

Dan Esgro

SAROD

Another prominent stringed instrument is the *sarod*, which is believed to be a descendant of the *rabab* found in Afghanistan. This instrument is most often played with a plectrum of coconut shell or ivory. The unfretted fingerboard is made of metal, and the main playing and rhythm strings and the sixteen sympathetic strings rest on a bridge that is fixed on a piece of hide.

Modern sarod, the instrument that brought my guru Allauddin Khan his fame.

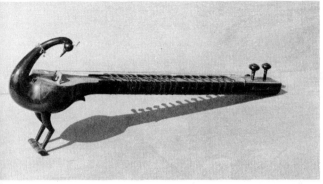

Taus or esraj with a carved and painted peacock at one end.

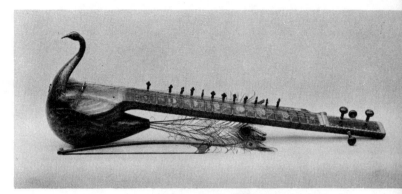

Peacock mayuri.

Two old harps. (Left) Viladi nada mandal. (Right) Suvar mandal.

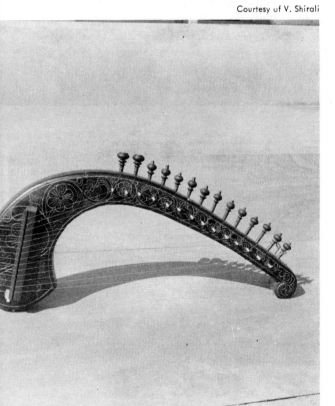

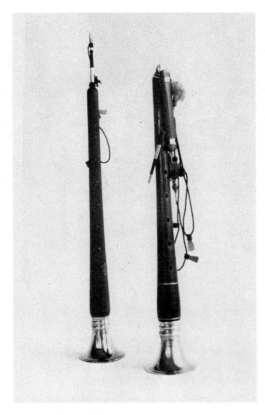

Two modern shahnai.

Tabla, the popular two-piece drum used in the North.
Eric Hayes

MURALI

The wind family includes a large number of flutes, usually made of bamboo, that come in many sizes and have varying numbers of holes. The flute associated traditionally with Lord Krishna is the *murali*, sometimes called the *bansari*, and Krishna playing his flute is a favorite theme in Indian art.

SHAHNAI

The other outstanding member of this family is the oboelike *shahnai*, which is thought to be an auspicious instrument and is often played outside a private home to celebrate house-warming, marriage, the birth of a child, or the sacred thread ceremony. It is also played for certain religious celebrations. Originally considered as more of a folk or popular instrument, over the past twenty-five years or so, the *shahnai* has gained in prestige, and it is now often heard in the concert hall as a solo instrument accompanied by an ensemble of drones and a drum.

TABLA

Of the multitude of drums that are found throughout India today, the most popular variety in the North is the *tabla*, which is actually two drums, each with one skin stretched across the top. The smaller of the two drums is the right-hand *tabla,* and the bass, left-hand drum is called the *banya*, though the two are called collectively *tabla*. The *tabla*, which can be tuned with a hammer and whose range is about an octave, has become popular only in the last two hundred years and is chiefly used to accompany *khyal* or *thumri* compositions and instrumental *gats*.

PAKHAWAJ

The drum that was preferred for accompanying the older, more heavy and serious *dhrupad* and *dhamar* singing and instrumental music played by the *been, rabab,* and *sursringar* was the *pakhawaj,* a one-piece drum made of clay with two faces or heads, tuned to different pitches. Today, however, the body of the *pakhawaj* is made of wood.

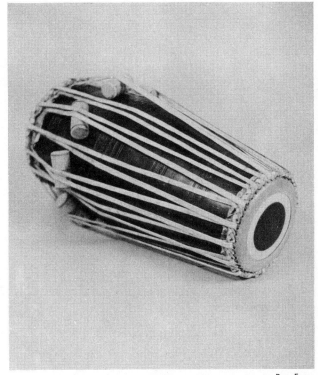

Dan Esgro

Pakhawaj.

A variety of drums: (upper left) *Tasha;* (upper right) *Duff;* (lower left) *Damaru;* (lower right) *the large drum is the huduk, the small one is the damaru.*

Courtesy of V. Shirali

Courtesy of V. Shirali

PERCUSSION

The percussion group (excluding drums, which are considered as a family apart) includes many kinds of bells, gongs, little cymbals, castanets, and the curious *jaltarang*—a series of porcelain bowls of graduated size, filled with water and played by striking the bowls with sticks.

A variety of cymbals and bells: (upper left) Khaj-tal, played by shaking and clacking together; (upper right) Jhanj, or hand cymbals; (below) Manjira, or smaller hand cymbals.

TWO

MY MASTERS

*The great Indian musicians,
innovators, and gurus*

THE BEGINNING
OF A TRADITION

Of the scholars, musicians, and patrons who made the contributions of highest value to Indian music over the past two thousand years, the first truly remarkable man was Narada. There were, in fact, quite a few Naradas, and there is a fairly widely accepted theory that "Narada" was used, more as a title than as a name, by a number of music scholars in ancient times. There is still some scholarly controversy as well over the dates of Narada's life, but most musicologists now agree that the Narada who is known to us by his great treatise on music lived in the first century A.D. He is celebrated for his book, the *Naradishiksha*, which treats in detail the principles and technique of the Vedic (*vaidika*) and post-Vedic (*laukika*) music.

In this work, the most valuable of all the *shikshas* (books of "trainings") of the period, Narada explains the notes, melody, and meter and describes music's sanctified and uplifting nature, which brings serenity and peace to the spirit of the listener. He deals with the three ancient scales (*gramas*), which were the basis of the old music, the five fundamental microtones that embody the sentiments and moods in their sounds; he dwells on the origins of the seven musical notes—said to derive from the different parts of the body. In his discussions, Narada brings up several types of *veenas* and tells how each is appropriate to a certain kind of music. Set down here for the first time was the fixed scale of the Vedic music (*samagana*)—the source of inspiration and development of all Indian music for more than two thousand years.

About the second century A.D. lived Bharata, whose dance-actor's handbook of the science of drama—the

Natyashastra—is one of the supremely valuable ancient texts we have on the theory of our music, and it is regarded even today with much respect. As in the case of Narada, it is believed that there were a number of Bharatas, and some say that this name was given as a title to great dance-actors. And so, this Bharata may not be the same Bharata Muni who is often mentioned in Indian mythology. The *Natyashastra*'s thirty-six chapters deal with information on stage performances; six chapters (28–33) are devoted specifically to the music associated with these dramas, and mention is made of music in other chapters. There are sections on the dancing and acting as well.

At this period in our history, music had already evolved to quite a high level, as we can see from texts on music written at the time. In about the sixth century B.C. a musical renaissance had taken place and a new and very well organized type of music—*gandharva*, or "celestial"—was devised by the scholar Druhina Brahma (who is sometimes also called Brahmabharata). Basing his great treatise on Brahma's work, Bharata, of the *Natyashastra*, carefully set down the essential laws and formulas of *gandharva* music. In this Bharata's time, *gandharva* music fell into three categories—sacred music played in the temples for rites and celebrations; music for the royal courts; and music used exclusively for dramatic presentations. Bharata discusses in great detail the *gandharva* music and explains every one of its components. The *gandharva* songs included the *dhruvā*, a religious type of song or hymn that was used in the operalike dramas, and Bharata speaks of these at great length in the *Natyashastra*. (One must be careful to distinguish between *dhruva* and *dhruvā*, with a long final "a," because the two are not at all the same either in structure or in use. *Dhruva* is a *nibaddha praband-ha* kind of song that developed at a later period—"*prabandha*" referring to a song not meant for dramatic performances—and *dhruvā* was used only for stage presentations.)

Besides giving extremely technical details on the elements of this music (such as discussions on the two *gramas* in use at the time, descriptions of the eighteen *jatis* [seven *shuddha* and eleven mixed] derived from

the two *gramas, tala,* and so on), Bharata narrates very completely every aspect of dramatic performances, which included dancing and music, like Greek tragedy or Western opera—staging, lighting, sets, kinds of auditoriums, and similar details. He tells of the instrumental ensembles, which included *veenas,* the *murali,* cymbals and various types of drums, that provided music for these plays and depicts the instruments, the arrangement of the players, and the process of tuning. To give an example of the thoroughness of this treatise, Bharata explains all the preliminaries of a stage performance, naming each of the separate steps: arrangement of the instruments, seating of the singers, vocal exercises for the singers, adjustment of the instruments for playing, tuning the string instruments, practicing the hand positions for keeping time, combined playing of the stringed instruments and drums. After all these preliminaries he describes, and quite a few more, the performance got under way.

THE NINE JEWELS

Kalidasa was a great poet-playwright who lived some time between the fourth and fifth centuries A.D., but his literary works are still read and very much appreciated today. Indeed, I have heard people mention Kalidasa on the same level as Shakespeare and Goethe; Rabindranath Tagore is the only other Indian literary figure of a comparable stature. In his dramas, Kalidasa incorporates many comments on music and dance; for example, he gives clear descriptions of various musical instruments, how they are used and how they are tuned, and he tells in detail of several types of dancing that were used in the dramatic presentations. Kalidasa lived in what is known as the Golden Period in Indian history, when the rulers of the Gupta dynasty were on the throne. During this time, classical dancing and, of course, music were enormously appreciated and encouraged in the royal court. The Maharaja Chandra-Gupta-Vikramaditya of Ujjain in the fifth century, a notable patron and connoisseur of the performing arts, kept in his court his "nine jewels"—nine of the finest representatives of the arts and sciences, and it is said that Kalidasa was one of his "jewels." At this time, many books were written on religion, politics, art, medicine, and astronomy, and these give us an excellent over-all view of the way of life and the development of culture in that period. The literary descriptions of the age are paralleled by stone sculpture in caves and temples that depict in extraordinarily vivid detail every aspect of human existence and are unmatched in their exquisite beauty and refinement.

Of the many scholars who lived in the centuries immediately after Bharata's time, the foremost is Matanga (some time between the fifth and seventh centuries A.D.), author of the *Brihaddeshi*, which is explained as an assemblage of regional musical forms of a mostly vocal nature called *deshi*. In the earliest centuries of this era, a type of music known as *deshi*, had been evolving parallel to *gandharva* and was taking in new *ragas* and songs and was using more instruments. As the *gandharva* music waned in popularity, the *deshi* music became more popular. Tunes of peoples from all the different parts of the country were being compiled and set down in the newer *deshi* system. (The *deshis* or *deshi prabandhas* were regional songs, but they were performed in a classical way.) Bharata had dealt with the *deshi* type of music in the *Natyashastra*, but Matanga expanded and completely defined it in the *Brihaddeshi*. This whole order of *deshi* music was remodeled and became the basis of another renaissance in Indian music. One of the beautiful things about Indian music is that nothing, no form, no style, is ever forgotten completely or abandoned. Rather, these forms and styles are modified and incorporated into the "new" system, so that our music is built up in layers, and each layer rests on and draws from the one beneath it. It is in the *Brihaddeshi* that we find the first definition of *raga* as we understand it today, though in earlier treatises, as we have already noted, the word *raga* was used in association with other basic scalar forms, such as *gramaraga* or *jatiraga*. It is an established fact that until about the time of Matanga, classical music was based on scale species whose foundations were

the modal structures called *jatis*, and it is now firmly believed that the *ragas* as we know them developed from the ancient *jatis*. Matanga speaks of many of the *ragas*, enumerating them and giving their characteristics.

In the musical heritage of North India, one of the foremost poets of distinction is Jayadeva, who lived in the middle of the twelfth century in the village of Kenduvilwa, now in West Bengal. Jayadeva is celebrated for his lyrical composition written mostly in Sanskrit (some liberties were taken with the language), called the *Geeta Govinda*, romantic and erotic poem-songs describing the love of Lord Krishna and Radha. These songs are in the *chhanda prabandha* style, "bound up" in meter, and each with its own designated *raga* and *tala*. Though the musical notation for each song is not included in the *Geeta Govinda*, the poem-songs have been quite popular and are sung even now by Hindustani and Karnatic musicians alike. These modern artists do not necessarily follow the *raga* and *tala* mentioned for each song in the work.

Sharangadeva, who lived in the early part of the thirteenth century, was an eminent scholar whose technical treatise, the *Sangeeta Ratnakara*, is still consulted and very much respected today. In this cardinal work, Sharangadeva discusses the broad range of musical forms, systematizes the old music theory, describes singing techniques of certain styles, dwells on the *prabandhas* (songs), enumerates one hundred eight different *talas*, and explains a multitude of musical terms, among them *grama*, *murchhana*, *shruti*, *jati*, and *alankar*. Sharangadeva, in the tradition of the scholars and commentators, set down his views and interpretations of musical developments from Bharata's *Natyashastra* through all the other outstanding musical treatises of ten centuries up to his own time. The *Sangeeta Ratnakara* is an astounding analysis of these ten centuries of music, as well as a complete up-dating and commentary on the music of Sharangadeva's own era. Our knowledge today of the *Sangeeta Ratnakara* comes from the version by Kallinatha, a scholar who, in the fifteenth century, wrote an extensive commentary on the work.

AMIR KHUSRU
AND THE "SEH TAR"

Shortly after the time of Sharangadeva, there lived an extraordinary innovator and genius, Amir Khusru, who was not only an unrivaled scholar and lover of music and skilled musician, but also a poet and statesman. He was of Persian lineage, but was born and brought up in India. He acquired his musical fame at the court of Sultan Allauddin Khilji, a Pathan ruler of Delhi, where he was a celebrated singer. Because of his musical talents and immense imitative powers, he was called Shrutidar, a name given to one who can reproduce any sound—musical or not—even if he has heard it only once. It is not unnatural that since he held such prominent positions, the historians of his time glorified him and gave him credit for many things that he really did not bring about. He is nonetheless responsible for a number of modifications of musical instruments, and in particular the sitar, for creating some *ragas* that are heard today, and for developing and popularizing some well-known styles of singing.

Many scholars believe that the sitar was in existence long before Amir Khusru's time, in diverse shapes in different regions of India. It was variously called *tritantri veena* (Sanskrit meaning "three-stringed"), *chitra veena* (seven-stringed), or *parivadini*. But it is an undeniable fact that Amir Khusru did make certain alterations and give the instrument a new name, "*seh tar*" (Persian for "three-stringed"). One of the innovations that he brought to the "*seh tar*" was to reverse the order of the strings, giving the instrument the present-day universal arrangement of the strings. Another ancient stringed instrument, the *been* or *veena*, still has its strings in the old "inside-out" order—that is, the main playing string is on the inside and the bass strings are on the part of the instrument that face toward the hand and the wrist of the musician as he holds the instrument. Another improvement that Amir Khusru brought to the sitar was to make the frets movable. (Frets are the metal strips or bars that go across the fingerboard of the instrument.) On the older instruments, such as the *veena*, the frets were fixed with wax and could not be moved; but Amir Khusru attached silken string or thin gut to the frets and tied them at the back of the sitar's neck, so that the player could slide them up or down. According to this method, the fingerboard was divided into the seven-note octave after eliminating some frets, and the frets could be moved up or down for the use of half or whole tones.

Before Amir Khusru's time, the classical songs (*chhanda prabandha*) were rendered in Sanskrit, which has the importance in the East that Latin has in the West. Sanskrit is often called "the language of the gods," and vast numbers of works on art, medicine, Hindu religion, science, and Indian culture have been recorded in it. Most scholarly texts on all subjects were written in Sanskrit until as recently as forty or fifty years ago. From Amir Khusru's time, the language of the classical songs changed from Sanskrit to Braja Bhasha, a Hindi dialect which is in use particularly in the region of Mathura and Vrindavan, and which lends itself well to musical settings.

Another of Amir Khusru's outstanding achievements was the cultivation and popularization of the *qawali* songs, which are still sung and appreciated today. Amir Khusru is said also to have set the groundwork for the *khyal* style of singing, some of whose elements were found in the *qawali* songs.

THE NORTH AND THE SOUTH

In the course of many centuries, two entirely different systems of music have arisen in India—the Hindustani system of the North and the Karnatic of the South. From about the thirteenth century, the musical systems of the North and the South split and continued along different lines, although they drew from one common heritage.

About the time of the fourteenth century, waves of invading peoples of foreign cultures swept across northern India, and eventually Mohammadan rulers took over control of that section of the country.

Under the new regime, a rather anticultural, even anti-Hindu policy was put into effect. Because of this, many scholars and musicians, disheartened by the situation, left the North and took up residence in other parts of India. Indeed, a great number of them, many of whom were devoutly religious Brahmins, fled to the South, where they felt their art and language would be better safeguarded and appreciated and cultivated to a much higher degree.

In the South, many musicians were in the service of Hindu rulers, and in many instances the temples also functioned as "patrons" for performing artists. Every temple had a large courtyard where concerts, discussions, and other programs could be held. In this way, there was a great deal of contact on the part of the common people with classical music. Anyone who pleased could attend musical programs given at the temples. In the North, on the other hand, classical music continued to be restricted mostly to the royal courts and to a small group of wealthy men who could afford to keep musicians in their households. Because of the openness of the system in the South and the musical interchange that was carried on, the Karnatic music developed in a highly organized manner, with very little irregularity in concept and approach.

Since vocal music is the basis of *all* Indian classical music, it is not difficult to understand why language played an important role in the evolutions of the Hindustani and Karnatic systems. Sanskrit was the language of the intellectuals, musician-scholars, and religious men. When the Mohammadan rulers came to power in the North, they were ignorant of the Sanskrit language. But what may seem like a mere linguistic difference on the part of the ruling Muslims was far deeper and amounted to a religious and cultural dichotomy. From this period on, Sanskrit no longer was the first language of Hindustani music, but was replaced, at least as far as vocal music is concerned, by the Braja Bhasha dialect.

In the South, apart from Sanskrit, the principal languages were—and are—Kanarese, Tamil, and Telugu, and great numbers of song texts were composed in both these tongues.

Another basic difference between the system of the North and that of the South is found in the presentation and approach to the music. Some Hindustani *ragas* that are played in the South are given altered names there. For example, the Hindustani *Jhinjoti* was renamed *Senjiroti* in the South, and *Raga Kafi* became *Raga Kapi*. Then, there are some *ragas* that use approximately the same notes in both systems but have entirely different names; *Raga Malkauns* of the North corresponds to *Hindolam* of the South, the Hindustani *Bhupali* and *Durga* are known respectively as *Mohanam* and *Suddhasaveri* in the Karnatic system. Some typical northern *ragas*, such as *Bihag*, *Khamaj* (or *Kamas*, as it is called in the South), and *Sindhi Bhairavi*, became quite popular in the South and kept more or less the same names. In many cases, too, a typical Southern *raga* may have the same name as a Northern one, and yet be quite different from it. The Karnatic *Todi*, *Bhairavi*, *Kanada*, and *Sahana ragas* are among these.

In general, Karnatic music is characterized by a far greater degree of precision than the music of the North, and it is based on a very strictly organized system. The percentage of fixed compositions played by artists is much greater, too. Embellishment on fixed forms is one of the prime elements of a Karnatic musical performance, whereas in the North, more stress is put on improvisation—reaching out beyond the basic forms. Perhaps because of the organization and logical arrangement in the Southern music, the Westerner often finds it easier to learn the Karnatic system, whether he is interested in vocal music, instruments, or the playing of the *mridangam*, the two-faced drum that is most popular in the South.

In the Karnatic system, instrumental music very closely follows the complete vocal pattern, even to the point of playing all the traditional song compositions in exactly the same way that a singer would render them. This certainly applies to such instruments as the *veena*, *venu*, or flute, and also to the violin. The violin has been the most popular bowed instrument in the South, functioning for the past three hundred years both as an accompaniment to vocal music and as a solo instrument in a master's hands. Its position is comparable to that of the *sarangi* in the North.

SHAPERS
OF KARNATIC MUSIC

Although this book deals primarily with Hindustani music, it would not be out of place to mention briefly some of the outstanding scholars and artists who helped shape the musical system of the South. Between the fourteenth and sixteenth centuries A.D., Vidyaranya, Ramamatya, and Vitthala all brought important innovations to their musical system. A pioneer in Karnatic music from the practical point of view rather than the theoretical was Purandhara Dasa, a composer of considerable importance in the sixteenth century, who is said to have written 475,000 songs, mostly in Kanarese and Sanskrit. Venkata-makhi, who lived in the early part of the seventeenth century, is famous for his scholarly work, *Chatur-dandi Prakashika*, and for his reforms in the scale system. Three musicians who all lived about one hundred fifty years ago are considered as the "musical trinity" of Karnatic music: Swami Tyagaraja, Muttu

Swami Dikshitar, and Shyama Sastri. Tyagaraja was a great composer and wrote all his songs in the Southern court language, Telugu. It is said that music flowed out of him like gushes of water out of a fountain. He was a worshiper of Lord Rama (an incarnation of Vishnu) and was a very pious man. All of his songs have as their subject Lord Rama and his accomplishments. These songs are known today as *kritis*, and at least one is traditionally included in any recital of Karnatic music. Dikshitar and Shyama Sastri both composed great bodies of songs, mostly in Sanskrit. These are beautiful, gemlike compositions in a slow or medium tempo and are, for the most part, religious songs. When we say "religious songs," we are not necessarily speaking of songs of a spiritual and holy nature, but rather of songs whose central characters are religious figures, such as Shiva, Krishna, or Rama. These godly characters are portrayed as human beings, with all the pathos, humor, and love of mortals. The songs can be rendered either with a religious intention or as a narrative of the gods' adventures.

Lord Krishna has offended Radha and been rejected for chasing other gopis. He now humbles himself before her. Radha's handmaiden encourages the girl to forgive him. Early seventeenth-century Rajput manuscript.

In a late miniature, Lord Krishna, traditionally represented as blue-skinned, walks with his love Radha in the idyllic groves of Vrindavan. The peacocks (foreground) are a symbol of longing and love.

The Metropolitan Museum of Art

THE GREAT REAWAKENING

The period of almost two hundred years following Amir Khusru is considered the "Dark Period" in Northern Indian history. Wars raged continuously, and cultural progress came to a stop. But then, parallel with the Renaissance in fifteenth- and sixteenth-century Europe, there came a reawakening in India's culture. In our musical history, the first outstanding name of this period is Raja Man Singh Tomar of Gwalior, who is chiefly known for his organization of the *dhruvapada* style of singing. With the help of some of the great versatile musicians known as *nayakas*, Raja Man revised the *dhruvapada* style of singing, a development of *prabandha* singing, and gave it new direction and shape. During the Dark Period this style had been kept alive by the Vaishnav sect, followers of Vishnu, who were saint-musicians in the city of Vrindavan, on the banks of the river Jamuna, just north of the central part of India. Raja Man brought the style back into favor and encouraged many new *dhrupad* compositions in praise of gods or goddesses or emperors. He also held music symposia and assemblies, and organized one of the very early schools of music.

Swami Haridas, a famous yogi, Hindu saint, and singer who belonged to this Vaishnav sect lived in Vrindavan most of his life and, though he was never attached to any royal court, he was known as one of the foremost musicians before and during the early part of Akbar's reign in the sixteenth century. Swami Haridas imparted his remarkable knowledge on musical subjects to Tan Sen, whose name stands out as the most highly respected in the entire Hindustani musical tradition of the North. Tan Sen's accomplishments and the force and effect of his music prompted many stories about him. The stories are all a conglomeration of historical fact and vivid legend that have been woven together and handed down from one generation of musicians to the next.

We have been told, for example, that thanks to the blessings of a Muslim saint, Hazarat Pir Mohammad Ghaus, in Gwalior a certain Brahmin and his wife had a son whom they named Ramtanu. The saint had

foretold that the child would become very famous when he grew up. As a young boy, Ramtanu showed no signs of fulfilling this prediction. He was, however, able to imitate any sound he heard. One day, when Swami Haridas and some of his disciples were camped in the forest, young Ramtanu hid himself behind a tree and roared like a tiger. The disciples were terrified, but Swami Haridas, who realized there were no tigers in that region, found the boy and recognized his extraordinary talents. He was so impressed with the boy that he asked permission from Ramtanu's father to take him as a disciple. And so, for ten years, Ramtanu stayed with the Swami. Then he joined the court of Rani Mrignaini, the widowed queen of Raja Man Singh at Gwalior, where the Muslim saint who had predicted his fame lived. At the royal court, Ramtanu fell in love with a beautiful Muslim girl and, encouraged by the Queen and the saint, the two were married. Ramtanu became a Muslim, and his name was changed to Ata Mohammad Khan. He returned to Vrindavan occasionally to learn at the feet of Swami Haridas and to enlarge his musical repertory. The Swami, who was quite old, soon died, and not long afterward the Muslim died as well, leaving all his fortune to Ata Mohammad. The young man acquired great powers of yoga and Sufi mysticism (a Muslim cult) from the Hindu swami and the Muslim saint. After having served several years at the court of Raja Ram, the ruler of Rewa, Ata Mohammad became the chief musician in the court of Emperor Akbar the Great at Agra and the first of the Emperor's "nine jewels." Emperor Akbar, like the great Gupta ruler Vikramaditya, was a patron of the arts all throughout his reign, and during his time much progress in music was made by scholars and performers, and the *dhrupad* style of singing reached its highest popularity and growth. Akbar gave Ata Mohammad the title of Mian Tan Sen, by which he has been known ever since.

Tan Sen is said to have had tremendous occult power and to have performed miracles through his music. By singing *Raga Deepak*, he was supposed to have been able to light the oil lamps, or by singing *Raga Megh Malhar*, to bring rain. Tan Sen was said to be *nad-siddha*, which means that he had complete mastery over sound, especially musical sound. He either created or, according to some scholars, popularized a number of *ragas* that are still associated with his name, such as *Mian ki Malhar, Mian ki Todi, Mian ki Sarang,* and *Darbari Kanada.* Tan Sen also invented a stringed instrument called the *rabab,* somewhat different from the Persian or Afghanistani *rabab,* and he called it *rudra been.*

THE DESCENDANTS OF TAN SEN

From Tan Sen descended two famous lineages of musical tradition (*gharanas*). One sprang from his son Bilas Khan and is known as the Rababiya *gharana,* because its members play the kind of *rabab* invented by Tan Sen. The other lineage stems from the family of Tan Sen's daughter Saraswati, who was married to a noted *been* player, Misri Singh (who was later renamed Nabat Khan, upon his conversion to Islam). This branch, called the Beenkar *gharana,* was named after the principal instrument its members employed —the *been.* Although Tan Sen and his family were converted to Islam, they maintained the sanctity and deep spiritual quality inherent in Hindus in executing the *rag alapana* either vocally or instrumentally and in singing the *dhrupad* compositions. They also practiced the Hindu, yogic, and Tantric exercises in order to have control of breathing, of the body, and of the mind.

Niyamat Khan, who later received the title Shah Sadarang, meaning "always colorful," was a musician in the court of Emperor Mohammad Shah in the first half of the eighteenth century and a member of the Beenkar *gharana.* As we have already noted, he was responsible for bringing the *khyal* style of singing to full bloom and for giving it the prestige that it did not have earlier. *Khyal* singing existed in a rough form in the thirteenth century at the time of Amir Khusru and was considerably improved upon in the fifteenth century when the Sharqui rulers were in power. Sadarang himself composed hundreds of thousands of *khyal* songs in almost all the different *ragas* that are still sung with much ardor.

Thanks to some of the descendants of Tan Sen who belonged to the Rababiya and Beenkar families, chiefly Nirmal Shah, Omrao Khan, and Bahadur Sen, many good instrumentalists emerged in the last half of the nineteenth century as outstanding musicians. The first two of these men were excellent *been* players themselves, and Bahadur Sen was a noted performer on the *sursringar;* all were very great teachers, or *ustads,* the word having much the same meaning as *guru.* They were responsible for guiding and nourishing many well-known players of the instruments they brought into vogue—the sitar, the *surbahar,* and the *sarod.* Among their disciples were Bande Ali Khan, a *been* player who established the Kirana *gharana* of the *khyal* singing style, Ghulan Hussein and his son Sajjad Hussein who were *surbahar* players, Enayat Hussein Saswanwale who was a *khyal* singer, Mithailal, a *been* player, Pannalal Bajpeyi, the sitarist, Fida Hussein, *sarod* player, and others too numerous to note here. The musicians mentioned here are among the great masters of the late nineteenth and early twentieth centuries who passed on the tradition of Tan Sen to their own disciples.

Mohammad Khan of the Rababiya *gharana* and Wazir Khan of the Beenkar *gharana* were the last of the giants belonging to the Tan Sen family and tradition, although Wazir Khan's grandson Dabir Khan is now living in Calcutta and is respected for his playing of the *been* and singing *dhrupad* and *dhamar* compositions.

Three truly eminent *dhrupad* singers of the early part of this century were Allabanda and his son Nasiruddin Khan, and Zakiruddin Khan (elder brother of Allabanda), whose grandsons, the Dagar brothers, have faithfully maintained the tradition of singing *dhrupad dhamar.*

Emdad Khan was one of the outstanding sitar players of this century and, inspired by the great *surbahar* player Sajjad Mohammad, he also took up this instrument. Emdad Khan's son Enayat Khan was one of the most sought-after sitarists of his generation. When he died in 1938, his son Vilayat Khan was only fourteen; he has since blossomed to become one of the prominent sitar players today.

Two great scholars and teachers of this century

have contributed enormously to the scientific development and cultivation of our music. The first of these is Vishnu Digambar Paluskar, a follower of the Gwalior *gharana* of *khyal* singers. Himself a superb artist, he became in the last part of his life an extremely religious, even saintly, man and then turned to singing mostly for devotional songs. Under his personal guidance, many music students became famous singers. Another of his contributions was a number of volumes of song compositions, mostly in the *khyal* style, notated in a system he himself evolved. Vishnu Digambar's primary achievement was the founding of schools of music, known as Gandharva Sangeet Maha Vidyalaya, in some of the major cities of India. Through schools, rather than through the direct *guru-shishya* system, it became possible for great numbers of young people to study our musical traditions. Until quite recently most of the professional musicians in North India suffered a very unfavorable reputation that was quite like that of the great painters in Paris at the turn of the century. They were respected for their art, but severely criticized and even shunned because of the degraded lives they led. Occasionally, similar criticism has been directed at some of the old jazz musicians of America. With the establishment of these music schools, boys and girls of good and educated families were once again encouraged to take up music.

The other name so vital to the bringing of classical music to the public throughout modern India is V. N. Bhatkhande, who in the early twenties founded the Marris College of Music in Lucknow, which is now called Bhatkhande Sangeet Vidyapeeth. This scholar introduced musicology along with musical training and organized many conferences and symposia which were attended by scholars of highest distinction. V. N. Bhatkhande had published many volumes of traditional *chizas* (Urdu for "song texts," or "compositions") and several books on music theory, and he devised a system of musical notation that is now the most generally employed for the graphic recording of Hindustani music. Though he was not a performer, he traveled widely and took great pains in collecting invaluable compositions of *dhrupad*, *dhamar*, *khyal*, and *tarana*.

MY REVERED GURU

A famous disciple of Wazir Khan and an extraordinary teacher and performer himself is Ustad Allauddin Khan of Maihar in Central India. This saintly and learned man became my revered *guru*, and it is to him that I owe my devotion and love for my musical training.

I saw him for the first time at the All-Bengal Music Conference in December, 1934. In contrast to the other musicians, who were wearing colorful costumes, turbans, and jewels, and were bedecked with medals, he seemed very plain and ordinary, not at all impressive. But even in my immaturity, it did not take me long to realize that he had qualities that far outshone the gaudiness of his colleagues. He seemed to shine with a fire that came from within him. Although I did not know enough about music then to discern his musical greatness, I found myself completely overwhelmed by everything about him. Baba has always been a strict disciplinarian with his students, but he had imposed upon himself an even stricter code of conduct when he was a young man, often practicing sixteen to twenty hours a day, doing with very little sleep, and getting along with a minimum of material things. Sometimes, when he practiced, he tied up his long hair with heavy cord and attached an end of the cord to a ring in the ceiling. Then, if he happened to doze while he practiced, as soon as his head nodded, a jerk on the cord would pull his hair and awaken him. From early childhood, Baba was ready and determined to make any sacrifice for music. Indeed, his entire life has been devoted to music.

Allauddin Khan was one of the sons of a quite well-to-do peasant family in Bengal. They did not have a great deal of money, but were very rich in the land they owned and the animals they kept. His family were Bengali Muslims, converted to Islam only three or four generations before. The village they lived in was predominantly Hindu, and they all spoke Bengali. And so, even though his family were Muslim, Baba knew all the ways of Hindus and was well acquainted with their customs and ceremonies. Later, he was to follow a way of life that was a beautiful fusion of the best of both Hinduism and Islam.

His father used to play the sitar for the family and for his own pleasure. And Baba's older brother, Afta-buddin, was a very talented and versatile musician who, too, did not perform professionally but played solely to express the music he felt within himself. In his later years, he became a very religious man and was revered equally by the Hindus and the Muslims who knew him. So it was natural that the musical inclinations of little Alam, as my *guru* was called by his family, were intensified by listening to his father with the sitar and his brother playing a variety of instruments, including the flute, harmonium (a small, boxlike keyboard instrument), *tabla, pakhawaj,* and *dotara* (a plucked-string instrument with two strings). Young Alam used to steal into the little music room at home to try to play some of his older brother's musical instruments—and was frequently punished for it. When his family realized that Alam had this burning love for music, they became worried that he might decide to be a professional musician and did not encourage him, for music was not thought of as a respectable profession for a young man. When young Alam wanted to leave his home and devote all his life to music, his brother, the influential one in the family, refused to let him go. The family much preferred that he take up regular studies in a school.

Baba has told us that by the time he was eight he could no longer take the strict discipline and enforced study of books. He hated studying and was constantly being punished for pursuing the thing he loved most —music. So, he left his family without saying a word and traveled to a nearby village, where he joined a party of traveling musicians led by a very famous player of the *dhol.* (Though the drums known as *dhol* or *dholak* are found all over India in different sizes and shapes, the *dhol* mentioned here is indigenous to Bengal. It is a one-piece drum with two faces and is played with the hand on the right side and with a stick on the left.) Baba told the musicians he was an orphan, and they accepted him into their group, feeling sorry for the lonely little boy. Then he traveled with the musicians as they toured, and they reached the city of Dacca, the capital of the present East Pakistan. While he was a member of this musical group, Baba had the opportunity to learn to play quite proficiently many varieties of drums—the *dhol, tabla,* and *pakhawaj*—and he also took up the *shahnai* and some other wind instruments—clarinet, cornet, and trumpet. During all the time Baba toured with this troupe of musicians and later stayed in Dacca, he did not communicate with his family. They were of course distraught when they realized he had left. They searched and searched for him, but finally had to give up.

BABA'S EARLY ADVENTURES

The first forty years of Baba's life were full of adventure, and he underwent many unusual, almost unbelievable, experiences through his intense love of music. Baba was never clear about how long he was with these musicians or how much time he spent in Dacca, but he says that he arrived in Calcutta when he was about fourteen or fifteen. I remember his telling me about the hardships he suffered there.

He went to one of the most famous Bengali singers of the day, Nulo Gopal, a very devout and orthodox Hindu. Baba instinctively thought it might be better if he said he was a Hindu himself when he approached this teacher, so he took a Hindu name. Nulo Gopal saw the tremendous ardor and talent for singing this boy had, but he warned Baba that he himself had learned music in a very old, traditional style and said that he would teach Baba only if Baba had the patience to learn in the same way. That is, Baba would have to learn and practice nothing other than the *sargams, palta,* and *murchhana* (solfeggio, scales, and exercises) for twelve full years. Only then would Nulo Gopal start teaching all the traditional compositions. This, he said, would not take a very long time, because Baba would already have a firm background! Baba did agree to the arrangement, and arduously devoted himself to his study, but unfortunately, after only seven years or so, Nulo Gopal died. Baba was so grieved by his death that, out of respect to his teacher, he took an oath never to take up singing as his profession. According to Baba, the excellent training he received from this *guru* in those seven years caused his musical sensitivity to grow to such a degree that he could notate in his mind as well as on paper any music he heard. This ability was to prove very helpful to him later.

During the seven years Baba was learning with Nulo Gopal, he took a job at the Star Theatre (run by Girish Ghosh, the father of Bengali drama) as a *tabla* player in the orchestra to make a little money, and he had some training in the playing of the violin from an outstanding Indian Christian teacher. Baba also participated in the frequent orchestral parties held by a prominent composer, Habu Dutt, who was the brother of the famed Swami Vivekananda. Habu Dutt had studied both Eastern and Western music and maintained an orchestra for which he composed in *raga* and *tala* framework; he used all the Western instruments as well as a few Indian ones. This later inspired Baba to create his own ensemble, the Maihar Band, which was quite famous for many years.

It was often frightening just to hear Baba talk about the hardships he suffered as a young man in Calcutta. The little pay he received at the Star Theatre and occasional extra income he got by playing a recital here or there all went to pay for gifts or offerings he brought to his teachers—fruits or sweets—in gratitude for their giving him lessons. Most of the time he had his one meal a day at some *anna chhatra*, a food dispensary provided for the poor by some rich families. (Until very recently, these existed in all the large cities as a common form of charity.) The rest of the day Baba either went hungry or nibbled at a handful of chick peas and drank the water of the river Ganges. He had no one particular place to stay. Sometimes he took a room in a cheap boarding-house, and other times he stayed in the stable of a wealthy family.

When he was in his twenties, Baba went to a city called Muktagacha, then in eastern Bengal, now in East Pakistan. It was here, at the court of Raja Jagat Kishore, that he heard the celebrated *sarod* player of the time, Ustad Ahmad Ali, and for the first time, he experienced the full effect of the musician and the beauty of the music. In his studies under Nulo Gopal, Baba had felt he was approaching the field of strict classical music, but when his *guru* died, he thought

he had reached only the threshold of the musical sanctuary. He realized he needed another good teacher to elevate him to a higher level in his playing and understanding. So, he decided just then, in the Raja's court, that he must take this musician as his *guru* and learn to play the *sarod*. Baba's burning desire to learn and a recommendation from the Raja persuaded Ahmad Ali to accept the boy as his disciple. When Baba began learning from Ahmad Ali, he gave up all his old dilettante musical interests and devoted himself solely to the *sarod*. The next four years or so were spent living and traveling with his *ustad*, serving him in every way, even cooking, and learning and practicing music as much as he could.

After some time, Ahmad Ali left the court and traveled to his home, the city of Rampur, taking Baba with him. By this time, Baba had learned a great deal of the art and technique of the *sarod* and had absorbed most of the knowledge of his *ustad*. Somehow, he felt that Ahmad Ali was a bit apprehensive about Baba's proficiency and was afraid that Baba might outdo him as a musician. One day, it happened that his *guru* called Baba and said that he had given him enough *taleem* (training) and praised him for achieving a fine standard of musicianship. Now, he said, it is time for you to go out and perform, and establish your own reputation, following the tradition of *sikkha*, *dikkha*, and *parikkha* (derivations from the original Sanskrit of *shiksha*, *diksha*, and *pariksha*, which mean training, initiation, and evaluation).

Since Rampur was the most important seat of Hindustani classical music, Baba was overjoyed when he learned there were almost five hundred musicians who belonged to the court of His Highness the Nawab of Rampur. Out of these, at least fifty ranked among the foremost artists and were famed throughout India. They included singers of *dhrupad*, *dhamar*, *khyal*, *tappa*, and *thumri*, as well as players of *been*, *sursringar*, *rabab*, *surbahar*, sitar, *sarangi*, *shahnai*, *tabla*, *pakhawaj*, and many other instruments. At the head of all these musicians was the truly great Wazir Khan himself, a member of the Beenkar *gharana*, and thus of the family of Tan Sen. He was the *guru* of the Nawab and, in his seat next to the Nawab's

53

throne, enjoyed a position that was unique at that time. After taking leave of Ustad Ahmad Ali, Baba went on a kind of musical "binge," and he met all the *ustads* and studied a little with a great many of them for a year or so. He was completely intoxicated with the ecstasy of meeting all these great musicians. After Baba settled down a bit, he decided he must finally go to learn from the greatest musician of them all, and the one about whom he had heard so many stories—Wazir Khan.

A GESTURE IN DESPERATION

Ustad Wazir Khan, a direct descendant of Tan Sen, was the greatest living *been* player of the time. Filled with enthusiasm and bubbling with hope, Baba went off to meet him, but the sentries who guarded Ustad Wazir Khan's gates, frowning at the young man's shabby dress and poor appearance, denied him entrance. In despair, young Allauddin Khan rather melodramatically decided that he would either learn from this great master or give up his life. Nourishing these severe thoughts, he bought two *tola* weight of opium with which to kill himself if necessary. But fortunately, he met a *mullah* (Muslim priest), who dissuaded him from such extreme measures and suggested another plan.

The *mullah* composed a letter in Urdu in behalf of the young aspirant, explaining how he had come all the way from Bengal especially to learn from Ustad Wazir Khan, and if that were to prove impossible, he would swallow a lump of opium and end his life. But there remained the problem of presenting the letter to the Nawab. While the spirit of desperation was mounting, young Allauddin happened to hear that the Nawab would soon be on his way to the theater, so he stationed himself on the road, hours ahead, and as the Nawab's vehicle finally approached, he threw himself down in front of it. The police dragged young Allauddin Khan away to face the Nawab, who, when he heard the whole story, was so impressed by the fervor of a young man ready

to use such grave methods that he called him to the palace to play for him.

Baba gave a very impressive performance on the *sarod* and on the violin, and then was asked if he could handle any other instruments. The Nawab was quite amused when Baba, replying, boasted that he could play any instrument available in the palace. So, all the instruments were brought out and, to the astonishment of everyone present, he did just that —one by one, he played them all, and quite deftly, too! The Nawab asked him if he had any other talents, and Baba said that he could write anything played or sung. The Nawab was overwhelmed when Baba did this easily on the first attempt. The Nawab then sang him a very difficult *gamak tan*, a complicated embellishment in a phrase. Fortunately, young Allauddin had detected that the Nawab was becoming a little annoyed at the thought that such a young man might know more than he, and so he meekly replied that such a *tan* would be difficult to write down. The Nawab was so pleased at this that, in a benevolent mood, he sent for Ustad Wazir Khan and recommended young Allauddin to him as a deserving student. The Nawab himself called for a large silver tray full of gold sovereigns, sweets, material for new clothing, a ring, and new shoes. All these were given to Wazir Khan on behalf of the disciple, and the binding ceremony between Wazir Khan as *guru* and Allauddin Khan as *shishya* took place on the spot.

As Baba has said, from the time he moved to Calcutta until he came to Rampur, he had communicated with his family and had visited their home several times. His family, hoping they could give him a reason to stay with them, forced him to take a wife on one of his visits, and later, had him marry a second time. (Muslims may marry up to four times.) But to their horror, Baba ran away from home on the day after each marriage ceremony. His fanatic love for music left no room for such things as marriage or a family then.

In his first two and a half years as a disciple of Wazir Khan, Baba more or less had the duties of a servant and errand boy to his *guru* and was not really being taught music by him. Baba was rather unhappy about this, but he still spent as much time as he could practicing what he had learned from Ahmad Ali and others on the *sarod*. Then one day, there came a telegram to him in care of Wazir Khan, asking him to come home immediately because his second wife had tried to commit suicide and was critically ill. She was an extremely beautiful woman, and the people of her village had tormented her, saying she could not keep her husband at home for all her good looks, and teased her to such an extent that in her unhappiness she tried to kill herself. Wazir Khan had the telegram read (it was in English) before passing it on to Baba. He was shocked and not a little angry to learn about this, because Baba had told him that he was completely alone and had no family. Immediately, he summoned Baba. After being interrogated, Baba tremblingly revealed the truth. When the great man heard the story, he was deeply moved. He realized that this was a young man with an unheard-of, abnormal desire to learn music, a love so strong that he would forsake anything else in life, including the love of two young and beautiful wives.

In tears, Wazir Khan embraced Baba, saying he had never realized any of these things, and he felt extremely sorry that he had not paid any attention to Baba in those two and a half years. Then he advised Baba to go home for a while, and as soon as he had straightened matters out, to return to Rampur. Wazir Khan promised that he would consider Baba as his foremost and best disciple outside of his own family, and said he would teach him all the secrets of the art of music that the members of Tan Sen's family possess. "I'll teach you all the *dhrupad* and *dhamar* songs," he said, "and the technique and different *baj* [styles of playing] of the *been*, *rabab*, and *sursringar*." He qualified his vow, however, by saying he could never permit Baba to play the *been*, because it is traditionally restricted to the Beenkar *gharana*—his family—and he warned that if Baba were to play it Baba would never have an heir and his family would die out. Then Wazir Khan further explained that it would be quite possible for Baba to use all the techniques and styles of playing the *been* on the *sarod*, and he agreed to teach him to play the *rabab* and *sursringar*, two instruments that were going out of use at that time.

Wazir Khan did indeed keep his promises. Baba told us that many years later, when he was serving His Highness the Maharaja of Maihar, one day news arrived that Wazir Khan was on his deathbed. Baba rushed straightway to Rampur to be with his *guru*. Wazir Khan blessed him before he died, saying that Baba's name and the names of his disciples would live forever and carry on the great tradition of the Beenkar *gharana* and the glory of Mian Tan Sen.

THE REMARKABLE "IMPURIST"

Few people have any idea of the contributions Baba has made to the world of music, especially in the instrumental field. Above all, I feel, he is responsible for enlarging the scope and range of possibilities open to an instrumentalist. He has led us away from the confines of narrow specialization that prevailed in our music really through the first quarter of this century. Until then, one player would do only music of a light and delicate nature, and another would perform only romantic compositions; some musicians were purely spiritual and others emphasized the "materialistic" side of the music—the wealth of embellishment. Because Ustad Allauddin Khan, as a young man, was taught by so many masters, he learned a variety of styles of singing and playing and acquired a good many instrumental techniques—wind and bowed and plucked-string instruments, and even drums. And so he very naturally incorporated in his playing of the *sarod* some of the characteristics of diverse vocal styles and of the playing styles associated with a number of different instruments. He is known mainly as a *sarod* player, but he also performed on several other instruments. He was equally well known as a violinist, and as he did with the *sarod*, he played the violin with his left hand. Three stringed instruments that he did not perform on in concerts are the *been*, the sitar, and the *surbahar*, although he was acquainted with their techniques.

Musicians who follow Baba's example may now choose from a great many vocal and instrumental styles—*alap*, *dhrupad-dhamar*, *khyal*, *tarana*, *tappa*, *thumri*—and synthesize, creating a whole new concept in interpretation and performance.

Baba faced much criticism in the beginning, as indeed, some of us, as his disciples, have been and are still facing. Early in his career, he was reproached for not playing "pure *sarod*" when he performed and was criticized for bringing other techniques into his playing. I myself, when I began public appearances, faced the charge of not playing "pure sitar" and of having *sarod* techniques in my music, because I had learned from a *sarod* player. And I remember clearly that even into the late 1930s, sitar playing was restricted to a very limited dimension, and the players kept to their favorite specialized areas of music. There were some who used a small sitar for the "authentic" sitar *baj* (here *baj* means style of playing) and played only medium-slow Masitkhani *gats* with simple *tans* (or phrases), a style of composition created by Masit Khan. There were others who played only medium-fast Rezakhani *gats* and still others who used a rather large sitar and played it more or less in the way one plays the *surbahar* (a large, deep-sounding instrument with very thick strings). I have heard the well-known sitarist Enayat Khan play the *alap, jor,* and *jhala* (first three movements of a *raga*) on the *surbahar,* then put aside that instrument and take up a small sitar to do the fast Rezakhani *gat.* His father, Emdad Khan, is known to have done the same thing.

The criticisms of "impurity" of style are likely to come from other musicians who use the same instrument, and they and their admirers can cause quite a storm of differing opinion. Also, musicians who do not belong to one strong and well-established *gharana* are often open to harsh judgments. A musician who is a member of a certain *gharana* may—and often does—change his style, enriching and expanding it after hearing other musicians and interpreting their ideas in his own way. But, if questioned about this, he has recourse to the shelter of his *gharana.* He can claim that there is a precedent for what he has done and trace it back through his own *gharana*'s traditions. Often, though, I am amazed that a musician who upholds the highest tradition can be cruelly criticized if he also happens to be a creative artist and brings about many innovations. The great Tan Sen and then

Sadarang and even Allauddin Khan faced this sort of criticism early in their careers, but later their "innovations" became part of our musical tradition, and were well established through their disciples. That is one of the beauties of Indian classical music—that since the Vedas it has never stood stagnant, but has kept on growing and being enriched by the great creative geniuses of successive generations.

As a teacher, Baba aims at perfecting the hand and finger technique of the student. No matter what instrument the student may choose, Baba insists that the student who shows promise should also learn to sing the *palta, sargams,* and other song compositions, carefully delineating the scope of the *raga* and its distinctive notes and phrases and correctly using the microtones, or *shrutis,* to give the proper effect to the music and make it come alive. The reason for this is, of course, that the basis of our music is vocal, and it is composed primarily of melody, of embellishment, and of rhythm; any melodic phrase, with or without a definite rhythm, that can be sung can also be played on an instrument, with each instrument's own features bringing a special quality to the sound. According to our tradition, even the instrumentalists are required to have a moderate command of the voice. This makes it easier for them when they take on the role of teacher to instruct their students, merely by singing the *gats,* or *tans,* or *todas,* or even the *alap, jor,* and *jhala.* Along with the ability to sing the melodies, Baba recommends that his students learn to play the *tabla* and acquire a good knowledge of *taladhaya* (rhythmics). In mastering the fundamentals, the student learns all the technique of properly handling the instrument of his choice, working in the particular idiom, tonal range, and musical scope of a given instrument by practicing scales, *palta, sargams,* and *bols* taught by the *guru.* Generally, Baba starts with basic *ragas* like *Kalyan* for the evening and *Bhairav* for the morning, first giving many pieces of "fixed music" in the form of *gats, tans,* or *todas* based on the *raga.* By "fixed music" I do not mean music that is written down as it is in the West; rather I am referring to what we call *bandishes,* which literally means "bound down," but in this context means "fixed." These are vocal or instrumental pieces, either traditional compositions or the teacher's own, that students learn and memorize by playing over hundreds, even thousands, of times, to be able to produce the correct, clear sound, intonation, and phrasing. Thus, Baba lays a solid foundation for the student to know the sanctified framework of the *ragas* and *talas*.

When the student, after some years of training, has fairly good control of the basic technique of the instrument and has learned a few more important morning and evening *ragas* (*Sarang, Todi, Bhimpalasi, Bhairav, Yaman Kalyan, Bihag,* and so on) and has some mastery of the fundamentals of solo playing, then he may expand his creative faculties and is encouraged to improvise as he plays. But he has to be careful not to impinge on the purity of the *raga*. That is, his playing must be correct both in technique and interpretation. The right feeling of a *raga* is something that must be taught by the *guru* and nurtured from the germ of musical sensitivity within the student. Unlike some other musicians, Baba has never been stingy or jealous about passing on to deserving students the great and sacred art that he possesses. In fact, when he is inspired in his teaching, it is as if a

Baba reprimands an erring musician with his cane at a concert given in his honor by the Maihar Band.

Eric Hayes

floodgate had opened up and an ocean of beautiful and divine music were flowing out. The disciple spends many hours simply listening to his *guru*, and then he endeavors to fill up the frame of a *raga* with improvised passages born out of the compelling mood of the moment or enlarged through his own attempts at improvisation as his understanding grows and he becomes more familiar with a particular *raga*. At first, the student may improvise only a fraction of his performance, but as his musicianship matures, so his confidence grows, and he improvises more and more. It is, in a way, like learning to swim. It is exhilarating in the beginning to feel your own body moving through the water, but you are afraid to swim far and there is always the fear of losing control somehow. So it is with a *raga*. You are always a little afraid at first that you will make mistakes, play the wrong notes, and go out of a *raga* or lose count of the rhythm as the *raga* carries you along, but your confidence keeps growing, and one day, you feel you have complete control over what you are playing. A truly excellent and creative musician of the Hindustani system will improvise anywhere from fifty to ninety per cent of his music as he performs, but this freedom can come about only after many many years of basic study and discipline and organized training (if he has a good deal of talent to begin with), and after profound study of the *ragas*, and finally, if he has been blessed with *guru-kripa*, the favor of the *guru*.

When I myself start to perform a *raga*, the first thing I do is shut out the world around me and try to go down deep within myself. This starts even when I am concentrating on the careful tuning of the sitar and its *tarafs* (sympathetic strings). When, with control and concentration, I have cut myself off from the outside world, I step onto the threshold of the *raga* with feelings of humility, reverence, and awe. To me, a *raga* is like a living person, and to establish that intimate oneness between music and musician, one must proceed slowly. And when that oneness is achieved, it is the most exhilarating and ecstatic moment, like the supreme heights of the act of love or worship. In these miraculous moments, when I am so much aware of the great powers surging within me and all around me, sympathetic and sensitive listeners are feeling the same vibrations. It is a strange mixture of all the intense emotions—pathos, joy, peace, spirituality, eroticism, all flowing together. It is like feeling God. All these emotions may vary according to the style and approach of playing and to the nature and principal mood of the *raga*. We Indians say that in a performance of our classical music, the listener plays a great role. It is this exchange of feeling, this strong rapport between the listener and the performer, that creates great music. But wrong vibrations emanating from egoistic, insensitive, and unsympathetic listeners can diminish the creative feelings of the musician. Although I am not a Tan Sen, at times I have seen miracles happen with my music. Perhaps my playing does not cause rain to fall from the skies, but it has made tears fall from the eyes of my listeners. The miracle of our music is in the beautiful rapport that occurs when a deeply spiritual musician performs for a receptive and sympathetic group of listeners.

A LEGENDARY TEMPER

Besides being famous for his performances and innovations in music, Baba was also very well known throughout the musical world for his temper. I was rather apprehensive about meeting him for the first time in person. But I still remember how surprised I was when I found him to be so gentle and unassuming, endowed with the virtue of *vinaya* (humility) in the true *Vaishnav* spirit. It is only when he is wrapped up utterly in his music that he becomes a stern taskmaster, for he cannot tolerate any impurities or defects in the sacred art of music, and he has no sympathy or patience with those who can. His own life has been one of rigorously self-imposed discipline, and he expects no less from his students. Baba's views on celibacy and especially on intoxication through alcohol or drugs are extremely rigid and severe. He strongly insists that the students follow *brahmacharya*—for the disciple, a traditional Hindu way of life that includes only the absolute essentials of material needs. This way, with no thoughts of fine clothes, fancy foods, sex or complicated love affairs or anything else that satis-

fies and encourages physical desires, the student can channel all of his powers and forces, both mental and physical, into the discipline of his music. Music, to Baba, is a strict, lifelong discipline that requires long and careful training, and if a student is not prepared to regard music in this way, he had better not take it up at all.

Unfortunately, Baba no longer travels or performs now, although on special occasions he may be seen playing the violin or conducting the famous Maihar Band (an ensemble of Indian and Western instruments) of which he is still the director. He also continues as Principal of the Maihar College of Music which he attends every day. In 1952, Baba was made a Fellow of the Sangeet Natak Akademi (National Academy of Performing Arts), and in 1958, he was awarded the Padma Bhusan, an honorary title for outstanding citizens, by the President of the academy. Viswa Bharati, Tagore's university, gave him the honorary degree of Doctor. Thus, honor and recognition came to him in the evening of his life, but he remains, following the saying in the Geeta, unmoved and unruffled as he pursues his work and the study of music, never bothering, never worrying or looking back. Baba himself believes he is well over a hundred years old, and his centenary has already been marked. His true age is not known, because records have not been kept, but what does it matter if he is over a hundred or nearing a hundred? What he has accomplished in his lifetime many others could not do if they had three hundred years to live. He is respected and well regarded by everyone, including the most orthodox Hindu Brahmins, as a *rishi*, responsible for safeguarding traditions, for developing, teaching, and passing on to disciples the art of music.

There are so many things one could add about Ustad Allauddin Khan. He belongs to a school that seems so far removed from our modern industrial era, and yet, in every way, he has been ahead of his time, injecting a new significance and life into Indian instrumental music. With him will pass an era that upheld the dedicated, spiritual outlook handed down by the great *munis* and *rishis* who considered the sound of music, *nad*, to be Nada Brahma—a way to reach God.

THREE

MYSELF

*The anguish of search,
the joy of discovery*

YYYYYYYYYYYYYYYYYYYYYYYYYYYYYYYYYYYYYYYYYYYYYYYY

I WAS BORN
IN BENARES

My own childhood was in complete contrast to Baba's. I was born on April 7, 1920, in one of our most famous cities, Varanasi (or Benares, as it is more widely known). Benares is the holiest of all our cities and is supposed to be one of the oldest in the world, dating back almost ten thousand years.

My early childhood was not a very happy time, and I was, except for the diversions I invented for myself, rather lonely. My father, a Bengali Brahmin from the village of Kalia in the Jessore district (now in Eastern Pakistan), had been a *diwan*, or minister, in the service of the Maharaja of Jhalawar for some years before my birth. Besides being a statesman, he was a great *pandit* in Sanskrit and philosophy and had studied the Vedas and the Vedic hymns and had learned to sing

dhrupad. When my father left the Maharaja's service in Jhalawar, a pension was arranged for our family, and he went to London to practice law. My oldest brother, Uday, also went to London then, to study painting at the Royal College of Art.

I remember, when I was very young, the family lived comfortably on the pension that had been provided for us, but after a little time, my mother had to regulate the household very economically. My father and Uday were still in London, and so there were just my mother and my brothers Rajendra, Debendra, Bhupendra, and I in the house in Benares. The two oldest of these three brothers were in school, and even I realized it was difficult for my mother to take care of the house and us and send the two boys to school. It would have been out of the question for my mother to work; but to have a little extra money, she used to go occasionally to an old pawnbroker, where

This lady musician in a Mogul court, shown in an eighteenth-century Rajput miniature, accompanies herself on a tamboura while singing.

she left jewelry and fine fabrics. When my father was in the Maharaja's service, my mother and the Maharani used to exchange presents. I used to watch my mother go to the trunks where she kept her gifts and take out a diamond brooch she had been given, or a *sari* woven with threads of gold or yards of the finest wools, and then, as we gave them over to the pawnbroker, she would weep quietly. Her sadness impressed me and upset me a great deal.

My mother was very much attached to me when I was small, because I was the baby of the family and was the only one who was around her constantly. She was a very sensitive and soft-spoken person, but had great strength within herself. In the years she spent in Jhalawar, she was one of the principal companions to the Maharani and always participated in the musical events held in the Maharani's private court. She had the opportunity to hear all the famous women singers of the time, and I remember even from my

very early years, she used to sing lullabies to me in her soft, melodious voice—the very beautiful old melodies and classical songs or songs from the dramas. Many of these songs I learned by heart and some of them I still enjoy singing.

My family was rather more musical than most, though music forms very much a part of the daily life in Bengal, the South of India, and to some extent, in the west, around Bombay and Poona. My father too had a deep love of music and was a musician of some proficiency. When he was studying Sanskrit and philosophy in Benares in his youth, he learned the old *dhrupad* style of singing from the famous *been* player Mithailal, a disciple of the Beenkar *gharana*. From authentic and traditional cantors throughout India he also acquired the profound knowledge of singing the hymns of the *Rig Veda, Sama Veda,* and *Yajur Veda.* Rajendra, the oldest brother at home when I was little, was also musically inclined. He was an active member of a social-cultural club and very often took part in its music sessions. They had a small chamber orchestra and used to produce their own plays every year. There were a few secondhand or borrowed instruments that Rajendra kept at home and practiced on once in a while—a flute, a small sitar in the corner of the room, a harmonium, and an *esraj* up on the shelf. As far back as I can remember, I used to love to sneak up and tickle the instruments while my mother was busy in the kitchen. I had the feeling I might be scolded for it if anybody found out, but later, I surprised the whole family by playing some of the songs I had heard Rajendra practice.

When I was eight or nine, a friend of Mejda's (my name for Rajendra, which means "middle brother") who used to come to the house taught me a number of Bengali songs, many of them written by our great poet Tagore. I had a pleasing voice and my family often asked me to sing some of these songs when we had guests at home. In fact, I became quite popular through my singing and frequently performed in assemblies or special programs at school. In the beginning, of course, I was very nervous and shy about performing in front of anyone, but my family encouraged me. Soon, I enjoyed singing and accompanying myself by picking out the notes on the harmonium's keyboard. We had a Gramophone at home and some records of instrumental music, some of Tagore's songs, and many religious songs and songs from the semiclassical musical dramas in Hindi and Bengali. I often used to imitate the records and sing along with them.

My early childhood in Benares has left me with many nostalgic musical memories. I can remember the thrill of waking up early in the morning, long before sunrise and, as I lay in bed, listening to the chant of the *Pujaris*, the priests of the temple of Lord Vishwanath (Shiva), as they moved along in procession for the bathing ceremony of Lord Vishwanath. Slowly, all in unison, they chanted as they moved, "*HARA HARA MAHADEVA SHAMBO, KASHI VISHWA-NATHA GANGA*," over and over. Sometimes I went by myself to visit the various temples; other times my mother took me to hear the *bhajans* (devotional songs) or the chanting of the Vedic hymns.

One of the most beautiful and impressive memories I have of Benares is the annual procession and worship at the temple of the goddess Durga, another manifestation of Shiva's wife Parvati. Every year around the time of *Dassehra* (September–October), we would awake about four in the morning, and I would go along with my brothers to the Durgabadi (temple of Durga). It was a two-mile walk, and we all started out with great enthusiasm, but usually it happened that one of my brothers or their friends would have to carry me more than half the way. We joined other small groups heading for the temple, and the little streams of people soon formed a great procession, carrying scented flowers of *bel*, *chameli*, and *juhi*, and burning incense. Some of the groups chanted Sanskrit hymns or sang devotional songs as they walked. There were people from all over India, singing in many different languages, and I could feel all around me the vibrations of intense religious love and devo-

The ringing of the bell at the temple of Shiva creates a religious atmosphere and signifies casting away evil.

At this same temple (in Benares) where I prayed as a child I listen to three Brahmins chanting Vedic hymns.

Eric Hayes

tion for the "seeing" of the goddess. This is known as the *darshan*, which literally means "seeing," but in this case means a "coming to see" a religious and godly figure whom we greatly respect and revere. When we arrived at the temple, we performed the rituals of the worship and viewed Durga, all adorned with flowers and special jewels and gold. Then we and the other worshipers were given little bits of fruits or flowers, sandalwood paste, or other special things. These were spread out and offered to the goddess, then bits of them were handed out on leaves to the worshipers.

Since my family was orthodox and very religious, it was natural for me to be easily moved and thrilled by religious experiences. To me, just as to any other Hindu child, all the gods and *avatars* (incarnations) were like wonderful people whom we knew well and loved very much. We used to hang up pictures of our favorites, like movie stars. In fact, until very recently, the most popular films in India were about the various gods and their adventures. My family were followers of Tantra and worshipers of the goddess Kali (another manifestation of Parvati), and I was by nature a great fan of Narayana (Vishnu). When I was given my own

The ghats along the sacred Ganges; behind the tumult, but still close to the waters, rise majestic palaces.

The Metropolitan Museum of Art

Eric Hayes

Hanuman the Monkey God leads the army, shown here on his tail, in triumph back to Ayodhya. In one hand he holds a banner, and in the other, a mountain with birds and animals. On his shoulder perches Rama-Chandra. Nineteenth-century illustration of part of the epic Ramayana.

slate and chalk, the first things I drew were my favorite godly characters. There were Chaturbhuj (four-handed) Narayana, Krishna playing on his flute, and Rama holding the bow and arrow, with Hanuman, the Monkey God, sitting at his feet. One of my best subjects was the goddess of learning, Saraswati, sitting on a white swan and playing the *veena*.

Often at the end of the afternoon, I used to wander out and watch the sunset from the *ghats* (banks) of the river Ganges. This is something that thrills me even today whenever I go to Benares, and fills me with a very deep spiritual peace that makes me forget all the material world. Lining the river are stone banks and stairs up to the city, and all along the way, on one side of the water, are the palatial houses that belong to *maharajas* or very wealthy families. Almost every house had its own *shahnai* (oboe-like reed instrument) player who used to come out for a few hours in the early morning and then for three hours or so in the evening. Everywhere the piercing sound of the *shahnai* was mixed with that of temple bells. Here and there small groups of people were singing and some were acting out a religious story, while others sat listening to a religious man. People came to bathe in the holy river and say their prayers, and at night there was the burning of the funeral pyres. These scenes turned my thoughts to birth and death and all the beauties of life, and to higher, more spiritual thoughts of religion. Often, someone had to come and take me home, almost by force, because I was so reluctant to leave these scenes, which provided some of the greatest moments of enjoyment I have ever experienced.

UDAY'S DREAM

It was at the end of 1929 that Dada (my eldest brother Uday) came back to India after almost ten years in Europe. He had gone to London hoping to become a painter, had received his degree, and actually turned out to be quite promising. But his artistic inclinations changed, and he turned to dance. My father was doing some experiments on the stage with Indian ballet in the middle Twenties, and he asked Uday to help him with some choreographical ideas and other aspects of production. Uday's career as a dancer began in a musical production that my father staged in London in 1924; I think it was the first Indian ballet produced in the West. Anna Pavlova, the famed Russian ballerina, came to one of the presentations and saw Uday perform. She was so impressed that she asked if he would help her produce two ballets she was planning, based on Indian themes. One was to be an Indian marriage depicted all through dance, and the other, a dance-narration of one of the stories about Lord Krishna and his love Radha.

My brother Uday, while he was still in Jhalawar with the family, had occasion to see many excellent male and female dancers performing in the *Kathak* style. He had also watched many folk dancers from the different regions of India and saw some of the dances of the aboriginal Bhil tribes. At the same time, he was very interested in the way the old dances had been represented in art, and he carefully studied the tremendous wealth of temple and cave art—both painting and sculpture—wherein performing dancers were portrayed in superb detail. Partly because he had seen so much dancing and had studied this temple and cave art, and partly because he had an inherent artistic sensitivity, dancing came as naturally to Uday as singing does to others. It is a rare thing for a person with no formal training to become a great dancer and a pioneer in the art as well.

Slowly a dream took shape in Uday's heart—to take a whole troupe of Indian dancers and musicians, representatives of our musical heritage, to the West. He understood then, that in order to realize his dream, he needed to return to his country to study more deeply the art and its history and to organize some precise plans. With this project in mind, he returned home in 1929 for a stay of ten or eleven months, during which he traveled all over the country, especially in the South, where the traditions of the dance are maintained at a high level. He studied and reviewed as much as he could of the noble style of the dance drama, *Kathakali*, and the most ancient style of dancing, *Bharatanatyam*. He also broadened his knowledge of folk and tribal dances and made a large collection of musical instruments, especially drums, from every region of India.

Uday came to Benares and told us about the troupe he was organizing and explained that he wanted all of us to join him and go with him to Europe. Uday was no more sure than we were that the idea would turn out well, or even that we had any talent, and the project was quite a large risk for him to undertake. He asked my brothers Rajendra and Debendra (Bhupendra had died a few years earlier) to participate in the activities of the troupe, as well as a beautiful cousin of ours, her father, a maternal uncle, and three or four outstanding musicians, among them Timir Baran, a well known *sarod* player and composer and disciple of Allauddin Khan. My mother was to come along so that she could take care of the household in Paris, where the troupe was going to stay and rehearse. I, of course, was included in all this, and it was understood that I would continue my schooling in Paris and might be able to join later on in the artistic activity. It took some time to convince everybody how well Uday's project might work out, and the decision to leave hung in mid-air for months. Rajendra was working toward his master's degree and would have to leave before his exams, and Debendra, who was also in college, would not be able to earn his bachelor's. For my part, I was very excited about the venture, and for months I shivered and trembled at the thought of the new life in Paris and could think of nothing else.

By the fall of 1930, we were en route to Paris. The trip was very long and has left me with strange impressions of the different cities we visited and the journey itself by train and boat. We traveled first to Bombay, where we spent four or five days. I was completely *bouleversé* by the entire city; it was the first time I'd seen tramways and big buses, and I remember the nauseating smell of petrol. Everywhere in the wide streets lined with immense buildings were people in Western dress and perfumed women in *saris* of glorious fabric and color. And there were even talking movies! From Bombay we journeyed by ship across the Indian Ocean and I was terribly seasick for a few days, but by the time we reached the Suez Canal, the water was very smooth. The Mediterranean was choppy and we were upset again, but when we arrived at Venice it all seemed to me a floating heaven, and I forgot about everything else. I could never have even dreamed up a city so beautiful. We were in Venice just one day, then we took the train to Paris. The transition from Benares to Bombay to Venice and finally to Paris was almost too much for my heart to bear. When I was quite young, my health had never been strong, and now all this excitement made my heart palpitate and caused me to feel continually feverish. For weeks I was sick with excitement.

A house had been rented for us, the Uday Shankar Company of Hindu Dancers and Musicians, some time earlier, and a friend and partner of Dada, Alice Boner, had already put everything in order before our arrival. Uday had sent his entire collection of instruments before we left India and, happily, they had all arrived intact.

Within a very short time after we were all settled, the rehearsals and training began, for we had had none before we left. Our rehearsals were held in one very large room of the house, and I was free to wander about and play on any of the little instruments. From the very minute they were unpacked, I used to gaze with wonder and marvel at the collection of drums and all the stringed instruments. The other members of our troupe often heard me picking out tunes on the sitar or the *esraj*, or experimenting on the *tabla*, and they would come over and encourage me, telling each other I had some real talent. I was delighted by their praise and very pleased; and, naturally, I worked even harder on my music. But even though I was encouraged by the other musicians, no one had time to sit down and teach me the techniques of any of the instruments or explain how they should be played properly. By listening very attentively to our little orchestra as they practiced, I soon found I could imitate rather well what they played. So, although I could play the correct notes, I had no idea of the correct position of the hands or fingering or any other basic elements of technique.

In another room of the house, all the beautiful costumes that we had sent from India were kept, for at that time, we had not yet started to design and sew the costumes ourselves, but ordered them from home. Later, one entire room was given over to copying and designing new costumes based either on ones we had or on Indian paintings or sculptures of dancers.

During the first months, everyone seemed completely filled with the enthusiasm of creativity. I will never forget how Uday looked, at the beginning and all through the eight years that we maintained the troupe. He appeared, really, like a god, and when he danced he was almost a god, filled with an immense power and overwhelming beauty. To me, he was a superman, and those years with him did a great deal not only to shape my artistic and creative personality, but also to form me as a total human being. It was Uday who taught me to understand and appreciate our ancient traditions in art and all our culture, and my apprenticeship under him in stagecraft, lighting, set design, and general showmanship was of great value to me many years later, when I myself produced ballets and musical dramas in India. Only one other man has impressed me as much as, if not more than, my brother Uday, and that is our great poet, painter, and composer Rabindranath Tagore, whom I saw for the first time in 1933, when we were back in India for a visit.

In 1938, Uday founded a great cultural center for all the performing arts in the mountains of Almora, in India, and if it could have existed more than the few years it did, all Uday's dreams would have been fulfilled and the center would have become internationally famous and attracted all the world's greatest artists. Uday started this culture center on almost twenty acres of land, and he constructed modern studios for dance, drama, and music, with built-in stages, costume rooms, workshops, and rehearsal halls. He brought in the best known *gurus* of India, among them Shankaran Namboodri, the greatest living *Kathakali* dancer, from whom Dada received his own dance training and the only real *guru* Dada ever had in his life. There were also Kandappan Pillai, one of the notable *Bharatanatyam* teachers, *Manipuri guru* Amobi Sinha, and even Allauddin Khan to supervise instrumental music. The center was an ideal combination of the old *ashram* type of school plus the modern workshop atmosphere one finds in some of the open-air institutions of the West. The teachers and students were all very close, and Uday, with his magnetism and strong personality, kept the entire complex functioning.

The most remarkable quality in Dada (Uday) was the infinite amount of Indian-ness in all his artistic creations. When I saw him dance and watched artists whom he had trained, I along with the others felt all the plasticity and fluid motion of the stone images from the temple and cave sculptures and paintings of Ellora, Ajanta, Mahaballipuram, Konarak, Khajarao and Bagh come to life. Uday's imaginative genius created a completely new, very pure and beautiful, but still totally Indian, style of dancing, taking the technique and essence mainly from *Kathakali* and also

from *Bharatanatyam, Manipuri, Kathak,* and several other styles of Indian folk and tribal dance.

Like other truly creative artists, Uday had to suffer a great deal of criticism in India and face the charge that his art was neither "traditional" nor "pure" in any one technique. To a certain extent, he is still confronted with the same accusations today, even though no creative dancer in India is free from his influence and most of them are his "students," either directly or indirectly.

His contributions in the realm of instrumental music are of no less consequence, and too few people are aware of the innovations Uday brought to music for the creative dance. Though he was not a performing musician himself, he knew exactly what he wanted the music to say and he knew just how to have it expressed. Even when he was a student, from seeing one step or position performed by the teacher, he could invent a hundred new things. When it came to special-effects music, Uday invented an entire new dimension in both concept and sound by using all sorts of classical, folk, and tribal drums, cymbals, gongs, and little finger cymbals like castanets made of metal or wood, and by devising new ways to play the traditional instruments—playing the *tamboura* with two sticks, for instance.

In the beginning, many of us did feel skeptical about Uday's music, but he would sit with us all, giving his suggestions and teaching us and patiently explain the musical effects he was trying to create, making the sound with his voice that he wanted each instrument to produce. A *B-O-O-M* here, a *ktink* there, and a *br-r-r-r-R-R-O-O-O-OM* on another instrument.

The aspect of Uday's approach that left the strongest imprint on my mind, even to the present, was his adamant refusal to use even a single Western instrument in his music; he very stringently adhered to his practice of using only those instruments that are traditionally found on the Indian subcontinent. That is, he did not feel it was out of keeping with his principles to use instruments from Java, Bali, or Burma, because the histories of these countries were strongly influenced by the old Hindu culture, and much of their dance and music traditions had been brought in from India in ancient times.

65

A NEW LIFE IN PARIS

For nearly two years in Paris I attended one of the French Catholic schools. It was so strange for me! First of all, because I was just learning French, I was placed in classes with children several years younger, and I didn't know very well how to get along with the other children. The boys seemed such brutes, strong and nasty little devils, so I preferred to spend my time with the girls. I fancied myself far more cultured than any of my schoolmates, and in many ways, I really was. The way the European children were brought up to behave was so unlike our Indian customs, and it was difficult for me to adapt myself to this new way of thinking and acting. I don't think I learned a great deal in those years in the French school, and I was happy when I finally was given permission to have private lessons instead and to spend the rest of my time either with the troupe rehearsing and touring or by myself, reading and inventing other things to keep busy. My mother went back to India in 1932, and at first I felt a little lost, but I soon adjusted to this not very happy kind of life. I spent much time listening to records of every sort of music—Indian, Western classical, even jazz—and took up more and more the life of a trouper. By the end of 1933, I was going on practically every tour we made.

Even when we were still in Benares, I had preferred more than anything else to stay alone and play with my brother's musical instruments, lose myself in thrilling stories, or act out plays in front of the mirror, taking the parts of the hero, the lover, the villain in turn. I had no brothers or sisters close to me in age, and there were no other children my age nearby. In fact, I had private tutors for some years and didn't go to a regular school until I was about seven. From then on, I carried around a whole world of imaginative fantasies inside myself, and the more books I read and the more plays and films I saw, the more intricate grew this invented universe. Much later, this fantasy world, my loneliness, and my efforts to grasp something unreachable all found expression through my music. From when I was quite young, I had a particular fascination for the stage and drama of all kinds. As I reflect on it now, I see that I really couldn't have done

anything other than be in show business, even if I had not become a musician.

When I was in Paris with the troupe, at the age of eleven or so, I began reading all the great classics of our literature whose stories every Indian is familiar with. I started with Bengali translations of our two vast Sanskrit epics, the *Ramayana*, which tells of the adventures of Rama, an incarnation of Vishnu, and the *Mahabharata*, whose main theme is the struggle between two families, one good, one evil, but which includes many other episodes, among them our favorite *Bhagavad Gita*, the dialogue between Krishna and the mortal prince Arjuna. The *Mahabharata* is many times longer than either of the Homeric epics, but I read the stories many times over. Through them, I learned all our beloved customs and traditions, and as I sat and read in our house in Paris, I could feel myself grow even closer to India and her ways. Within these epics lay the whole world—all the drama, romance, humor, pathos, the science fiction and the scientific theory, all the beauty of the mortal and the grandeur of the divine. Then, I read some of the stories of the Puranas, a huge collection of ancient tales dealing in a wonderfully entertaining way with every aspect of Hindu customs and ideas. Some of the stories of the Puranas are also mentioned in the epics, but here they are told with very elaborate detail. One of my favorites was the story of Krishna in his childhood. A story that impressed me deeply was the life of Siddhartha Buddha and the fact that he had so much, yet was able to renounce everything and still live within the world.

As my French improved, I tried to finish some of the books we had been reading in school, novels of Victor Hugo and Anatole France, but it was less of an effort for me to read detective stories and comic books. I was making progress in English too, but I still much preferred to read in Bengali, not because it was easier, but because it brought me closer to my home, my people, and the ways I was used to.

Although I may have been too young to read them with full understanding, I devoured works of distinguished Bengali authors, such as Bankim Chatterji, whose novels taught me some of India's history in a colorful, entertaining way. These and the plays of

D. L. Roy were far better, I thought, than any history class in school. Through Roy's plays, I learned of happenings in the Muslim and other periods, and acquired a very fanciful and romantic view of history. My favorite stories were those of Sarat Chandra, and I must have read every one fifteen or twenty times. His books made me very much aware of being not only an Indian, but a Bengali, and they showed me *my* Bengal—the people, and the villages, the warmth, the old traditions, and every aspect of these people to whom I felt so close. Events of our past and affairs of the present that I never could have been aware of otherwise in Paris were revealed to me through all my readings.

So, while I was in Paris, a very strong national— even regional—feeling was developing in me, as so often happens when one is away from his homeland. I poured over all Uday's books with pictures of the cave and temple art, volumes and volumes of them, and I absorbed all the stories that explained each illustration. I really fell in love with India and its past, and so it was easy and most natural for me to take up music, and especially dance in the beginning, based on our ancient tales.

I was hungry for anything in Bengali, and I grabbed up all the magazines and pictorial reviews that came from home. Weeklies and monthlies I consumed and even subscribed to some of our children's magazines. I absorbed all our traditions and ways of thinking from these books and periodicals, and they created my whole world.

When I was thirteen or fourteen I began to read Tagore—his essays, poems, plays, and short stories. Many of them went over my head at first, but I enjoyed them nevertheless. Some of his thematic poems, based on Jataka stories (Buddhist period) moved me even to tears, and the beauty of all he wrote deeply penetrated my spirit. When our troupe came to India on tour for the first time, we all went along with my brother to Shanti Niketan in Bolpur, near Calcutta, which is a large center established by Tagore himself. Tagore was there, sitting in a huge chair like a king, or like a majestic lion, with those piercing, clear eyes. We all went up and did the *pranam* before him and he gave his blessing to everyone. When I went up

before him, I remember he said one thing to me: "Be great like your father and your brother," and when he put his hand on my head, a magical thrill went all through me. I have never seen a man living in such beauty. Tagore's family, extremely cultured, literate, and handsome people, were like feudal lords, almost like royalty. And he gave everything away to found his institution. It was to be a general college, as he first conceived it, with classes held in the open air, in natural surroundings something like the old *ashrams* of the saint-sages. Because of Tagore's dynamic magnetism, many noted *pandits* and scholars came to the school and offered their services. Seeing this giant of a personality at his school was one of the rare experiences of my life. As time passed, I read Tagore's works with more understanding and am still discovering wonderful new ideas in his writing. As many say, it takes more than one lifetime to know Tagore.

After 1934, when the troupe was constantly on tour and the house in Paris could no longer be considered our headquarters, I was not able to spend as much time with books, and the enchantment of reading so many of our ancient stories and other beautiful works was broken. For the next three years or so, my tastes in literature turned more to the occult and the religious. Lives of the Hindu saints and yogis and other religious figures, mostly written in Bengali, intrigued me, and I read quite a few books on Tantra and spiritual yoga. At this age, I was extremely impressionable and romantic in nature, and these books had a strong effect on my thinking. I had great dreams and plans for myself—I was to become an important religious figure or a noted yogi, and from reading about the history of my country and its contemporary problems I viewed myself as a political leader and drew up elaborate plans, even designing ways to bring an end to enslavement to the British. I saw myself, too, as an actor, as a musician, as a dancer.

In my role as member of Uday's troupe, I was soon able to play various instruments to accompany the dancers, mostly sitar and *esraj*, and later I experimented for a while with the *sarod*. With Uday as my teacher, I learned a few small roles to dance with the ensemble. I was the Monkey God and wore a mask, and also danced the little part of the Snake-Devil. As

I grew taller, physically, and as my dancing improved, I was given more important roles, and was already recognized by the critics for my dancing ability. Then, when I was sixteen, I had my first solo dance, which I choreographed myself. Its subject was Chitra Sena, a character in the court of the god Indra, who was a famous *gandharva* or celestial dancer-musician. My solo, which lasted about four minutes, was based principally on the *Kathak* style of dancing from northern India, where a lot of fast, intricate footwork and body movement are used. It is something like tap dancing and the effect is achieved not with shoes but with little bells worn on the ankles. The solo got wonderful notices from the critics, and I was much admired for my dancing performances in general.

Often while we were rehearsing in Paris during those first years, famous Western musicians would come to watch us or to talk to Uday about music. Georges Enesco was a friend of Uday's and on his frequent visits to our house, he seemed fascinated by Indian music. At that time, Yehudi Menuhin, who was still a boy in short pants, was his student, and we had the opportunity to go and listen to one of his rehearsals. Andres Segovia, master of the classical guitar, was also very interested in our music, and he too visited us occasionally. I was just beginning to have some idea of Western classical music and was fortunate in hearing the very best artists perform. We saw Toscanini and heard Paderewski and Casals, Heifetz and Kreisler. I remember hearing musicians arguing about their favorite violinists, Kreisler or Heifetz, and I can still hear the sound of Kreisler's bow. Once at the Paris Opera there was a special event at which Chaliapin, the Russian basso, sang, and we had center box seats. When he sang, I felt the rumble of his voice vibrate inside me and the chandeliers seemed to shake. We had at home an excellent record collection, through which I became well acquainted with many symphonies, concertos, and solo compositions. My interests were not limited to classical music, though. I loved French accordion music, and I listened to a lot of flamenco and Spanish music; and in some of the restaurants I got to hear Russian balalaikas and Hungarian music. Later, as we toured, I got to know the folk music of many countries, as well as compositions of their classical composers.

Often, when musicians came to our house to see Uday, they expressed their views on Indian music. Many of them had heard it only as the ensemble of our troupe played it—that is, music primarily for dance, which is not at all the same as Indian classical instrumental music. The short dance items lasted from three to eight minutes, and the longer ones, balletlike compositions in which we all danced, took about fourteen minutes. For these numbers, the music was a mixture of tribal, classical, ballet, and popular, but interspersed among the dances were solo, purely classical instrumental pieces. Even so, these items, which lasted only eight or ten minutes, could give only a small suggestion of the nature of our classical music, since in a recital of this music in India one piece may last several hours. So in part, the opinions of these Western artists on Indian music were not adequately supported by actual musical experience. I heard them say our music was monotonous and grating and not pleasing to the ear. After listening to it, some of them said how interesting and exciting it was, but "it did go on and on so." Others asked, "When do you start and when do you finish?" or complained that it was too repetitious. I realized later that one of the things that upset them most was the lack of modulation in our music and the fact that we do not employ harmony or counterpoint. I was both hurt and infuriated when I heard what some of these Western artists had to say, and I was sorry they could not understand the greatness of our music. This lack of understanding motivated me, in later years, to explain our music and talk about some of its characteristics to my own concert audiences.

BABA JOINS THE TROUPE

Our troupe made its American debut in 1932, and the excitement of our first visit to New York has never been equaled. Early on a fine morning we came out on the deck of the ship, and there, through the mist, was the Statue of Liberty and the skyscraper giants disappearing into the clouds. Our week in

New York was like a fantasy. I was completely intoxicated by Broadway and all the lights and nonstop cinema. I spent all my days at Loew's, the Rivoli, and the Paramount, reluctant to miss one cartoon, newsreel, or vaudeville act. In New York, we heard jazz played live for the first time; there were Duke Ellington and Louis Armstrong, so young and spirited. Our troupe, managed by Sol Hurok, performed in a very good theater near Broadway, and on our later tours, we performed in Carnegie Hall. From that first tour, I also remember Chicago very clearly. It was winter and Lake Michigan was frozen over, and I was amazed to see so many people walking and skating over the ice in the freezing wind. At the time, in the early Thirties, our troupe had the warmest receptions and greatest successes in two countries—Germany and, most of all, in the United States.

In 1934 we returned to India to tour there and study for nearly eleven months. I had some lessons in the *Kathak* style of dancing in Calcutta, and I seriously studied the *Kathakali* style with *guru* Shankaran Namboodri, also in Calcutta. I was very much interested in dance at that time and had made great progress, and I had no doubts about my fame and my future career as a dancer. Of course, I kept up my interest in instrumental music and preferred the sitar to other stringed instruments. But still, the sitar was only a kind of hobby, and I considered myself as a dancer before all else.

Even so, destiny was at work, and slowly, slowly, I began to be increasingly attracted to instrumental music and particularly to the sitar. I was already quite an admirer of Vishnudas Shirali, who became one of the musical directors of Uday's troupe and who played the sitar with a beautiful, melodious hand. When we were in India in 1933 for a short tour, I heard a nephew of the troupe's other musical director, Timir Baran, play the sitar. The boy was older than I, and his speed and technical virtuosity amazed me. His playing inspired me to such an extent that on our next trip to Calcutta I resolved to become a disciple of his teacher, the famed Enayat Khan. And so, when we came back to India in 1934, everything had been arranged and I was to become the student of Enayat Khan. The night before the *ganda* cere-

mony (our custom of tying the hand of the disciple to the hand of the *guru* with a symbolic thread), I suddenly became very ill and was sent immediately to a hospital, where they found I had a severe attack of typhoid. Of course, it was impossible then for me to learn from Enayat Khan and the ceremony had to be canceled. Perhaps it was coincidence, but it seems to me that I was not meant to become his disciple. We have a notion that one is destined to be the disciple of a certain *guru* and it is impossible to try to change it or to go to anyone else. Indeed, it was later in that very year, at the All-Bengal Music Conference, that I first met Allauddin Khan, the man who was to become my *guru*. Other events concurred to bring me closer to the sitar in that year. Toward the end of 1934, a wonderful sitar player, Gokul Nag, joined our troupe for a short time and very much impressed me with his artistry. He was another who did much to reinforce my growing interest in the sitar, although I did not take lessons from him.

Uday too had been present at the All-Bengal Music Conference and had heard Allauddin Khan. He was thinking then that he would like to have one of India's most eminent musicians join the troupe and come to Europe as a soloist, and Allauddin Khan seemed the perfect artist to ask. Negotiations began, and Baba agreed to come with us if he could bring his little son Ali Akbar, who was two years younger than I. Plans were made; we were to go to Burma, then Singapore and Malaya, Hong Kong, Japan, and from there to San Francisco, then Baba was to meet us for the tour in Europe. But while we were in Singapore, a telegram came for Uday with the message that our father had died in London. We returned immediately to India and spent some time with our mother. Our tour plans were revised, so that we were scheduled to spend a few weeks in Bombay working on final rehearsals and then set out for Europe via Cairo, Alexandria, Tel Aviv, Haifa, and enter Europe by way of Greece and Bulgaria.

Ustad Allauddin Khan came and joined us in Bombay, bringing Ali Akbar. I remember one day Ali Akbar went to my maternal uncle Matul and told him how he had dreamed of his mother and was feeling depressed and did not want to come to Europe with Uday's troupe. Matul was the only person in the whole troupe who had developed a friendship with Baba and could talk with him openly. He went to Baba and told him what had happened with Ali Akbar, and Baba finally decided to let Ali Akbar remain in India with his mother.

The day came when we were due to sail, and we all felt the sadness of the departure. My mother, who had come to Bombay to see us off, was going to remain in India, and already, she was feeling the loneliness of our absence. Somehow, she and I both had the premonition that we might not see each other again. While we stood on the pier, getting ready to go aboard the ship, she took my hand and put it in Baba's hand and told him, "I'm not going with you, and I don't know if I'll ever see my child again, so please take him and consider him as your own son." We all had tears in our eyes as we said goodbye, and as it happened, it was the last time I saw my mother.

Baba stayed with our troupe for nearly a year, and during all those months, I was his guide, interpreter, helper, and special companion. I suppose he missed Ali Akbar very much, and so he gave to me all the love and affection that would have gone to his son. While we were traveling, especially, I used to take care of Baba, finding the right restaurants and the proper kind of food for him. As a devout Muslim, he does not eat pork; but, like a Hindu, he does not eat beef either. One day, I remember, I wanted to do something special to please him, and recalling that he occasionally enjoyed smoking, I went out and bought him a pipe and pouch for tobacco and a lighter. When I presented the gift to him, instead of being pleased, he flared up in one of his unreasonable, furious angers. "Have you come to do the *mukhagni* with this?" he demanded. (The *mukhagni* according to Hindus is the ceremony of placing the first fire in the mouth of a dead man on the funeral pyre and is performed by the eldest son.) "I'm not one of those *gurus* you can buy," he raged.

But most of the time, he was very gentle with me. He knew how serious I was about learning instrumental music, and I got him to begin teaching me the basics of sitar and voice. Sometimes, he would become upset and grow angry when I was learning,

because, although I was a good student, he felt that dance was uppermost in my thoughts. It angered and hurt him that I should be "wasting my musical talent" and living in glitter and luxury. Baba insisted that this was no way to learn music from him, not in these surroundings, and he swore I would never go through the discipline and master the technique of the sitar. Tauntingly, he called me a "butterfly" and made some very cruel remarks about my constant girl-chasing, my dandy's tastes in clothing, and all my other interests outside music—painting, writing, and reading. He often said, *"Ek sadhe sab sadhe, sab sadhe sab jaye,"* which means if you do one thing properly and very well, then all other things will come easily later, but if you start with too much, you end up with nothing.

All the same, Baba enjoyed teaching me and I knew it. When he was nice to me, as he usually was, I learned very quickly and well, but when he was angry, I got stubborn, thick-headed, and dull and refused to learn. It must have been because I had never been scolded by anyone, even as a little child.

In the summer of 1936, we spent a few months at Dartington Hall, in Devonshire, England, a beautiful, open place, where Uday planned to work on a few new ballets. I had a great deal of time to pratice on the sitar and have lessons with Baba. This was the first time I played scales and exercises and not just whatever pleasing melodies came into my head, and all summer I worked on the exercises and fixed compositions and learned many songs. Inside me, I sensed something new and very exciting; I felt that I was coming close to music and that this music is what I was meant to devote my life to. But then in the fall, Baba had to leave us a bit earlier than had been expected and go back to India. At the time, there was a great turmoil brewing inside me—sometimes I thought I would continue with my dancing and become a truly great performer; everyone said I was well on my way. And then something within me would pull me the other way and say music, music. For many months I was torn between staying with Uday's troupe and giving up everything and going off with Baba to learn the art of music. In a way, it was unfortunate for me that Baba left so soon. Had he been with us just another month or so, I might have come to a decision sooner about my musical dilemma. Baba often repeated to me before he left that, although I had much talent and he would love to teach me, it would be possible for me to learn with him only if I could give up the sparkle and easy fame of my artist's life in Europe and come to the little town of Maihar, where he lived, and spend many years with him. And often, too, he expressed serious doubt that I would ever be able to take myself away from the glamorous life in the West.

When Baba left us, for some reason, I went back more strongly than ever to dancing and received much praise for my efforts, and I even put aside the sitar in favor of a *sarod*. I was soon able to perform on the *sarod* with our ensemble and also did some sitar solos, for, in the year with Baba, I had learned enough technique to understand what I was doing and had absorbed enough to use what I had been taught. Baba had encouraged me with the sitar because I was already acquainted with it and knew how to handle it a little, but when he left, I picked up the *sarod*, because his own playing of it had impressed me so much and I wanted to imitate him.

THE LONG ROAD TO MAIHAR

It was a year and a half before I saw Baba again, and throughout that time I was filled with worries and questions and indecision, and there was really no one I could talk to about it. Uday was quite convinced that I should keep up dancing as my primary interest, but he thought a few months with Baba wouldn't do me any harm. At this time, Uday was planning to disband the troupe and establish his center for the performing arts in India. He thought I could get a solid musical background with Baba, then come back and assist him at the center.

We finished our last tour and the troupe returned to India in May, 1938. While we were still in Paris, in the fall of 1936, a telegram arrived from India informing us of the death of our mother. A small house had just been completed for her in the village

of my maternal grandfather near Benares, and at the time, two of my older brothers were with her. The news greatly saddened us, and me especially, because I had seen her so little since she returned to India in 1932. We had always been extremely close and had been able to speak very freely to each other. So, when we came back to India in 1938, I went straight to this little house of hers.

Back in India, with no immediate plans, I thought of a religious event which, for lack of time and opportunity, I had neglected for many years; and I decided this was the time to go through with it. This is the sacred-thread ceremony that initiates a young Brahmin boy into the religion. Usually it is performed between the ages of seven and twelve, and although I was much older than that, I wanted to have the ceremony performed. In the month of May, my head was shaved, and I prepared for the initiation into Brahminism. Each initiate must spend a few weeks or even longer living like a monk, eating special food, and abstaining from all material things. I spent nearly two months living this way, free of worldly matters, before I returned to my normal life.

Before we came back from Europe, I had been secretly corresponding with Baba, who again told me he would be happy to have me learn from him, if I could abandon my fancy ways and come to Maihar, not just for a few months, but to stay. I said nothing to Uday about this correspondence, but he promised me that I could go and stay with Baba while he looked for a site for the cultural center.

When my religious duties were over, I prepared to leave for Maihar. It was about a day's journey away, and Rajendra accompanied me to the village on a day in July. As we traveled, I was all in a turmoil inside. I felt as though I were committing suicide and knew that I would be reborn, but had no way of knowing how the new life would be. I was extremely nervous and afraid of Baba's legendary temper, having seen a few small samples of it when he was with the troupe. Hundreds of doubts swept over me, and I wondered if I would be able to stay and go through all the discipline, because I knew very well my own sentimentality and my inability to bear a harsh word from anyone. And although I myself had made the decision to go to Maihar, I felt like a lamb being led to the butcher. When I arrived, Baba was really shocked to see me so transformed. My head was still shaven, and I wore simple clothes of very coarse material. With me I had brought one tin suitcase with a few belongings and two blankets with a pillow rolled up inside them. I had changed myself to the opposite extreme from the boy Baba had known in Europe, partly because I sincerely felt that I had to give up a great deal if I wanted to devote myself to music, and partly because I felt this new self would please Baba. In a way, there was some play-acting on my part, leaving behind my dandy's habits and living as I thought I *should*. But I could see right away that Baba was pleased with me.

I went and stayed in the little house next to Baba's, and in the beginning it was very difficult for me. Maihar was just a small village, and it was very quiet. Alone at night in my house, I was frightened when I heard the howling of the jackals and wolves nearby, and the deep croaking of the frogs and all the racket of the crickets. After eight years of luxurious living in Europe, it took me months to accustom myself to sleeping on the cot made of four pieces of bamboo tied together with coconut rope. Every morning, I remember, a maidservant used to come in very early to tidy up and put the water on for tea and prepare a little breakfast. After I'd been in Maihar for some time, another student came and stayed with me, but Baba beat him on the second or third day and he ran away. At least thirty different boys came to share the little house with me, but none of them ever stayed longer than a week or ten days because they could not bear Baba's temper and strict discipline.

"GO—GO AND BUY BANGLES!"

I was quite lucky to have already spent a year with Baba when he was traveling with Uday's troupe. In that time I had gotten to know him quite well—all his little weaknesses and the peculiarities of his nature. Some of these poor boys who came to Maihar

had no idea how to interpret Baba's moods. Normally, he was the humblest, gentlest person imaginable, filled with *vinaya*, like a devout follower of Vishnu. But often, when he started teaching, he turned into a violent, irascible follower of Shiva and would not tolerate one little slip from the student. He even used to scold the *maharaja* who employed him! I really have the record, though. Baba never once struck me or even raised his voice to me. Well, just one time.

Once, when I had first come to him and he was teaching me an exercise, I was not able to play it correctly. "Ha!" he exclaimed, "You have no strength in those wrists. *Da, da, da,*" he cried, as he smacked my hands. Well, I had been trying my best, and I felt terrible that he should be angry with me. From my childhood, no one had ever spoken angrily to me, although I was quite spoiled and sometimes behaved badly. So when Baba raised his voice to me, I began to get angry myself, rather than frightened. "Go," he taunted me, "go, go and buy some bangles to wear on your wrists. You are like a weak little girl! You have no strength. You can't even do this exercise!" That was enough for me. I got up and went to the house next door where I had been staying, packed my bedding and belongings, marched off to the railroad station, and bought a ticket home. I had just missed a train and had to wait a while for the next one. In the meantime, Ali Akbar came running up and, seeing my bags, asked what happened. "I won't stay," I told him. "He scolded me today." Ali Akbar looked at me incredulously and asked if I were mad. "You are the only person he has never laid a hand on. We're all amazed by it. Why, do you know what he's done to me? He's tied me to a tree every day for a week and beaten me and even refused me food. And you run away because he gives you a little scolding!" Adamantly I insisted, "No, I will leave on the evening train." Ali Akbar persuaded me to go back to the house with him, and I temporarily set my bags down again in my room. By then, he had told his mother what happened, and she told Baba. Ali Akbar came to tell me they wanted me to have lunch with them, and when I went into the house, Ma (Ali Akbar's mother) said to me, "Come. You are leaving soon, but just go and sit with your Baba for a few minutes." I went over to him and did a *pranam*, and I saw that he was cutting out a photograph of me and putting it into a frame. Neither of us said a word, but I saw that he was moved. After a little while, I finally said, "I am going today." Slowly, he looked over at me, and asked, "Is that all? I mean, I just told you to wear bangle bracelets and it has hurt you so much that you are going to leave?" I had tears in my eyes already, and had never seen him like this. He stood up and came over to me, and said, "You remember at the pier in Bombay how your mother put your hand in mine and asked me to look after you as my own son? Since then, I have accepted you as my son, and this is how you want to break it?"

Naturally, I didn't leave Baba after this scene. And ever since, whenever he felt angry because of something I had done, he would go and beat someone else.

In a way, Baba was extremely autocratic in his method of teaching. Often, he would be seated on a mat with some pillows on his hard sofa-bed, smoking a *hookah*, a big Indian pipe that goes *hubble-bubble*, when a student came in. He would say, "Sit down. Sit down on a chair." Now, one had to understand what he meant by that. If he was in a good mood, perhaps he really wanted the student to take the chair. But if he was in a bad temper and said, "Oh, sit down in that chair there," the poor unknowing student would sit down and Baba would jump up and hit him with the top of his *hookah* and shout, "See! He sits on a chair right in front of me. Hah! He think he is my equal!" It *was* really very difficult to know just what Baba wanted people to do.

At first, I was very uncomfortable and unhappy with Baba in Maihar. My concentration suffered, and I found my mind wandering after only a few hours of work, yet I felt I was atoning for my eight years of materialistic living in the West. I thought I had lost many years and was trying to make up for what seemed to me a waste. Of course, I realized later that the experiences of my childhood in Europe had been very helpful.

It did take a few months, but I got used to the quiet, disciplined life with Baba. Usually I would wake up about four o'clock in the morning and have a quick wash, not the regular bath, and drink a cup of tea. I took my sitar and practiced the basic scales until six o'clock or so. Then I had my bath, did the morning worship that I practiced since my sacred thread ceremony, and ate two boiled eggs and a piece of Indian bread. After the little meal, I practiced the exercises or whatever I had learned the previous day, so I could play it well when I went to Baba later on. Everything had to be memorized, of course, because, except for some small reminders about the music, we don't write anything down—neither the notes nor any of the formal instruction. It must all be absorbed right away by the hands and the mind. A little after seven, I took my sitar, trembling and apprehensive, and crossed the little garden to Baba's house, where we would work for two or three hours. Sometimes he gave me a very difficult thing to learn, and the lesson would take only half an hour; then, I would go and practice for another hour or two, trying to play it properly. Baba realized immediately that, mentally, I was quite advanced in the music. But my hands were far behind, because I had spent so little time learning and practicing the basics. I used to hate the scales and exercises; it was a spiritual torture to me, because my hands could never catch up to the idea of the music inside my head. I went through months of depression when I felt I was getting nowhere, but when my technique improved, I learned extremely quickly. Baba would be inspired, and a half-hour lesson often lasted three or four hours. In the beginning, although I had great respect for Baba, I didn't completely understand what he wanted from his disciples. He is a teacher in the old style, demanding of the student total humility and surrender to the *guru*, a complete shedding of the ego. The disciple is only the receiver, and what he is being taught is all he should consider; he must not judge the *guru*, and must not criticize.

I would have a small meal in the midmorning, and a rest, then I would practice again for several hours. There was a late-afternoon session, too, with Baba, once I had acquired some proficiency in the exercises and had begun learning some of the basic *ragas*. Although Baba knew all the techniques of playing the sitar, he did not play the instrument himself. He therefore taught me mostly by singing what he wanted me to play and learn. This is often done with our music, because by imitating the voice one can get a deep insight into the *raga* and a better understanding. To learn the correct finger strokes for plucking the sitar's strings, I first learned the spoken syllables that are used to identify each stroke; then it was easy to play them as Baba called them out—"*Da, ra, diri, darar.*" To teach a slow part (*vilambit*), Baba usually sang; but for the faster, more intricate *gats* and *todas* he used the stroke syllables. Often, too, he sat with his *sarod* and played what he wanted to teach me, but this was difficult for me, because the tonics of sitar and *sarod* are not the same. Eventually, I devised a way of adjusting my tuning so that the two instruments could work together. This later inspired Baba to take me along to the music conferences with him, where I sat in the background as his disciple when he performed, and I was permitted to play a little from time to time. Many years later, this brought up a new idea that Ali Akbar and I developed—the *sarod*-sitar duet known as *jugalbandi*. Baba also taught me, and his daughter Annapurna as well, the technique of the *surbahar*; and later she and I performed duets with this instrument.

The only entertainment I had was going for walks along the river or on the lovely hillside, for there were no cinemas or "city" diversions. Often Ali Akbar accompanied me, and we would spend hours walking and discussing all our ideas. I used to tell him of my adventures in Europe, and he spoke to me of the problems he had. We would return to the house by dark and all have dinner about seven-thirty, then spend a few more hours practicing.

Most often, Baba taught me alone; but later Ali Akbar, and sometimes his sister Annapurna, would join me for the sessions. Ali Akbar and I became very close, even though I was two years older than he. When I came to Maihar and saw him after nearly three years (he had been in Bombay with us before we left for Europe in 1935), I was greatly surprised and pleased at the progress he had made in his music, for it had never before seemed to me that he had much enthusiasm for playing the *sarod*, and I knew the almost incredible degree to which Baba carried his strictness with him. Ali Akbar told me he had been compelled to practice for fourteen to sixteen

hours every day, and there were times when Baba tied him to a tree for hours and refused to let him eat if his progress was not satisfactory. Ali Akbar was born with music in his veins, but it was this constant rigorous discipline and *riaz* (Urdu for "practice") that Baba set for him that has made Ali Akbar one of the greatest instrumentalists alive.

After I had made some progress with my music, there was a period of several years when the three of us—Ali Akbar, Annapurna, and I—all sat with Baba and learned from him together. He would start to teach us, singing such serious and beautiful *ragas* as *Lalit, Multani, Yaman Kalyan, Bihag, Mian ki Malhar, Darbari Kanada*, and sometimes he would just go on teaching for three or four hours and lose all perception of the passage of time. Many times we cried because of the intense beauty of the music, and no one would think of disturbing the spell.

ON MY OWN

After I had been with Baba in Maihar for several years, a marriage was arranged between his daughter Annapurna and myself. Baba did not want me to stay in a separate house, so I moved into his house, although somewhat reluctantly, since an Indian feels awkward about living with his in-laws. It was difficult to argue with Baba, but I made a very strict arrangement whereby I would take care of all my own expenses except for providing food.

Even so, I had my financial problems. When I first went to Maihar, Uday had been very understanding and had sent me money regularly, but when he realized I was not coming back to help him at the center, he was hurt and more than a little angry and stopped sending me an allowance. Then for a few years I took small loans, but didn't really manage very well. By the second year of my training, Baba gave me permission to perform alone at some of the small music festivals and to accompany him when he went on concert tours, sitting with him and playing *tamboura* or a few lines on the sitar when he looked over at me. This was almost like being taught on the stage and was very good training. I was lucky in that, having spent all my childhood in an atmosphere of music and having already had Baba's training and guidance during the year he spent with our troupe, I was able to perform much earlier than even a good student normally does. When I started with Baba in Maihar I had almost ten years of background—playing sitar, *esraj*, flute, and drums, as well as dancing and being generally acquainted with the stage and show aspects of performing artists' lives. In December, 1939, after only one and a half years of training, I went along with Ali Akbar to the Allahabbad Music Conference, where I had my first real success.

During the seven years I spent in Maihar, besides going with Baba when he gave concerts, Ali Akbar and I went to Uday's center several times for a few months, and once Uday left Almora and went on a tour with his dancers, and I went along for a while, but I felt somewhat reluctant about dancing again.

Then Baba arranged for me to give radio recitals for the state-controlled All-India Radio in Lucknow. I was to do a regularly scheduled broadcast to be presented twice a week about every two months. This was a very important opportunity for me, because performing within a specific time limit was excellent training for the concerts I was to give later. Here, too, my childhood background in show business was a great help. I traveled back and forth, all the way to and from Lucknow, to do these recitals, until 1944. Each day I spent at the radio station's studio, I did three or four sessions, and my programs were well proportioned and included a variety of styles.

Late in 1944 I left Baba and the little town of Maihar with my wife and son Shubhendra, who was about three, and went to Bombay. Though Baba was reluctant to let me go, I felt it was time, after seven years of training with him, for me to work on my own and build a career for myself. And even though my early period of training with Baba was finished, I continued to visit him for two or three months every year until 1949, and after that, I went to see him in Maihar as often as I could, and occasionally he came to see us for a few weeks.

The next few years in Bombay were a bitter time

for me in many ways while I struggled to earn a reputation for my playing of the sitar and enough money to maintain my household. I did some work with film scores, but received very little for it, since my artistic creations somehow were never on the commercial side of the film industry. Except for a few engagements at the major music conferences (or festivals) in Calcutta and other large cities, I had to depend financially on the performances I gave for the music circles. These music circles, a wonderful institution we have in India, are private organizations run by membership; they sponsor musical evenings for which they ask one distinguished artist and his accompanists to perform. The programs the circles give are held in small halls and usually start about nine or nine-thirty in the evening. A dais is set up along one wall for the musicians, and chairs are placed against the other walls, but nearly everyone squats on the floor. The audience is made up of connoisseurs and real lovers of Indian music, people who know the music well and can follow every subtle detail of *raga* and *tala*. It is frequently so inspiring to play for such an audience that the concerts go on for many hours. I can remember performing for audiences who did not want me to stop, and the concerts were not finished until five or six in the morning. Of course, this is exceedingly strenuous on performer and listener alike! In spite of the fact that the music circles pay the artists much less than the major music festivals or other public concerts, I, like all other musicians, found it a great pleasure to perform for these warm, receptive, and understanding audiences.

Also while I was in Bombay, I played for a number of "private programs"—that is, I was invited to perform in the home of a *maharaja* or a very wealthy citizen. For these performances, I received a little more money, but my music was supposed to serve more as entertainment and background music. Very often, when I went to one of these gatherings, the guests sat comfortably in deep sofas, smoking and drinking, and carrying on spirited conversations, and paying no attention whatever to the music. Many musicians, I discovered, were willing to tolerate this because they were well paid for performing for such people, but I could never stand for this kind of atmosphere. I started my own personal rebel movement, insisting that either everyone sit on the floor or a dais be brought for me and my accompanists, and I asked everyone to keep silent and give their full attention to the music, not smoking or drinking as they listened. Sometimes, these audiences were surprised, but they cooperated.

When Uday closed his cultural center at Almora in 1944, a number of the musicians and dancers who had been with him joined the Indian People's Theatre Association in Bombay. They told me about the group and the creative opportunities they found there, and a few months later, I was asked to join the association as the musical director of all stage activity—that is, ballet productions. Apart from my teaching and directing in the group, I as well as my colleagues would be free to continue other musical activities outside I.P.T.A. Since I realized this position would give me an excellent creative outlet, I did not hesitate to join.

The group I was to work with lived in a beautiful old mansion with an immense garden in the suburbs just outside Bombay. There were boys and girls from all over India, working, learning, practicing all together, even taking meals in a common dining hall, squatting on the floor Indian style. I immediately liked the group and was inspired by its busy, interested, and creative atmosphere. Some of my time was spent teaching music to the young people, but my major efforts went into composing the score for the ballet that was in the works, entitled *India Immortal*, which was a cultural and political history of India shown all through dance.

When I joined this "cultural squad," as it was called, I was already aware that it was being financed and sponsored by the Communist Party of India, but I made it quite clear that my only interest was in artistic creativity and that I did not want either to be given orders by the Party or to be involved with politics in any way. I was given full assurance that I could devote myself completely to music and would not have to participate in any political activity. The first four or five months with the Indian People's Theatre Association were a happy and productive time for me. I was very inspired, and the music just flowed out of me. In a very short time, I completed

the ballet music and found myself altogether satisfied with it.

Very soon after I finished the ballet music, I was commissioned to do the scores for two films, *Dharta ke Lal* ("Children of the Earth") and *Neecha Nagar* ("The City Below"). Both were of a sociopolitical nature and were very interesting to work on. Generally, music for Indian films, both then and now, means a group of songs—that is, ten or twelve songs are composed for each film, and no importance is given to the background music. In these two films I tried a new approach, putting great stress on the incidental music and having it follow the feeling of the narrative and emphasizing the drama. I used only Indian instruments, either solo or in ensembles, whereas most other film scores called for an assemblage of Western instruments and rarely took advantage of the sound of our own Indian instruments. The films, forceful and stimulating, but on a rather naïve level, were not at all commercial and could not be considered by any means "box-office successes," but the connoisseurs of film and music did recognize and appreciate my efforts to develop a new approach in handling the score. Because neither of the films was very successful, those associated in their production did not have much of a chance for further work in films, and this was the end of my film career as well—for the time being. Many years later, when I went back to film scoring, I again tried my idea of using only Indian instruments and Indian classical and folk forms for the incidental music. This time the idea caught on, and it was taken up by many other music directors.

India was going through serious political upheavals in 1946, and when I returned to my duties at the Indian People's Theatre Association after doing a concert tour and completing the film scores, I found the troubles reflected in the "cultural squads." At first I had felt so happy and free there, but now orders came from the Party boss to do new plays and ballets based on current political topics—from their point of view, of course. Everywhere we toured with our ballet, I saw that artists, writers, and folk musicians in other chapters of I.P.T.A. had joined the group because of its political attraction for them, and not only for the artistic opportunities it offered. I grew more and more unhappy with the way things were turning out and finally decided to leave I.P.T.A. in the summer of 1946.

I and four of the others who had left I.P.T.A. were offered the chance to take charge of a new ballet production the Indian National Theatre was preparing. The dance was based on Pandit Nehru's famous book, *The Discovery of India*. The Indian National Theatre provided us with dancers, musicians, and funds, and we began rehearsals in the summer of 1946. In a few months, the production was ready, and we took it to Delhi for the important Asian Conference the following spring. By the time we had done several performances in Bombay, my brothers Rajendra and Debendra and our two colleagues who had come from I.P.T.A. with us all decided it was time for us to undertake an independent venture and start our own group. That way we would be free to function as we pleased and would not have to answer to the politically affiliated directors of the various cultural groups. In the summer of 1947, then, we five formed the India Renaissance Artists and, acting as its directors, enlisted several dozen musicians and dancers to take part in our dance production. The ballet was an improved and elaborated version of *The Discovery of India* and we were lucky that Panditji gave us his permission to do the historical work in dance form —and gave us his blessing on it as well. We portrayed the early Dravidian period in India and the Vedic era, and went through the history of India, even to Gandhi's death, and showed the development of our entire culture, our politics, and our art. With high enthusiasm we directed all the rehearsals and even made all our own masks and costumes. The ballet was a tremendous undertaking for us, and so we were gratified by our successes in the two-week tour to Calcutta and then two more weeks in Bombay. I felt my own creative powers expanding and maturing, but I'm afraid the same was not true of my sense of business, for some misunderstandings arose between our two colleagues and us three Shankar brothers that brought about much unfortunate publicity, and we were forced to disband the India Renaissance Artists.

NO STRENGTH, NO HOPE, NO WILL

In the next few months I underwent the worst struggles of my life, both materially and spiritually. Many of the artists who had been performing in the India Renaissance Artists and who were now out of jobs were living in our house, and we brothers felt that we had a commitment to take care of these people and feed them for the time being, since they had originally given up good jobs to join us in the I.R.A. And so it happened that I, through the few concerts I was giving at the time, was the sole supporter of nearly thirty-five people. Concert opportunities then were few, and I was on the verge of offering myself to various societies to perform, even though I would not have chosen to give concerts for them ordinarily. I had no strength left, no will, no hope, and I felt that I was failing completely as an artist and as a person. Things had reached such a point that I had resolved to take my life. Our house was near a railway, and I planned in elaborately grotesque detail how, at a certain moment, I would hurl myself under an oncoming train and end my miseries. I prepared a letter for Rajendra and one for the police, saying that no one but myself was responsible for my death. The day I had chosen for my fatal move had nearly arrived, when I received news from a friend that the Prince of Jodhpur had come to Bombay for a visit and wanted to hear me play. I had met this Prince a few years earlier at the College of Princes at Ajmere, where I had gone to perform along with Baba. The Prince set the time for my performance, and I was told that I would receive a large sum of money for it.

The performance was scheduled for the evening, and in the morning of that day I took my sitar and began to practice. I remember very well how dejected I was that I had not been practicing lately, and as I held my sitar and played, I kept thinking this might be the last concert of my life, and I cried and cried as I thought of the people I loved and cared for, who would mourn for me after my death. Even the people who didn't like me personally, I thought to myself, would weep for me when I died and would say, "Too bad. He was such a promising artist. . . ." My musings grew increasingly dramatic as the morning turned to afternoon.

Then, while I was sitting and practicing, someone knocked at the gate and came in to speak to me. Very humbly, he explained that he was not speaking for himself; he was traveling with his *guru*, and his *guruji* had to go to the bathroom! The man recognized me, since I was sitting with my sitar, and he became even more apologetic for disturbing me. I dried my tears and began to ask a few questions. I learned that this man's *guru* was a *mahatma* ("great soul") known as Tat Baba. I immediately got up and became very attentive, for I had heard this name before and had been told that this man was a very great yogi and a saintly person. The fellow went on, explaining that just as they were passing by our house, the *guru* had asked him to stop the car so that he could go into the nearest house.

Performing the deeply moving ceremony of greeting Tat Baba by anointing his head with sandalwood paste and presenting him with offerings of flowers and garlands.

Eric Hayes

And quite simply, that is how I met the person who changed the course of my life—not only on this one day, but many times thereafter. When I saw him, I was completely overwhelmed by his appearance. He looked like a young man of thirty, full of youth and life and light. His head was completely shaved and he wore a long robe of sackcloth or burlap, from which he got his name. (*Tat* means "sackcloth.") His very aspect moved me to tears and filled me with a great peace. I asked if I could offer him some fruit, but he took only tea. He sat there with his tea for about twenty minutes, hardly speaking, and when he did, he expressed his thoughts in a very strange and abstract way. Then he asked me if I would play the sitar for him, and overjoyed, I took up my sitar, ready to perform. "No, no; not now." And he asked me to come at eight that evening to the house where he was staying. I just looked at him and said yes, completely forgetting my arrangement with the Maharajkumar and all thoughts of money.

That evening I went and played for Tat Baba, and he sat, totally absorbed in the music. I had tears in my eyes as I played, and I was very deeply inspired by his presence. When I stopped playing, after an hour and a half, I realized that Tat Baba was in a trance. There were only Champak Lal (the man who owned the house) and one or two of the *guru's* disciples in the room, and we all sat quietly for a few minutes. When the *guru* came back to the physical reality of the room where he was sitting, he got up without speaking and went into the adjoining room. In a couple of minutes, he called me to come in. That half hour was the first time I spent alone with him, and we had not, of course, had much chance to speak before. Tat Baba spoke to me of many things. He said that the tests in life are sometimes extremely hard, especially when one has to face cruel and envious men who have a will to destroy others. "No one," he said, "can stand up against this unless he is blessed with strength by his *guru*." He kept silent for some moments and I was too awestruck to make a sound. "Wipe away all your worry," he counseled. "You are still going to go through a period of difficulty, but everything will be all right." His next words surprised me: "The money you missed tonight will come back to you many times over." And I realized he knew all about my concert for the Maharajkumar. Looking deep into my eyes, as if he knew of my plan for suicide, he warned, "Don't do anything foolish. Be manly and have patience." He asked me to return to see him in two days, and then he sent me home.

On the way home in the car, Champak Lal told me many things about Tat Baba. I learned that he was a *trikal gnyani*, which means that he has the knowledge of the past, the present, and the future and has gone through all seven stages of attainment, or *siddhi*. My companion informed me that, although Baba does not perform magic or tricks, or show off his occult powers, like the usual yogis of a lower standard, everyone was very much aware of his great inner strength. He said, too, that though Baba looked so youthful, he must be well over a hundred. This he explained by citing the names of many of his disciples who were all over sixty years of age and who had been Baba's disciples from their childhood. Filled with wonder, I listened to story after story about this fabulous person, but I must confess that I did have a few doubts and could not help noticing the ardent, almost blind, love that all his disciples had for him. Of his age, I was completely convinced a few years later, when I met some other of his disciples, all in their late sixties and seventies, who said they had been with Tat Baba since childhood and that their fathers before them had been Baba's disciples. Perhaps it is odd, but I never wanted to ask Tat Baba about any of these tales, and I never seriously doubted him, even after he initiated me in Delhi a year and a half later. Deep within me, I knew how great and powerful he was. When he accepted me as his disciple, he spoke, or "sowed," the *beej mantra*, the sacred words, into my ear, and these words are still alive within me. (This initiation is not the same as the ceremony in music where the thread is tied to symbolize the binding of the *shishya* to the *guru*.)

In the two and a half months after I first met Tat Baba, we saw each other often, and I noticed the strangest things began to happen to me. Money started to flow in, and suddenly I had invitations to play three concerts a week. So many offers came

from Calcutta that I decided to go there and stay for a few months. And many little everyday problems were solved. Trouble I had had with my ears since childhood disappeared and has bothered me only once or twice since then. Most important, within me I felt a new, special strength, a surge of power.

Tat Baba never showed me any gross miracles, but I felt his miraculous powers in many apparently trivial occurrences. Even while I was still seeing him in those first few weeks, long before I was initiated, I felt very strongly his love for me, and he constantly repeated he was with me, supporting me, giving me strength. I remember once he said to me, "Do you think that incident of stopping at your house to go to the bathroom was a coincidence? Or perhaps that I couldn't have waited a few minutes more? People like us can control all our bodily functions for days! It was destined that we should meet. I had to come to you." Since that time, even to the present, I have seen many miraculous things happen in association with Tat Baba, but I have taken them for granted, as things that will naturally result from the thoughts or actions of such a person, and I have never been surprised.

A PARROT
SIPPING TEA

There is one incident I remember that impressed me enormously. I was supposed to be leaving soon for Calcutta, and Tat Baba had already left for Girnar, the Mountain of the Lions, in the region of Gujerat or Pushkar in the North, or some other favorite stopping place of his. One day, well after his departure, all of a sudden one of Tat Baba's disciples came running up to my house, calling out, "Baba has come! Baba has come!" and he said that Tat Baba was at the house of one of his disciples. "But," he went on, "he hasn't come in his own body. He has come as a parrot."

I felt this was just a bit too much, and I reflected on the fanatic love of Tat Baba's disciples and said to myself that this time their devotion had gone beyond its limits. To the disciple, I expressed none of these doubts, but patiently asked for some details of this incredible event. It seemed that a beautiful green parrot had flown out of nowhere into the house of one of Baba's disciples and settled in the room where Baba always sat when he visited, on the couch that was reserved for Baba alone and upon which no one else sat, out of respect for the *guru*. The parrot went straight to this couch and would not move from it. At first, they tried to shoo it away, but when they saw the parrot had no intention of being displaced, they decided to try to feed it some little seeds and bird food. The parrot refused. The woman of the house came into the room with a cup of tea for someone, and the parrot left the couch, flying straight over to the tea, and began to take little sips from the cup. Then, the woman recalled a vivid dream she had had, where Baba appeared as a parrot and said, "What's the matter? Don't you recognize me?" and then told her that he would visit her house and remain for three days. The parrot remained on the couch and sipped the tea, for Baba lived on practically nothing but tea, and pecked at a vegetarian dish that had been prepared for him.

When the disciple finished telling me the story, I ran all the way back to the house with him, and if I hadn't seen the parrot myself, I would never have believed it. By the time I arrived, there were hundreds of other people at the house making a terrific commotion. I went and did a *pranam* to the parrot-*guru*, along with all the rest of the visitors. And indeed, this amazing parrot stayed there on the couch for three and a half days receiving disciples and visitors, then suddenly flew up and disappeared out the window. I knew that often if Tat Baba had some message for one of his disciples, he would come to him in a dream and speak. But this was extraordinary.

Tat Baba is unlike many other holy men, who establish their own little colony in a forest and remain there all their lives. He prefers to travel and, with his peripatetic *ashram*, he numbers thousands of people as his disciples. In different parts of India, he is even known by different names. He never stays very long in one place and has no set itinerary. If you ask him if he will be in a certain place next week

or tomorrow or this evening at seven, he does not know. Sometimes, he wears very expensive Western suits and drives a huge car, or sometimes his body is covered with dirty rags and he is filthy and unshaven, or sometimes he will travel first class on the railroad and reserve a whole car for himself and his companions.

Once, I recall, I was to participate in the ceremonies celebrating the opening of a new radio station. I was scheduled to play and was just resting a bit in my room at the government guesthouse and preparing for the concert. Quite unexpectedly, the door swung open and a strange character sauntered into my room. The light was shining in my eyes and I could not very well make out who this person was. He was dressed in a very smartly tailored Western suit and greeted me with a loud and emphatic "Hel-lo," grandly sweeping a hat from his head as he saluted me. Then I recognized him—Tat Baba, of course! He had come, just like a child, to show me his new clothes. He was with a party of people who had no idea who he really was, and they had all come for the opening ceremonies of the station. He told me to act as if I were just a friend and to behave very good-naturedly, taking my cues from his own conduct. And indeed, if I had some trouble trying to treat him as just another person, I could scarcely control myself when I heard him laughing and making crude jokes and being met with the same coarse behavior by those who were with him. He is a great prankster and loves to put on disguises, acting like another person, deliberately hiding his true nature.

When I first met Tat Baba, as I said, I was perplexed by the way he spoke and by the way he phrased answers to his disciples' questions. I myself could never approach him with a direct question, but if I was ever in his company and had a question in my mind, the answer always happened to come up as if by chance when he spoke in conversation either to me or, more often, to someone else. This is one of the remarkable qualities in his mental power: he speaks to another person and directly answers my unasked question. The very words he chooses, too, are put together in a strange way. He has a wonderful punning ability, and the sounds of one word suggest similar sounds of another and another and another, and the words run on in a mad string that somehow makes sense in an abstract way.

To me, Tat Baba is not so much like a living person, but rather like a great force, and I can always feel him with me. At first he gave me just the *beej mantra* and never told me to suffer any hardships for him. He knows me, my life and my background, and he says he will not tell me to do this or not to do that, for he knows that I shall, just by myself, do everything that has to be done. He has encouraged me, though, to practice yoga for the body, to keep it in tone. Recently, Tat Baba has been kind enough to initiate me into even higher secrets of yoga and meditation in which special *mantras* have to be repeated, taking care to maintain the correct posture of sitting and the correct breathing, and placing each sound of the *mantras* in the different *chakras* of the body. The effects of this second initiation are miraculous, and I find that I am filled with great bliss and undergo many beautiful spiritual experiences. At these times, I feel as if I could completely give up the materialistic side of my life, but, as Tat Baba tells me, the time is not right yet, and I still have to go through the process of my *karma*. Then, one day, of my own accord, I will be able to give up all my materialistic pursuits and devote the rest of my life to religious contemplation and helping others acquire spiritual strength. I have learned so much from him, just by sitting and listening. He claims it is this *guru mantra* that does all these beneficial things, constantly working in the mind of the disciple, directing him. When I was living in Delhi, he often came to stay with me, and now that I am based in Bombay, he comes once or twice a year, and I meet him as often as I can. In spiritual matters, Tat Baba is my only *guru*.

From my childhood I have been attracted to those great saints and yogis who were almost legendary figures. A distant aunt of mine used to charm me with stories of the miraculous feats performed by Tailangi Swami, Kathia Baba, Bijoy Goswami, and many others. Then, as an adolescent in Europe, when I was with Dada's troupe, I went through a period of avidly reading books on Ramakrishna Paramahamsa and his great disciple Vivekananda, who was the first to bring the message of the Hindu religion to the West. When Vivekananda came to the West in 1893, to a conference of all the religions of the world in Chicago, he was given three minutes to speak, and he spoke for three days! Two saints whom I never met but whose lives fascinated me were Shri Aurobindo and Ramana Maharishi. I read and knew so much about these powerful saints that I felt as if I really did know them. Later, when I was grown, I met a number of other impressive and powerful yogis and have been blessed by them and have been asked to play the sitar for them as well.

Though I may never surrender myself to these saintly people as a disciple, I am very pleased to meet them and pay homage to them. One of them who has impressed me by her warmth and goodness is the lady-saint Mata Anandamai, or "Mother Full of Joy," who is really like a mother to me. Then again, there are many small-wonder-workers whom I have seen operating since I was young—men who can read minds or tell the future, or who give out talismans—but they have never made a very favorable impression on me. One of the greatest religious events for devout Hindus is the Kumbha Mela, a vast gathering of saintly people from all over India, something like a religious convention. The Kumbha Mela takes place every twelve years, when certain constellations of stars coincide in a particular position.

In January, 1966, I was fortunate to be able to attend the Kumbha Mela. Assembled there were hundreds of thousands of monks and religious men and women from all over the country. There was one man believed to be three hundred years old, and there were scores of religious "showmen" and magicians, but there were also a few of our very great saintly Hindus. Every morning there were processions of these saintly and godly people, on their elephants, to the bathing place in the rivers. The presence of these people gave an additional aura of holiness to the sacred bathing place. The entire area of the meeting ground, three miles square, was covered with brightly colored tents—big tents for the outstanding figures and smaller tents for their disciples. The biggest tents belonged to the religious heads, those with the best showmanship and organizing abilities, some of whom speak English and have traveled widely outside India. Quite a few of these important people asked me to play the sitar for them in their private tents, but I was not able to accept most of the offers. I did, however, play for a short time for the group of religious men in the tent of Maharishi Yogi, about whom I had heard only outside India, in such places as Sweden and California. Before his extraordinary rise to fame through his association with many famous stars—and his subsequent downfall—I was impressed by his ability for organization and for communicating with the Western mind. His system of meditation seemed to guide many young people away from the use of drugs. I also played in the tent of the lady-saint Mata Anandamai where I was deeply inspired by the beautiful religious atmosphere and the many bearded holy men who were seated all around me.

Once, I remember, I experienced an ecstatic feeling of spiritual bliss when I played for the great living saint, the Shankaracharya of Kamakoti Peetham. We were in Madras, in the mango grove adjoining a house, and I played under the scorching sun of high noon. The saintly man was sitting on a small mat on the ground and a mat had been spread for Alla Rakha and myself. The saint's elephant was standing quite near, eating grass, and there were multitudes of ants creeping over the ground. When I started to play, all these things evaporated from my mind, as if I were in a trance. First, I played *Raga Todi*, and then Alla Rakha's tabla joined me for another *raga*, and miraculously, our instruments never once went out of tune—an amazing thing since we were in the direct sun. When we finished playing, there was a long hush. The only sound was the back and forth swush, swush of the elephant's trunk sweeping up grass. And the Shankaracharya remained lost in a trance-like state.

COMPOSITIONS IN THE SOUND OF INDIA

All-India Radio, the government-sponsored broadcasting network, offered me a twofold job in New Delhi near the end of 1948, as the director of music for the External Services Division and as the composer-conductor for their proposed new instrumental ensemble. Never before had any performing artist been offered such a responsible, respected, and high-salaried position by any government organization. The promise that I could work on creative and experimental lines attracted me to the post, and I went to New Delhi to take up my duties in February, 1949. I was to help the program executive and the program assistant, both administrative officers, in planning all the productions dealing with music in the External Services programs, whose broadcasts are beamed to countries in Europe, the Middle East, Africa, Southeast Asia, and the Far East. I found great encouragement there for my orchestral pieces, the incidental music I did for radio plays, and for musical dramas. The ensemble I worked with consisted of the sitar, *veena, sarod, sarangi, vichitra veena,* flutes, *jaltarang* (china bowls of different sizes filled with water and played with sticks), *tabla, dholak,* and many other kinds of drums, cymbals, and percussion instruments. The early musical experiments I did when I was with Dada's troupe in Europe later had motivated me to try ballet music and film scores, and now I was determined to experiment further in compositions of a predominantly Indian nature—that is, pieces that retained as much as possible the Indian character and the quality of Indian sound.

The different kinds of compositions I worked on fell into a few basic patterns. One of my composing methods was to take a *raga* and, treating it with as much classical purity as possible, have the entire ensemble play it as if it were being improvised. For instance, I took such *ragas* as *Darbari, Mian ki Malhar,* or *Puriya,* and had the ensemble play the whole *alap* and *jor* movements as we play them on solo instruments, followed by a piece within a *tala* framework. The entire composition was fixed, and the musicians followed me as I conducted. The effect was altogether breathtaking and new, and it sounded as if the whole piece were being improvised, even though the musicians had a complete score in front of them. There was no counterpoint or harmony in these pieces, nor did all the instruments play together all of the time. Instead, I tried to take full advantage of the quality, color, tone, and range of each instrument, and I had each one play separately or along with another complementary instrument in different parts of the composition. After some time, when the musicians had come to know my technique and were quite confident of their playing, I would call on a few of them, one at a time, who were good solo performers to improvise occasionally.

Another of the techniques I experimented with at the time was composing a piece based on one of the light *ragas*, mostly used for the *thumri* form, such as *Piloo*, *Khamaj*, or *Kafi*. Keeping the spirit of the *ragas*, I used them as the groundwork for romantic, bright, lilting pieces with exciting rhythms and lively melodies. Occasionally in these compositions, I even used a very free kind of counterpoint, where one group of instruments played against another, executing different phrases with any number of rhythms. Actually, this was nothing new, since this kind of "counterpoint" is more like a very close dialogue between the two artists in a recital of classical music.

The most exciting compositions I did—the ones that got the loudest and most enthusiastic reception from audiences—were based on the pure folk style, using regional tunes and all the different kinds of folk dances. I also did a large number of program, or thematic, compositions: the life of Buddha, some fairy tales for children, and episodes from various eras of Indian history. I also orchestrated some well-known poems of Tagore and composed background mood music for drama. In these thematic pieces, I kept strictly to the theme, spirit, period or region from which the subject came. Naturally, I was completely free to utilize any instruments I chose, including Western instruments that I used for special effects. I could take any styles and any forms of music and very freely work them into the compositions. Even if a classical *raga* was used at some point, I could leave it intact to sustain a mood or mix it with several other *ragas* in quick succession for another kind of effect.

After about three years with the External Services, I changed over to the Home Services Division of All-India Radio. There, I was very pleased to be able to organize a larger ensemble that was known as Vadya Vrinda, or National Orchestra, with which I continued to work for the next few years. This orchestra was very much like the instrumental ensemble I had been working with earlier, only it was considerably enlarged. In particular, the string section had been greatly augmented and now included many Western instruments of the violin family.

In my childhood, so often had I heard Uday refuse to use one single Western instrument in the troupe's orchestral ensemble that his adamant and repeated refusals made a strong impression in my mind. But as my musical senses matured, especially while I was with All-India Radio, I slowly came to change my attitude and realized that Western instruments, especially violins and their relatives, could portray Indian music most beautifully and, in fact, had been used in India by outstanding musicians for many years. I was first attracted to the idea of the violin playing Indian music when I heard Baba perform on it in his own superb way. Later, I heard some masters from the South playing Karnatic music on the violin, and then I was convinced that the instrument is quite capable of bringing out all the delicate nuances of Indian classical music. A Westerner, however, would probably be surprised at the way an Indian violinist sits on the floor and holds his instrument at a seemingly odd angle to the body. I found, too, that in an orchestral piece where a certain bass quality is required the cello and double bass add to our music a full body and richness of tone. Since I became aware of these possibilities, I often use all the members of the violin family in my various types of orchestral compositions.

PUSHKIN'S LOOK-ALIKE

During the years I was associated with All-India Radio, I was free to perform at all the important music conferences throughout India, and at the end of 1954 I went to Soviet Russia as one of the members of the first Indian cultural delegation sent out of the country. Our group was composed of about forty eminent dancers and musicians representing different styles

Satiajit Ray and I at a scoring and recording session of the Apu trilogy.

from all over India, and we were sent by our government for a two-month tour as part of a cultural exchange with the U.S.S.R. We were given spectacular treatment—almost as if we were diplomats—wherever we traveled, and our performances were very well received. Though I had been almost everywhere else on the European continent on my previous tours, this was my first time in the Soviet Union, and I was quite excited about it. I was especially thrilled to see *Swan Lake*, *Romeo and Juliet*, and *Giselle* and other ballets performed at the Bolshoi Theater in Moscow. While we were in Tiflis, Georgia, where we had been invited to see the Georgian folk ensembles, I was surprised to hear one of my own orchestral compositions performed—a tone picture of a camel caravan. And the Georgian musicians were very pleased to play it for us. Wherever we went in Russia, I noticed

that many times when people saw me and were introduced to me, they made a remark to their companions about me, and I always heard the same word. I soon realized that they were saying Pushkin, and were all marveling how much I resembled him. In fact, a film director even approached me with an offer to play Pushkin in a film he was doing!

Also during the time I spent with All-India Radio, I had the chance to do the scores for some films that became quite successful not only in India, but all through the West. *Kabuli Wala* won a special prize for its music at the Berlin Music Festival, and *Pather Panchali*, the first film done by Satiajit Ray, became a classic of Indian cinema. In this film, there is a perfect blend of excellent acting and directing, story, music, and photography. Ray won international fame in no time and was considered one of the best film directors in the world. I did three more scores for Ray's films later; two of them completed the trilogy of which *Pather Panchali* was the first. Though Ray improved and became more mature in his directing with each picture he made, I, along with many others, think that *Pather Panchali* is still one of his best creations. Though it may be technically less perfect than his later films, it has a naturalness, a lyricism, a spontaneity, and a charming lack of sophistication that combine to give the film a beautiful unity.

THE VINAYA OF YEHUDI MENUHIN

In 1951, I had the opportunity of meeting a great Western musician who soon became a close friend —Yehudi Menuhin. He had come to India for the first time, and soon after his arrival in Delhi, where he was to give several concerts, my dear friend Dr. Narayana Menon held a musical soirée at his home for Yehudi and asked me to play. I had seen Yehudi for the first time in the early Thirties, in Paris at his rehearsals, but never got to know him, although his teacher Georges Enesco often visited our house. Yehudi experienced Indian music for the first time that evening at Dr. Menon's house, and he was obviously deeply moved. I had never before seen a Western classical musician respond so emotionally to our music, not just show interest in its technical aspects. This reaction of Yehudi's to our music and my own reaction to his personality were the beginning of a beautiful friendship between us. While he was still in India, I heard him give a concert of Bach and Bartók—a piece Bartók composed for him. And he also had a chance to hear several other Indian musicians, from both North and South, perform. Since that first trip, Yehudi has been so taken with Indian music that he is still writing and speaking of it, studying it and trying to understand it better.

A few years later, in 1955, in conjunction with a special India Week celebration at the Museum of Modern Art in New York, Yehudi undertook to arrange for me to come and perform. Unfortunately, I was not able to come to New York then, but sent Ali Akbar and the young *tabla* player Chatur Lal in my place. I have performed on the same stage as Yehudi many times, though not with him; there was the UNESCO celebration in 1958 and the Commonwealth Festival in 1966. And then at the Bath Festival in 1966, of which he was in charge, we played our first duet. The Bath Festival had commissioned a young German composer to do a piece for us, but while we were rehearsing it, the music did not seem satisfactory. We kept the beginning of the piece more or less as it was, and I rewrote the rest completely, keeping only *Raga Tilang* as the base. This we did in just three days! And the piece was an immediate success. When we did the recording of it soon afterward, I again rewrote it completely, and called it "Swara Kakali." I also composed a short solo piece for Yehudi based on the morning *Raga Gunakali* and called it "Prabhati" which means "of the morning." Yehudi had never played Indian music before, and in this short time his efforts to play with as much Indian spirit as he could were really praiseworthy. In the latest duet that I have composed for us, based on *Raga Piloo*, which we played at the United Nations in a celebration of Human Rights Day, December 10, 1967, he really grasped the spirit of the music, and I am sure that, as we played, the audience was as aware of this as I was.

Human Rights Day concert at the United Nations; Yehudi and I perform duets accompanied by Alla Rakha, with Kamala playing the tamboura.

Courtesy of United Nations

Courtesy of United Nations

Yehudi and I are rehearsing with high spirits at my home in New York before the United Nations concert. While playing Indian music, Yehudi always observes our custom of sitting on the floor.

Yehudi takes great pleasure in working on a piece with me and rehearsing it, the two of us together. I compose the music spontaneously and he writes it down; and then, while we are practicing, it is a joy to see this superb musician shedding all his pride and awareness of self and accepting like a child or like a devoted student my teaching and my music, although he is superior to me in age, experience, and fame. After every rehearsal, he jumps up and embraces me, and I can feel how much love he has for our music. Since my childhood, he was my idol and hero, and now he calls me his *guru*. I find in Yehudi the inherent quality of *vinaya* and the desire to search for knowledge, for, besides his fascination with our music, he is deeply interested in Indian philosophy and yoga. I think he has done a great deal to awaken in Western classical musicians an intense curiosity about India's classical traditions. He is an ideal example for music students all over the world.

REACHING WESTERN EARS

After I came to Delhi in 1949, I was amazed to find that there was very little appreciation of our classical music in the city, in spite of the fact that Delhi traditionally produced many fine musicians. In the beginning I was staying at the home of Sir Shri Ram, the respected industrialist, and at the request of a few friends, I began holding musical soirées in the adjoining mansion that belonged to his brother, Sir Shankar Lal. For these programs, some of the time I played solo pieces, and other times I asked a staff artist of All-India Radio or a visiting artist to play or sing. Occasionally I asked for some contributions to help bring in other fine artists to perform for the group, whose members soon numbered almost one hundred fifty. Some of the members of this informal group were inspired to start a regular music circle, and so the Jhankar Music Circle of Delhi was formed. For the next two or three years, I was its arranger and director. Later, the same group broadened further and became the Bharatya Kala Kendra.

From 1950 until I left Delhi half a dozen or so years later, I performed some musical experiments that made me feel even more strongly that I had to bring my music to the West and try to give Westerners some insight into our vast musical heritage.

At the time, I was quite friendly with some ambassadors, counselors, and ministers in numerous foreign embassies in India, who loved music and wanted to know more about the music of India. From just listening to concerts, they told me, they felt they had no real knowledge or understanding of our music. One evening, I was performing in the home of the Belgian Counselor for a group of diplomats, and thinking that they may not know exactly what to expect and listen for, I gave my listeners a short talk on the music before my recital, and then gave explanations of the *ragas*, *talas*, and the scales that we use, before I did each individual piece. Everyone seemed pleased to have even a brief explanation of the music they heard so often around them. From some of the diplomats who were present that evening, a group was formed that was to meet once or twice a month at various officials' homes for recitals and talks on Indian music, and in no time, the group included fifty or sixty enthusiastic music lovers.

Often, my childhood experiences in Paris came back to me, and I thought of the artists who had called our music repetitious and uninteresting. I wanted to correct these impressions and help Western listeners understand what we played. Fortunately, I knew enough about Western music to give my explanations in terms which these people were already acquainted with and to make comparisons between the two musical systems. At the same time, I came to understand better the Western mind and the kind of explanations it required. The success of these explanations and the enthusiasm of these small audiences of Westerners encouraged me in my plans to go to the West with my music and try to promote a better understanding between the two musical heritages.

In 1956 I left All-India Radio. I wanted very much to travel outside India, to Europe and especially to the United States, and had formulated some definite plans. I had made contact with a European agent, who arranged for a few concerts in London and some other cities in England. When in September, 1956, we left for Europe, I was aware that I was taking a big risk with this adventure, but I had already decided to bring Chatur Lal with me as *tabla* player and N. C. Mullick to play *tamboura* and to help take care of my sitar, which he himself had constructed. By the time we reached London on the first part of our tour, some contacts had already been made, we found, by Indian student organizations in Germany, and there were also several concerts arranged for us in other European cities.

By these first concerts we earned very little money, and so we had to be as frugal as we could, living economically and staying in small hotels. Much of the time on the tour, I felt terribly humiliated and hurt, because, for me, it was almost like going back twelve or thirteen years to the hard days in India when I was just starting my career. We generally played in small halls with a seating capacity of five to six hundred, and even so, the halls were seldom full. The audience was usually more than half composed of Indians who had moved to the West. Although these audiences were small, they were especially appreciative of our music. Inadequate promotion and publicity, as well as a relative lack of popular interest in Indian music, kept our audiences limited to people who were already familiar with our music —mostly these fellow countrymen living abroad and a small number of Westerners who were acquainted with Indian music through visits to our country or study of other aspects of Indian culture. In Germany I found the warmest audiences of all Europe, though even there the audiences were by no means large. I was hurt most in Paris, the city I loved so in my youth, because I was met with a hard coldness, except on the part of a very few, and found little rapport between us musicians and the listeners. In the next few years on my tours in the West I went through the same hardships and spiritual difficulties—small but warm audiences and ridiculously low earnings—but I kept my spirit of mission and found a little improvement in the audiences' reception and appreciation with each successive visit.

Some good friends had booked a number of programs for us in New York, Philadelphia, and Boston, and so I came back to the United States after nearly twenty years, in October, 1956. I had been looking forward to coming to the States, on my own this time, and was excited about the trip. My first concert, at the Y.M.H.A. in New York, was surprisingly successful and got quite good notices from the critics. There were a few other performances in New York during the next couple of months, including one at Town Hall which was, like almost all my other performances, arranged through friends without the help of a proper agent. Some Indian friends set up

a few programs for us then in Los Angeles and San Francisco, and so we toured to the West Coast. None of these places was new to me, but still, coming on my own after such a long time and performing for such a different kind of audience, I saw things from a new perspective. I noticed quite a change in the country itself—so much more affluence and self-assurance, and the attitude of the young people seemed to have changed so much since the war.

From the first, I considered California with its mild climate and lush greenery one of the most beautiful and stimulating places in the world. The city of Los Angeles, in particular, excited me because it seemed so diverse and animated—a city with many different faces. This attraction for Los Angeles prompted me eleven years later to open a branch of my school of music there. In Bombay, I established my Kinnara School of Music in 1963, with the idea of teaching the style of instrumental music used by the Beenkar *gharana* that I had learned from Baba. I felt that it was necessary to continue the old *guru-shishya parampara*, but in combination with modern approaches to teaching. In my dreams I saw a school run on the basis of the old *ashrams*—a small but complete community somewhere beyond the city, with some very talented disciples—not too many—and a carefully chosen group of *gurus* to teach the different styles of singing and of instrumental music. I even had plans for thorough training in yoga for all the disciples and some classes in Sanskrit, which is necessary for research and work in the old scriptures.

In recent tours to the United States, and especially to the West Coast, I found many young people with a great desire to learn the music of India. And even in India, over the past five years or so, I have seen many young people from the West who have come to study our music. Some of them come to study with the help of fellowships, and others have saved up enough money to make the trip alone. But I have seen too often that by the time these eager students have settled down in a city, found a teacher, and started to assimilate the new atmosphere, their time is up. Most of them returned to America none the wiser, at least in relation to music. It was after seeing all these young people that I thought of starting a branch

Lou Mack

Yehudi comes to visit Kinnara, my school of Indian music in Los Angeles.

of my school in America. I immediately decided on Los Angeles as the site for it and made all the necessary arrangements. Classes opened at the end of May, 1967, in very modest quarters; but the school has grown since then, and we have had to move to a larger building. Smoking is not permitted on the school premises, and everyone is required to take off his shoes before entering the school. There are no chairs, so students have to sit in the Indian manner, and they must also learn the proper greetings that are exchanged with the teacher.

My purpose in starting the school was to give young men and women a chance to learn the fundamentals of our music before going to India for further study. The curriculum concentrates on three main disciplines—voice, sitar, and *tabla*, though there are also quite a few students studying flute and *sarod*. In addition to the basic technical training, we give

the students a thorough knowledge of the history and development of our music, along with the legends, mythology, religion, and cultural heritage of the past, and their links with the present. All this is accomplished through talks, lectures, demonstrations, books, periodicals, and other kinds of informal "texts." I am trying not only to teach the music of India but also to emphasize the many aspects of our culture and customs that are so closely associated with the music. Of course, all this is only the first step toward the dream I cherish—founding *ashram*-like institutions outside the cities, where the training in music will be accompanied by studies in philosophy and the scriptures, and the students will live according to the strict discipline of *brahmacharya*. Americans, perhaps more than anyone else, I think, are ready for this discipline, for several reasons. First, after achieving tremendous affluence, they have had more than their fill of material things now. Then, most importantly, there is the problem of the young people and their search to find the way to peace, harmony, and love. Theirs seems to be a revolt against the Western ways of life, but I find they are good at adapting to other customs, and the traditions of India seem most attractive to them now, in spite of the strictness and discipline they call for.

AROUND THE WORLD

My accompanists and I returned to Europe in May, 1957, and during our three-month tour on the Continent, our reception was very much as it had been at the beginning. This time, we also performed in Belgium and Holland, and we were pleased that the reception in Germany was noticeably warmer. It was quite an adventure in those days to make such a tour; and when it was over, I felt that it had been successful in many ways—but not financially. When I returned to India I decided to continue using Delhi as my home base, though I knew I would be spending a lot of time traveling, since I was in demand for many concerts all over the country. I even made a short trip back to Europe at the end of 1957—for just three weeks—to do the music for a Swedish film.

Early in 1958 I undertook rehearsals for a new musical production in Delhi, sponsored by the Triveni Kala Sangam institution. The production, which I called *Melody and Rhythm*, portrayed the entire panorama of Hindustani music through both an orchestra and a choir, the ensemble consisting of nearly a hundred artists. The choir sang in all the different styles —*dhrupad, dhamar, khyal, tappa, tarana, thumri*— and there were also a few solo pieces. The orchestra performed pieces ranging from strictly classical to folk, and I even had them do some lullabies, *bhajans*, and popular songs. The show was sensational and turned out extremely well; I was especially pleased that Baba was at the opening performance and that he came to embrace and bless me. At another performance, Nehru (or Panditji, as we called him with affectionate respect) was present. When the curtain came down after the beautiful, soothing lullaby, the audience, hushed by the peaceful quality of the music, was unable, for many moments, to applaud. It so happened that Panditji, who was sitting in the center of the balcony, had completely fallen asleep. Many people saw him thus, and they grew even more aware that they should not applaud lest it awaken their beloved Nehru. After the show's finale, he was so excited, he came straightway up on the stage, embraced me, and congratulated all the artists.

That same year I headed a delegation of musicians and dancers for a tour of Japan. I had been more than a little excited by the prospect of visiting the country for the first time, and I was dazzled by all that I saw there when we arrived. I was amazed to see how this nation had achieved a remarkable material prosperity and, at the same time, had kept alive its ancient culture and artistic heritage. And I was very amused to find how truly a "man's country" it is. We all enjoyed our six weeks' stay in Japan, and our performances in Tokyo and other cities were very warmly appreciated.

Since then I have been on tour almost constantly and have visited many new places and revisited many that I already knew. Everywhere I find the same growing enthusiasm for our music and the desire to understand it better. I came to the United States in late 1961 and 1962 to do a long tour, performing in all the principal cities across the country, and returned again in 1964 and 1965. Indeed, I find that I am in the States more than once every year, and the country has become my second home. In Europe, I performed at the Leeds Festival, the Prague Spring Festival, and the Edinburgh Music Festival in 1963. The Edinburgh Festival gave a big boost to Indian music in Britain, since that year special attention was given to India and Indian events. For the first time, the *Manchester Guardian*, the *Observer*, and *The Times* all took a newly respectful attitude toward our music, which pleased me very much. Little by little, since I began my tours of Europe and the United States, I had seen the audiences change and improve each year, but after the Edinburgh Festival the general

Three musicians with whom I have worked in close rapport: Kamala, who plays the tamboura; Ali Akbar, with whom I have brought about many musical innovations, shown here with his sarod; and Alla Rakha, whose brilliant tabla accompaniment has won him many enthusiastic fans.

Tony Roberts   Courtesy of American Society for Eastern Art   Dan Esgro

attitude became extremely warm and very, very encouraging.

Apart from my listeners in India, I find the closest rapport in the United States, and I am overwhelmed by the amount of love the Americans show me and by their willingness to learn and to listen. Everywhere I go—New York, Los Angeles, St. Louis, Chicago, Boston—I find the same enthusiastic appreciation for something far deeper than a fad. England too is wonderful now, and Paris, which had been a difficult place until recently, has opened up at last! Rome receives me warmly, and Switzerland, I was surprised to find, was equally receptive to our music. The Scandinavian countries, as I had expected, were particularly responsive and alive, even in the most northerly part, in Lapland. It is the young people, I think, who create this wonderful feeling, and in each country I visit I see that its young people look and behave like all the rest of the young people all over the world.

In India, of course, I find audiences of people of all ages who have a profound understanding of our music. In some small villages in the western part of India, or in the South, or even in my own province of Bengal, I have found the very best audiences. These attentive lovers of music refuse to leave me, and when they inspire me, it is my greatest pleasure to play for them for perhaps seven or eight hours continuously. Unfortunately, my audiences in India's large cities are usually not so understanding or receptive, and I am sometimes confronted with a certain lack of discipline. For a number of years, now, I have been urging Indians to take on a more considerate attitude in their listening. I have been criticized in my country for being "Westernized," because I ask that concerts begin on time and that audiences listen in silence and with proper decorum (although occasional spontaneous appreciation at the appropriate time is very inspiring). Unlike the West, most Indians have not yet learned the value and importance of time, and when it comes to attending concerts, people do not hurry themselves. I argue that, if they can manage to arrive on time when they have to catch a plane or train, and even when they go to a movie, why is it that, for a concert of their own music, they will walk

in forty-five minutes after the music has begun?

It is not just the audience, either. The one who organizes the concert assumes it will not begin on time, so at the last minute, carpenters are still banging their nails on the stage, and technicians are setting up microphones around the dais, but still the carpenters have not finished with their work! And then—the artists! For some reason, many of our great performers think it below their dignity to arrive on time, and they make a point of coming in half an hour late. For the past ten or fifteen years I have been the "bad guy" because I want to change all this, and I have been criticized and torn apart by audiences and critics alike. Now, though, I think concert procedures in the big cities are beginning to improve. The saddest thing was, I felt, that the members of the audience came and went as they pleased. In the West, I usually begin my concerts with a short piece, then play a longer one, then after the intermission, play the main piece. But in India, tradition has it that the opening piece must be a long *raga*—one to two and a half hours in length—and so, if I were to ask people to remain outside until the first number is finished, I would lose my audience!

My alternative was to begin the concert with a shorter item, asking latecomers to come in when it was over. But this, my critics complained, is un-Indian! The fact is, however, that this is the very procedure they use in the South for concerts of Karnatic music. At first, some members of my audiences would walk into the hall in the middle of a *raga*, talking and roving about, the chairs flapping until they sit down. Then, all the how-are-you's and have-you-been-well's to their neighbors. Such carelessness and gossiping, and even peanuts with shells cracking, and popcorn! And if there was some important official sitting in the front—I was finished. While the music was being performed, he was being entertained by the "organizer," who brings tea on a tray, sandwiches, and little things to eat. Many times I was so disturbed by this that I had to put down my sitar and wait for the people to finish their tea. Of course, sometimes they were ashamed and immediately sat up, ready to listen to the music, but at other times they just sat and finished their tea. How could I be ex-

pected to perform with all that commotion going on?
Music is music, I said, and it has to be listened to
with attention and concentration. There is nothing
"Westernized" about coming to concerts on time or
keeping still while the music is being performed. But
now, I think, the situation is improving.

A BEATLE
IN BOMBAY

What I call the great sitar explosion began in early
1966—at least, that is when I became aware of it,
when I went to Britain. The special attraction to sitar
suddenly came about when the Beatles and the Rolling
Stones and some other pop groups used it in record-
ings of their songs. Until then, I had never heard any
records of these groups, but I knew vaguely that they
were young popular singers.

Then, in June, 1966, at a friend's house in London,
I met George Harrison and Paul McCartney, of the
Beatles. I found them to be very charming and polite
young men, not at all what I had expected. George
talked to me about the sitar and said that he had been
very much impressed with the instrument and its
sound and my playing of it since he first heard me. I
told him that after hearing so much about his accomplishments, I would like him to show me what he had
done with the sitar. With an awkward and childlike
expression, he said shyly that it was really not very
much. I was struck by his deep humility. George explained to me he had had no real training with the
sitar, but had done some experiments with it on his
own, using his knowledge of the guitar as a background, and he expressed, very sincerely, his desire to
learn from me to play the sitar. I carefully explained
to him that one must undergo many long years of
study and practice of the basics before one can play
even a single note properly. He understood all this
perfectly and said he was prepared to go through the
years of discipline. I invited him to come to India with
his wife, Pattie, to study and spend some time with
me. He accepted enthusiastically. He asked me to his
beautiful house in Esher, outside London, and a few

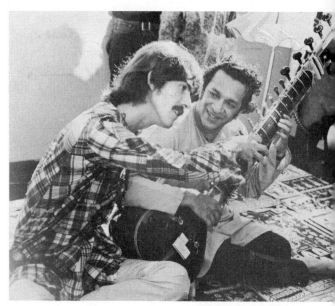

Courtesy of Kinnara School of Indian Music

*George Harrison, my Beatle student, visits Kinnara in
Los Angeles for sitar lessons.*

days before I had to leave England, I gave George his
first lesson in Indian music. I found him to be quite
sensitive and quick. I visited him once more before
leaving for India, when he had requested me to play
for a few mutual friends and, of course, the other
three Beatles. I always feel inspired when I play for a
small, close group and especially for musicians—no
matter what tradition or country they belong to. And
that evening, as I was accompanied on the *tabla* by
Alla Rakha, I felt very happy with my music, and my
little audience responded very warmly as we played.

After I returned to India, George wrote and said he
would be able to come and spend six weeks with me. I
was pleased and wrote back telling him to grow a
mustache and cut his hair a bit so that he would not
be recognized immediately. When we went to pick up
George and his wife at the airport in September, we
found that the mustache trick had worked—no one
recognized either him or Pattie at first, although there
had been a lot of publicity about their visit in the
papers. They registered for a suite at the Taj Mahal
Hotel under a false name, but as it turned out, one

young Christian page boy happened to recognize them and truly, within twenty-four hours, almost all Bombay came to know that George Harrison was there. In another day or so, huge crowds of teen-agers gathered in front of the hotel, headlines appeared in the papers about George's arrival, and my telephone started to ring nonstop. One caller even pretended to be "Mrs. Shankar" and demanded to talk to George. She changed her mind when I took the telephone myself.

I could not believe it when I saw this mad frenzy of young people, mostly girls from twelve to about seventeen. I would have believed it in London or Tokyo or New York—but in India! And I realized that young people in our big cities like Bombay or Delhi are no different from other young people of the world. Some of these girls stood for eight or ten hours outside the hotel, screaming at me to send George down and furiously yelling for him. After a few days, I knew the situation was going to get even worse. I couldn't teach and George couldn't practice with all those young people screaming down in the street. Things reached such a state that we had to call a press conference to explain that George had not come as a Beatle but as my disciple, and he asked to be left in peace to work on his music with me. Then, we went to Kashmir and Benares and a few other places and spent the rest of his visit in relative quiet. In his lessons, I had George practice all the correct positions of sitting and some of the basic exercises. This was the most that one could do in six weeks, considering that a disciple usually spends years learning these basics. Even so, George came to understand the discipline involved, and since then he has realized how difficult it is to play the sitar and has said that it would take him forty years to learn to play it properly. On my subsequent visits to London, I have been able to give him a few more lessons, and I spent more time with him on a visit in early 1967, and then we were able to work a few more days when we were all in Hollywood that summer. Though I know he is very serious and sincere about Indian music, I realize that George is part of a group, that he is a Beatle first, and that his commitment as a Beatle takes much time and energy. We shall see how much of himself he will be able to devote to the sitar.

HIPPIES AND PROBLEMS

Many people these days think that Indian music is influencing pop music to a high degree. But my personal opinion is that it is just the sound of the sitar and not true Indian music that one finds in pop songs. Except for a few groups who I think are musically creative and adventurous, pop musicians are using the sitar in an extremely shallow way, just as a new sound or gimmick. Though the sitar is being exploited now by pop groups on both sides of the Atlantic and will no doubt continue to be used this way for some time, those who sincerely love Indian music as *classical* music should not be upset by this. One instrument can serve many styles of music. The guitar, for instance, has been used in so many different types of music, including pop and rock, but that has not affected or modified the traditions of playing the classical guitar. And then, there is this "electronic sitar!" It is supposed to be a new invention, but I have been listening to people play electric sitars for the past twenty-five years in India, and I was presented with several of them by various manufacturers in Delhi and Bombay quite a few years ago. Though I myself have never used an electric sitar for serious concert performances, the instrument has been widely used for some years now in film music and different forms of popular music in India.

The Beatle scene and the sitar explosion brought me immediately into a position of immense popularity with the young people, and now I find myself adored like a movie star or young singer. But I have had to pay for this. On the one hand, I have been facing criticism from the very "traditional" people in India who say that I am commercializing and cheapening my music with the pop influence and lowering my standards of playing the sitar. These charges I have had to face mostly in my own country, but also to some extent from classical musicians abroad. On the other hand, I was confident about one thing: I knew I would be able to present the correct perspective of our music to young people all over the world so that they would have a better understanding of it. I love these young people very much, and since they know I love them, they listen to me and are very receptive.

Now, I am glad that this is indeed what is happening; but few people are aware of what I have gone through for the last two or three years, trying to explain to my audiences that Indian music is not related to pop or rock music, and cannot be hailed with hooting, catcalls, and whistles, and a lot of frenzy, but that it is classical in nature and must be listened to with the same serious attitude that one brings to a Bach concert or a program of Mozart or Beethoven. Over the past year or two, I have noticed an immense change in the attitude of my audiences and I feel now that these young people do understand what kind of music they are listening to.

Along with the teen-agers, there was another large group, known as "hippies," who became my zealous admirers. I found it even more difficult to bring them to an understanding and appreciation of our music from the correct viewpoint. The reason for this was, I felt, that many of them were involved with various kinds of hallucinogenic drugs and were using our music as part of their drug experiences. Though in the beginning I was hurt by their approach to Indian music as a "psychedelic," spiritual, and erotic experience, I later realized that it was not wholly their fault. I discovered that a few self-appointed American "gurus" had been propagating misinformation over the last few years about India, saying that almost all the noted ascetics, thinkers, and artists in India use drugs. These "gurus" went as far as saying that one cannot meditate properly, play music, or even pronounce the sacred word OM unless one is under the influence of such drugs.

It was, of course, gratifying to see that many people loved India and all its culture; but their expression of this love was superficial, and their understanding of India's ways was very shallow. Wearing beads and bells and flowers and carrying joss sticks came across as a mimickry and a mockery of the real thing. I remember having seen even at our most holy festival, the Kumbha Mela, many of these long-haired characters from America and Europe, and in this huge assembly of religious people, I saw that very few of these young people directed themselves to the good

and saintly persons, but instead were satisfied—even overjoyed—to spend their time at the feet of the original "hippies" of the world, the aghoris and nagas. Naga, which should not be confused with the Naga tribal people in the extreme northeastern part of India, refers to the sect of religious men who go naked or semi-naked, and then they become aghoris when they dwell near the burning ghats where the bodies of the dead are cremated and practice a variety of filthy rites. Their philosophy is that in the material world there is neither good nor bad; nothing pleases them, nothing disgusts them. This way, they try to free themselves from any bonds to the gross world. Through the centuries, there have been some truly remarkable saints and siddhas (men who have acquired beneficial occult powers) who emerged from this group, but the majority of them never attain a state of holiness. Most of these aghoris and nagas are more or less religious showmen; they keep their hair long, their naked or semi-naked bodies are nearly always unclean, and they have what we call jata, hair left to grow as long as it can, unwashed for years and years, and all tied up in kinky knots. In recent times, even the little purity that remained in their philosophy has been perverted. Indians generally consider these men with some fear, because they seem to be devil-worshipers and have no clean godly powers. It is these people whose lives often depend on drugs and alcohol, and the hippies almost instinctively turned to this sort of religious group. India now is overrun by unwashed, rebellious young people, and it is really sad to see these young Americans and Europeans from good families and backgrounds who are trying to find some kind of spirituality and peace of mind this way in India. They do not realize that it is not the true Indian religion, philosophy, or thinking that they are following, but that these are some of the openly perverted and degenerate schools of thought they are drawn to because of the association with drugs and, to some extent, sex.

On one of my recent visits to the United States, several young men came to me to learn the sitar. When I first saw them, their appearance filled me with pity—they looked pale and anemic and had shiny, glazed eyes, their hands shook before their dirty bodies and they showed a strange, unnatural nervousness. When I found later that some were quite talented, I felt even sadder. I learned then that apart from habitually smoking marijuana, these boys were also taking LSD, methedrine, and heroin. I tried to be sympathetic and explained to them that first they had to get rid of these habits before I could consider teaching them. But they answered me with the same words I have heard from hundreds of others since—that they feel so much more "aware" through drugs, that they are so much more spiritual, and that the drugs have opened up something inside them, and everything seems much more beautiful. The next phase of our conversation was, as I had expected, a criticism of their parents, their society, and government policies. I spoke with these boys for a long time, discussing their frustrations and complaints, trying to have them see the situation from another point of view.

Often I, too, am overcome by the hatred, the jealousy and envy, the wars, all the ugliness that is part of our world. I try to live in beauty and goodness; I seek out all that has a quality of inner beauty, and I am immediately repulsed by anything ugly that sends out bad vibrations. Over the years, with the help of my *guru*, I have tried very hard to create and build up within me a kind of beauty and spiritual strength, so that I always have this to turn to when the harshness of the world becomes too depressing. It is this inner beauty that I have worked so long to create that I try to reveal through my music and share with all my listeners.

SATISFACTIONS

Over the last few years, I have come to understand young people much better, and I have found some remarkable people among the somewhat more mature hippies. These are the people, many of them with an excellent education or practicing knowledge of one of the arts, who after years of academic and disciplined lives, have tried to "expand their minds," as they put it, trying to find a more meaningful experience through drugs. Personally, I have *never* considered

Eric Hayes

A never-ending round of press conferences! This one was given in Calcutta on a recent trip.

drugs to be any help in understanding oneself and the world around one, but I can now accept some of these people because of the maturity of their attitude and the awareness of what they are doing. But even so, it hurts me deeply to see young people take to this easy escape from any *sadhana* found in disciplined hard work. I have had a great deal of contact with such young people, especially among the students at my school in Los Angeles and in the music courses I taught at City College of New York during the fall semester of 1967. I have tried to make them understand through affectionate, but strict, teaching that their initial approach to Indian music, in many cases, was wrong, and even their approach to Indian religion and thought, and to the other disciplines of life was not altogether correct. The students listen to me with care, and I have had good results with many of them.

So often these students have come to me and said, "We have no one to look up to. We cannot respect our parents or teachers or even the government and the law." I am grateful for the love and respect of these young people, and I feel that through my music I have been able to bring them a little closer to the thoughts and traditions of India. So, of course, the

95

problems of young people are considerable, and perhaps I do not know what is the best way to solve them, but I am sure these rebellious young people seeking answers must be handled with love and understanding more than anything else, and they must have good examples and ideals set before them to follow. Already, over the past months, I can feel a change in them, an improvement that is very gratifying.

I have been facing a surprising problem with some of my concert audiences since about 1965, especially in England. I found many young people who were "high"; sitting in the front rows of the hall, they were altogether in another world. Often, too, they sat there in front of me carrying on indecently with their girl friends or boy friends, and many of them even lit cigarettes (if that, in fact, was what they were) whenever they pleased. Their conduct disgusted me, for too many people in this dazed stupor send out bad vibrations that are extremely upsetting.

As in my young days in India, I started my own rebellion against these rebellious youths. I had to put down my sitar and explain what the music stands for and what it means to me and my *guru*, and what it meant to his *guru* and all the generations of musicians who have handed down these sacred traditions to us. I told them how one must be clean and solemn in body and mind to be able to produce this music, and that one must be in the same frame of mind to *listen* to it.

Only then can it work its magic, without need of any outside stimulus. Till rather recently, I have often had to request that members of my audiences stop smoking and sit up properly and listen to the music with respect and reverence, but I am now happy to note that things have changed to such an extent that this problem has practically disappeared. My audiences everywhere are so much more clean and respectful, serious and receptive—especially in the United States. It warms me to hear high government officials or other eminent people tell me that I am a good influence on the young people of their country. And I am pleased now when older men and women come to me after performances and thank me for doing so much for their sons or daughters. What could be more satisfying?

It is ironic that in these very same moments I am being criticized in my own country for "prostituting" my music and commercializing it, for being a big hero only to the hippies, for associating my music with drugs, and for encouraging dissatisfied youths from the West to flock to India. But the hippies are dead, as they have officially declared, and I am convinced that young people all over the world, after generations of restriction, and then years of abuse of their new freedom, are now slowly settling down, and with a clear awareness, will show us the way to attain peace, harmony, and love.

FOUR

A MANUAL
FOR THE SITAR

After reading all I have said about the *guru-shishya-parampara* and its very personal method of teaching, the reader might very well ask in what way an impersonal beginner's manual could be helpful to the student of the sitar. To this I would say that if a person with some musical talent is very eager to learn the sitar but cannot find a teacher, and if he is intelligent, sensitive, and patient, he can learn some of the fundamentals through such a manual—the proper way of sitting, the positions of the hands and fingers, the tuning and placement of the instrument. He can also master the very first and most important part of learning, by practicing the scales and exercises, and he can acquire some basic knowledge of the essential *ragas* through the *sargams*. Then, when the student goes to a teacher to take up deeper and more serious study of the instrument, he will already have some understanding of the sitar and the nature of Indian classical music.

The ten primary *thats* of the Hindustani system and their ten corresponding *ragas*.

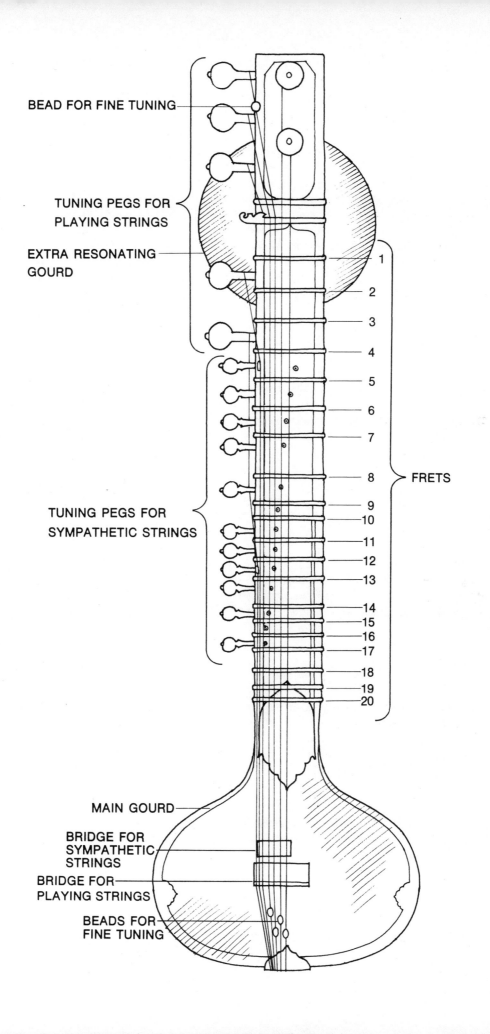

BEAD FOR FINE TUNING

TUNING PEGS FOR
PLAYING STRINGS

EXTRA RESONATING
GOURD

1
2
3
4
5
6
7
8
9
10
11
12
13
14
15
16
17
18
19
20

FRETS

TUNING PEGS FOR
SYMPATHETIC STRINGS

MAIN GOURD

BRIDGE FOR
SYMPATHETIC
STRINGS

BRIDGE FOR
PLAYING STRINGS

BEADS FOR
FINE TUNING

GENERAL CHARACTERISTICS AND CARE OF THE SITAR

Sitars are generally fashioned from teak wood. They have six or seven main playing strings and anywhere from nine to thirteen sympathetic strings, with the exception of student sitars, which have no sympathetic strings. Many sitars have an extra resonating gourd (see the diagram on page 99). They have anywhere from nineteen to twenty-three frets; nineteen is the standard number, but I recommend the addition of a twentieth fret so that the upper octave Ma (Ṁ) can be played without pulling the string.

The sitar is a very fragile instrument and should be handled with great care at all times. The following points should be observed in caring for the instrument:

1. As much as possible, do not subject the sitar to drastic and abrupt temperature changes. Do not store the sitar near radiators, heaters, air conditioners or windows.

2. When not being played, the sitar should be kept in a substantial cloth bag that will cover the entire instrument. It is a good idea to have a plastic bag made, which will cover the cloth bag and keep out any moisture.

3. The sitar should be kept either lying on the floor (frets facing up) or propped in a corner (frets facing in to the corner). I feel that it is safer to keep the instrument in a corner.

4. As with any finely made stringed instrument, it is a good idea periodically to relax the tension on the strings. Every six weeks or so *loosen* the strings, but *do not let them go completely slack*, and leave them that way overnight. Some tension must be kept on the strings or the bridges may move, which would alter the sound of the sitar.

5. The sitar should be kept clean and dust-free. A clean cloth can be used for wiping the exposed surfaces of the instrument. A one-inch-wide paintbrush with two- or three-inch bristles is very good for dusting under the strings and bridges.

The Strings

Steel and bronze wire are used for sitar strings. The following gauges are recommended: (The gauges are given in English Imperial Gauge, but equivalent gauges are available.)

String	Tuning	Material	Gauge
1	Ṃ (see page 99)	high carbon steel (music wire)	30
2	Ṡ	bronze	27
3	P̤	bronze	25
4	S̤	bronze	21
5	P	high carbon steel	32
	(The fifth string can be left off entirely to facilitate playing of the bass strings)		
6	S	high carbon steel	33
7	Ṡ	high carbon steel	34
Sympathetic Strings		high carbon steel	34

Stringing the Sitar

Sitars will generally come with strings on them, but if the gauges are incorrect or any strings are broken, a new string should be prepared and placed on the instrument in the following manner:

1. An eye large enough to fit over one of the pegs at the bottom of the instrument should be made in the end of the string (see below).

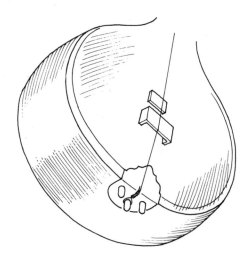

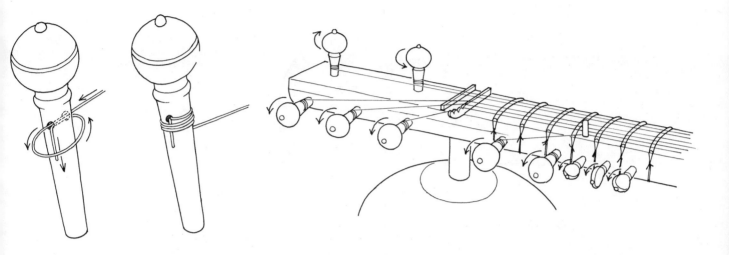

2. The other end of the string should be fed through the hole in the tuning peg (as shown above left and center) and doubled back around and through again. The loop should be pulled in close to the peg, and the string should be wound onto the peg in such a way as to clamp down the end of the string that is sticking through the peg. The strings should be wound onto the pegs in the directions shown above, right.

3. The placing of the sympathetic strings is quite an involved process and will seem difficult at first. The end of the string without the eye on it must be threaded *under* the large bridge, *over* the small bridge, and *under* the frets, to the proper hole in the neck of the instrument. The tuning peg must be completely removed from the neck and the end of the string fed down through the hole. The end of the string can be extricated from the inside of the neck by means of a small piece of wire hooked at the end (see diagram below). A fairly large paper clip bent into the shape shown is ideal for the purpose. Feed the string into the peg in the manner shown above.

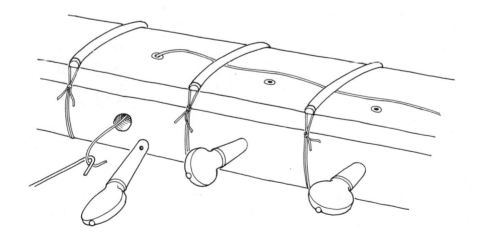

INDIAN MUSICAL NOTATION AND ITS NEAREST WESTERN EQUIVALENTS
(The sitar is tuned to C sharp.)

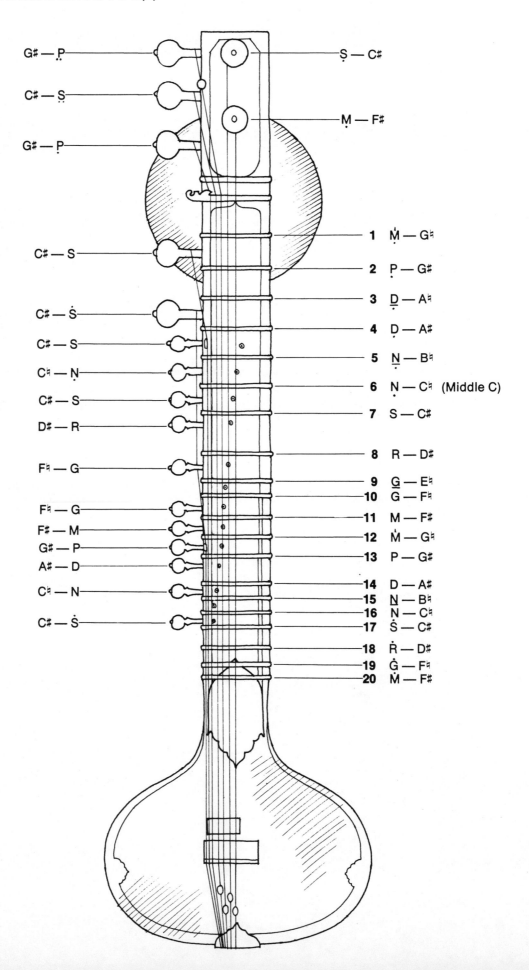

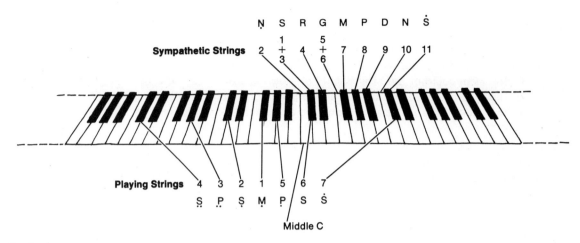

N S R G M P D N Ṡ

Sympathetic Strings 2 1
                        + 4 5
                        3   + 7 8 9 10 11
                              6

Playing Strings 4 3 2 1 5 6 7
                 Ṣ Ṗ Ṣ M P S Ṡ

Middle C

Tuning the Sitar

Due to the great variation in size and quality of sitars it is difficult to prescribe a tuning that will be ideal for all sitars. Depending on the size and strength of the instrument, the SA (S) may vary anywhere from B natural to D natural. C sharp is a fairly standard SA (S) for sitars and the diagram on the facing page shows a sitar tuned in C sharp. The student should experiment with different tunings to discover which SA (S) produces the best sound on his instrument. If the student is not familiar with the corresponding Western notation that appears in the diagram on page 102, the diagram above of a piano keyboard may be of assistance.

Moving the Frets

As the student will readily discover, *komal* RI (R̲), *komal* DHA (D̲), *komal* ṘI (Ṙ̲), and *komal* GA (G̲) cannot be played when the frets are in their normal positions (for C-sharp tuning, shown on page 102). If these notes are used in the exercise being played, the fret that normally produces the *shuddha* (natural) note — i.e., R, D, Ṙ, and Ġ, the 8th, 14th, 18th, and 19th frets respectively — must be moved back toward the main tuning pegs into the proper position to produce the note desired. To do this, place the instrument upright on the floor with the back of the neck facing you. Place the index fingers on either end of the fret and the thumbs on the fret cord (shown right). Slide the whole unit (fret and cord) slowly and evenly into place. To return the fret to its original position, repeat this process.

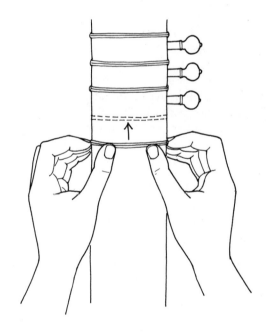

The Playing Position

The importance of maintaining a proper position while playing the sitar cannot be overemphasized. Although there are a number of variations, I find that the two positions shown in photographs A and B are the most satisfactory. Women may prefer the position shown in photograph B. The following points should be taken into consideration in finding a position both practical and attractive:

1. The main gourd of the sitar should rest on the sole of the left foot.
2. The face of the instrument should be perpendicular to the floor.
3. The neck of the instrument should be at an angle of approximately 45 degrees from the floor.
4. The right forearm and the right thigh should press against the main gourd and hold the sitar in position. The beginning student may find it easier to support the instrument by sitting with the right knee raised. Care should be taken to make sure that the right knee does not obstruct the left hand when playing on the upper octave frets.

Important to Note:

(a) *The left hand does not support the sitar.* The student should be able to hold the sitar in the proper position without using the left hand at all.

(b) *In the proper position, the student will not be able to see clearly the fingers of the left hand on the frets.* The beginner may pull the instrument closer to his body or lean over its neck in order to place the fingers properly, but the student should get accustomed to judging the placement of the fingers while looking at the back of the neck.

The Right Hand Position

1. The right thumb should be pressed firmly on the edge of the neck between the main gourd and the final fret. The thumb should not move up and down the neck or be taken off the neck while the instrument is being played (see photographs E and F).
2. The *mizrab* (plectrum) is worn on the right index finger. The corners should fit over the sides of the last joint of the finger, and the striking tip should project approximately one-fifth to one-fourth of an inch from the end of the finger (see photograph G). The *mizrab* should fit quite tightly on the end of the finger to insure that it will not move from side to side while playing. The student will find the *mizrab* quite painful to wear at first and may, for the first week or two of practice, wish to use the type of *mizrab* that has a plastic coating on the corners. The uncoated *mizrab* should be worn as soon as the student has gotten accustomed to the pressure. Once the usual callus is formed on the index finger, the *mizrab* has a better hold.

The Left Hand Position

1. The two left hand fingers primarily used are the index and middle fingers, which we will refer to as 1 and 2 respectively. The fingers should be held in a graceful and relaxed manner.
2. The tips of the fingers should press on the string just behind the fret and not directly on top of it, to avoid muffling the sound (see photograph H).
3. The thumb should press lightly on the back of the neck in a position directly parallel to the index finger (see photograph I).

Note: As a general rule, all *arohana* (ascending) and *avarohana* (descending) passages are to be played with the index finger (1). The middle finger (2) is used only to play the highest note in any given passage and for certain types of ornaments. (Fingerings are given in all of the exercises, so that the student can readily understand the application of this principle.)

A. Basic Playing Position

B. Alternate Position: Right Knee Raised

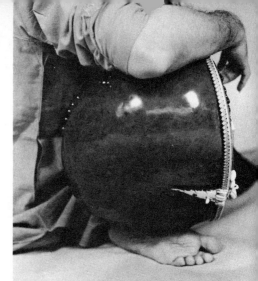

C. Main Gourd Rests on Right Foot

D. Sitar Face Perpendicular to Floor

E. Position of Right Thumb

F. Right Thumb Always Stays in Position

G. Mizrab Worn on Right Index Finger

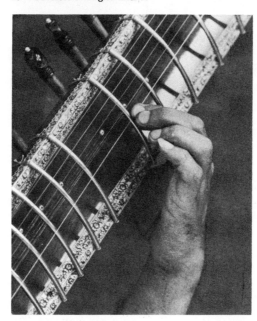

H. Fingers Press Behind Fret

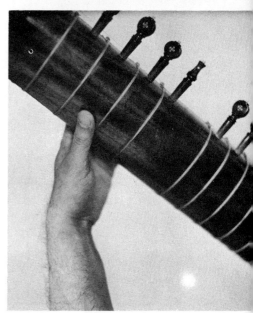

I. Position of Left Thumb

EXPLANATION OF NOTATIONAL SYMBOLS

Symbol	Name	Placement in Notation	Explanation
S, R, G, M, P, D, N,	*svara*	S R G M P D N Ṡ	These letters are abbreviations of the North Indian solemnization syllables, Sa Re Ga Ma Pa Dha Ni. These syllables are the equivalent of the Western Do Re Mi Fa Sol La Ti. When practicing the exercises, the student should think in terms of Sa Re Ga, etc., not Do Re Mi or C D E.
‿	*matra*	S R GM G	A *matra* is a beat or pulse. *Matras* in any given exercise are of equal duration. If there are two *svaras* or notes contained within one *matra* sign, they should be played at twice the speed of a single note per *matra*. If there are three notes in a *matra*, they should be played three times as fast as a single note per *matra*. If there are four notes, they should be played four times as fast, etc.
—	Rest	S —R G—M G	Rests and notes within a given *matra* are of equal duration. If only one rest is contained within the *matra* sign, nothing is played during that beat. If there is one rest and one note in a *matra*, the student should pause for half a beat and play the note for half a beat. The same principle applies when there are three or four or more notes and rests contained in a single *matra*. **Note:** The fingers should not be lifted from the string during a rest. Every note should sound until the next note is played.
·	Octave Sign	(a) Ṇ Ḍ Ṇ (b) Ṡ Ṙ Ġ	(a) When the dot appears below the note, it should be played in the lower octave, that is below Sa (Ṡ) on the seventh fret. (b) When the dot appears above the note, it should be played in the upper octave, that is, above Sa(S) on the seventeenth fret.
—	*komal*	S R̲ G̲ M P D̲ N̲ S	Indicates that one should play the note that is half a tone lower than the natural *(shuddha)* note (that is, when the symbol appears below the note Ga (G̲) one should place the finger behind the ninth fret rather than the tenth fret. Likewise, when the symbol appears below Ni (N̲) one should place the finger behind the fifteenth fret rather than the sixteenth.) **Note:** When *komal* Re (R̲), *komal* Dha (D̲), *komal* Ṙi (Ṙ̲) and *komal* Ġa (Ġ̲) are to be played, the eighth, fourteenth, eighteenth and nineteenth frets respectively must be moved back toward the main tuning pegs to the correct position to produce the note that is half a tone lower than the one produced by the fret in its original position (see diagram on page 103).
ˈ	*tivra*	G Ḿ P D N	Indicates that one should play the note that is half a tone higher than the natural note (that is, when the symbol appears above Ma(Ḿ) one should place the finger behind the twelfth fret rather than the eleventh). **Note:** This symbol appears only over Ma(M); all other note changes are indicated by the *komal* symbol. *Sa(S)* and *Pa(P)* are never raised or lowered.
ǀ	*da*	S R G M P ǀ ǀ ǀ ǀ ǀ	This symbol indicates an inward stroke of the *mizrab* executed by moving the index finger toward the thumb.

EXPLANATION OF NOTATIONAL SYMBOLS

Symbol	Name	Placement in Notation	Explanation
—	*ra*	S N D P M — — — —	An outward stroke of the *mizrab* executed by moving the index finger away from the thumb.
ᵥ	*diri*	SS RR GG or S R G ᵥ ᵥ ᵥ ᵥ ᵥ ᵥ	A *mizrab* stroke executed by playing *da* and *ra* in rapid succession.
· — ǀ	rDa	S S — S S or S S — S ǀ ǀ · — ǀ ǀ ǀ · — ǀ	When the dot appears before the *bol* figure *ra da* (— ǀ) (*da, ra* and *diri* are referred to as *bols*), it indicates *ra* should be played with a weak stroke and *da* should be played with a strong stroke. **Note:** When reciting *bol* phrases such as those on page 135, this figure should be pronounced "Ruh Da."
c	*chikari*	S — R — G — M ǀ c ǀ c ǀ c ǀ	Indicates a *ra* stroke on the *chikari* strings. In a *bol* phrase a *chikari* stroke is pronounced "Ya." Example: The *bols* for the first *sargam* on page 141 would be *da ra da ra, da ra da ra, da ya da ya, da ra da ra, da ya da ra*, etc.
,	Accent	P D N , D N Ṡ , Ṡ N D P	The comma is used to delineate groupings. The first note of every group should be played with a *da* stroke and should be slightly stressed.
⌐¬	*krintan*	⌐R S Ṇ S¬	*Krintans* are melodic figures produced by actions of the left hand fingers alone. For descriptions of individual *krintans* see the exercises on page 132.
⋀	*zamzama*	⋀ ⋀ R S R S	When this symbol appears above a two-note figure, it indicates that the figure should be repeated, that is, R S (with ⋀ above) is played R S R S. When the symbol has three peaks (⋀⋀) instead of two (⋀) the notes should be repeated three times, that is, R S (with ⋀⋀ above) would be played R S R S R S. See the exercises on page 134 for execution of *zamzama*.
⌒	*meend*	S R͡ G M	The notes contained under this symbol are produced by pulling the string with the second finger. See the exercises on page 137 for execution of *meend*.
∿	*gamak*	S̃ R̃ S̃ R̃ S̃ R̃ S̃ R̃ S̃ ǀ ǀ ǀ ǀ ǀ	*Gamaks* are performed by pulling the string from one note to the next and back again in rapid succession. See exercises on page 140 for detailed description of *gamaks*.
x	*sum*	x ǀ 13 14 15 16 ǀ 1 2 3 4 ǀ	Indicates the first beat of a *tala* or rhythmic cycle.
o	*khali*	o ǀ R S N D ǀ P M G R ǀ S	After the *sum, khali* is the most important point in the *tala*. The divisions of a tala, for example 4-4-4-4, 3-2-2, 4-4-2-2, can be demonstrated by a system of clapping and waving the hands. *Khali* is that point in the cycle where a wave of the hand is used. Examples: *Teen-tal* 16 beats Divisions 4-4-4-4 clap wave x clap o clap ǀ 1 2 3 4 ǀ 5 6 7 8 ǀ 9 10 11 12 ǀ 13 14 15 16 *Rupak-tal* 7 beats Divisions 3-2-2 wave o clap clap ǀ 1 2 3 ǀ 4 5 ǀ 6 7 (*Rupak-tal* is a very unusual *tala* in that *khali* is on the first beat of the cycle.)

GENERAL INTRODUCTION TO THE EXERCISES

The exercises contained in this manual will give the student a grasp of the fundamental techniques of sitar playing. A great effort has been made to try to explain and notate everything as clearly as possible, so that bad playing habits will not be developed. The student should unquestionably have a teacher, but given the scarcity of competent sitar teachers outside of India and the great popularity of our music abroad, people seriously interested in our music may be able to gain some insight into its performance by carefully studying the following exercises.

The following points should be observed while studying these exercises:

1. The exercises should be studied in the order in which they appear.

2. Each exercise should be memorized and mastered before proceeding to the next one.

3. Each exercise should be repeated over and over again without pausing between repetitions.

4. There is no pause between the ascending (arohana) and descending (avarohana) portions of any exercise.

5. As the student will readily discover, most of the exercises (*murchhana, palta, bol, krintan, zamzama, meend,* and *gamak*) are comprised of small melodic patterns that are repeated on each successive note of the scale. In notating the exercises, we have placed a vertical line between the patterns to help delineate them so that they can easily be applied to each successive note of the scale. This line does *not* indicate a pause. The rhythm should remain steady for the entire exercise.

6. In each of the exercises, at least the first two patterns and the final pattern of the ascending and the descending portions have been given. The arrow is used to indicate that the student should repeat the pattern on each successive note of the scale in the manner exemplified by the first few patterns, until the final pattern is reached.

7. The exercises should be practiced very slowly at first. Every note should be clear and precise and fingering and plucking notations should be followed exactly. Once the exercise is absolutely clear and completely memorized, increase the speed step by step.

SAPAT AND MURCHHANA

Murchhana and especially *sapat* exercises are the most basic and important exercises for the beginning sitar student. Once they have been thoroughly mastered, all of the *paltas* and *sargams* should come quite easily to the student. The student should always begin a practice session with these exercises. He should first familiarize himself with the notes of the scale and be able to play the complete scale from P to Ġ without difficulty before attempting to play the embellishing notes that are indicated. Once this has been accomplished the following explanation of the embellishing notes should be studied:

(A) The type of embellishing note that is notated in front of the main note is written like this:

$$P - {}^{N}\widehat{D} - N$$

but the rhythmic values of the notes are actually

$$P - \widehat{ND} - N$$

The string must be pulled the proper amount with the first finger so that when the string is plucked, the embellishing note, in this case N, will be heard *on the beat*, not preceding the beat as one might think by looking at the notation. The string should then be returned to its original position at such a rate that the main note, in this case D, will be reached in the middle of the beat. (See the *meend* exercises on page 137 for a complete description of the technique of pulling the string.)

(B) The type of embellishing note that is notated after the main note is written like this:

$$\widehat{G}^{M} - \widehat{R}^{G} - \widehat{S}^{R}$$

but the rhythmic values of the notes are actually

$$\widehat{GM}\,\widehat{RG}\,\widehat{SR}$$

The difficulty with this figure is that it should actually *sound* like

$$G\ M\ R\ G\ S\ R$$

In trying to play this figure the beginning student will usually play something that sounds like this:

$$\widehat{G} - \widehat{M\,G}\,\widehat{R} - \widehat{G\,R}\,\widehat{S} - \widehat{R\,S}\,N$$

which is not correct.

After pulling to the embellishing note, the student must move the finger directly to the next main note so that the first main note is not heard again in passing. This is a very difficult technique, but it is absolutely essential.

Sapat

Exercise 1.

Arohana (Ascending)

Left Hand (L.H.)	1		1		1		1		1		1
Notes	P	⌣	ᴺD	⌣	N	⌣	S	⌣	ᴳR	⌣	G
Right Hand (R.H.)	I	c	I	c	I	c	I	c	I	c	I	c
	(Da)	(Chikari)	(Da)	(Chikari)	(Da)	(Chikari)	(Da)	(Chikari)	(Da)	(Chikari)	(Da)	(Chikari)
Fret	2		4		6		7		8		10	
Western equivalent if the sitar is tuned so that C sharp is Sa.	G-sharp		A-sharp		C-natural		C-sharp		D-sharp		F-natural	

L.H.	1		1		1		1		1		1
Notes	M	⌣	P	⌣	ᴺD	⌣	N	⌣	Ṡ	⌣	Ṙ
R.H.	I	c	I	c	I	c	I	c	I	c	I	c
	(Da)	(Chikari)	(Da)	(Chikari)	(Da)	(Chikari)	(Da)	(Chikari)	(Da)	(Chikari)	(Da)	(Chikari)
Fret	11		13		14		16		17		18	
Western	F-sharp		G-sharp		A-sharp		C-natural		C-sharp		D-sharp	

Avarohana (Descending)

L.H.	2		1		1		1		1		1
Notes	Ġᴹ	⌣	Ṙᴳ	⌣	Ṡᴿ	⌣	Nˢ	⌣	Dᴺ	⌣	Pᴰ
R.H.	I	c	I	c	I	c	I	c	I	c	I	c
	(Da)	(Chikari)	(Da)	(Chikari)	(Da)	(Chikari)	(Da)	(Chikari)	(Da)	(Chikari)	(Da)	(Chikari)
Fret	19		18		17		16		14		13	
Western	F-natural		D-sharp		C-sharp		C-natural		A-sharp		G-sharp	

L.H.	1		1		1		1		1		1
Notes	Mᴾ	⌣	Gᴹ	⌣	Rᴳ	⌣	Sᴿ	⌣	Nˢ	⌣	Ḋᴺ
R.H.	I	c	I	c	I	c	I	c	I	c	I	c
	(Da)	(Chikari)	(Da)	(Chikari)	(Da)	(Chikari)	(Da)	(Chikari)	(Da)	(Chikari)	(Da)	(Chikari)
Fret	11		10		8		7		6		4	
Western	F-sharp		F-natural		D-sharp		C-sharp		C-natural		A-sharp	

Exercise 2.

Arohana

L.H. (Use 1 at all times unless 2 is indicated)

Notes	P	ᴺD	N	S	ᴳR	G	M	P	ᴺD	N	Ṡ	Ṙ
R.H.	I	I	I	I	I	I	I	I	I	I	I	I
	Da	Da	Da	Da	Da	Da	Da	Da	Da	Da	Da	Da
Fret	2	4	6	7	8	10	11	13	14	16	17	18

Avarohana

L.H. 2

Notes	Gᴹ	ṘG	Ṡᴿ	Nˢ	Dᴺ	Pᴰ	Mᴾ	Gᴹ	Rᴳ	Sᴿ	Nˢ	Dᴺ
R.H.	I	I	I	I	I	I	I	I	I	I	I	I
	Da	Da	Da	Da	Da	Da	Da	Da	Da	Da	Da	Da
Fret	19	18	17	16	14	13	11	10	8	7	6	4

Exercise 3.

Arohana

L.H.

Notes	P	ᴺD	N	S	ᴳR	G	M	P	ᴺD	N	Ṡ	Ṙ
R.H.	—	—	—	—	—	—	—	—	—	—	—	—
	Ra	Ra	Ra	Ra	Ra	Ra	Ra	Ra	Ra	Ra	Ra	Ra
Fret	2	4	6	7	8	10	11	13	14	16	17	18

Avarohana

L.H. 2

Notes	Gᴹ	ṘG	Ṡᴿ	Nˢ	Dᴺ	Pᴰ	Mᴾ	Gᴹ	Rᴳ	Sᴿ	Nˢ	Dᴺ
R.H.	—	—	—	—	—	—	—	—	—	—	—	—
	Ra	Ra	Ra	Ra	Ra	Ra	Ra	Ra	Ra	Ra	Ra	Ra
Fret	19	18	17	16	14	13	11	10	8	7	6	4

Exercise 4.

Arohana

L.H.

Notes	P	ᴺD	N	S	ᴳR	G	M	P	ᴺD	N	Ṡ	Ṙ
R.H.	I	—	I	—	I	—	I	—	I	—	I	—
	Da	Ra	Da	Ra	Da	Ra	Da	Ra	Da	Ra	Da	Ra
Fret	2	4	6	7	8	10	11	13	14	16	17	18

Avarohana

L.H. 2

Notes	Gᴹ	ṘG	Ṡᴿ	Nˢ	Dᴺ	Pᴰ	Mᴾ	Gᴹ	Rᴳ	Sᴿ	Nˢ	Dᴺ
R.H.	I	—	I	—	I	—	I	—	I	—	I	—
	Da	Ra	Da	Ra	Da	Ra	Da	Ra	Da	Ra	Da	Ra
Fret	19	18	17	16	14	13	11	10	8	7	6	4

Murchhana

Exercise 1.

Arohana

L.H.
Notes: D̥P D N S R G M P P̂D M̂P Ĝ M R̂G Ŝ R N̂S D̂N P | **2**
R.H.: | — | — | — | — | — | — | — | — | — |

L.H.
Notes: N̂D N S R G M P D D̂N P̂D M̂P Ĝ M R̂G Ŝ R N̂S D | **2**
R.H.: | — | — | — | — | — | — | — | — | — |

Ŝ N S R etc.
| — |

R̂S R G etc.
| — |

Ĝ R G M etc.
| — |

Continue this pattern on successive notes of the scale

L.H.
Notes: M̂G M P D N Ṡ Ṙ Ġ Ĝ M R̂G Ŝ R N̂S D̂N P̂D M̂P G | **2**
R.H.: | — | — | — | — | — | — | — | — | — |

Avarohana

L.H.
Notes: ĜR G M P D N Ṡ Ṙ R̂G Ŝ R N̂S D̂N P̂D M̂P Ĝ M R | **2**
R.H.: | — | — | — | — | — | — | — | — | — |

L.H.
Notes: R̂S R G M P D N Ṡ Ŝ R N̂S D̂N P̂D M̂P Ĝ M R̂G S | **2**
R.H.: | — | — | — | — | — | — | — | — | — |

Ŝ N S R etc.
| — |

N̂D N S etc.
| — |

Continue this pattern on successive notes of the scale

L.H.
Notes: D̥P D N S R G M P P̂D M̂P Ĝ M R̂G Ŝ R N̂S D̂N P | **2**
R.H.: | — | — | — | — | — | — | — | — | — |

111

Exercise 2.

Arohana

L.H.
Notes: ᴰP̣ Ḍ Ṇ S R G M P |
R.H. | — | — | — | — 　　　2

L.H.
Notes: ᴺḌ Ṇ S R G M P D |
R.H. | — | — | — | — 　　　2

ˢṆ S etc.
ᴿS R etc.
ᴳR G etc.

L.H.
Notes: ᴹG M P D N Ṡ Ṙ Ġ |
R.H. | — | — | — | — 　　　2

Avarohana

L.H. 　2
Notes: Ġᴹ Ṙᴳ Ṡᴿ Nˢ Dᴺ Pᴰ Mᴾ G |
R.H. | — | — | — | —

L.H. 　2
Notes: Ṙᴳ Ṡᴿ Nˢ Dᴺ Pᴰ Mᴾ Gᴹ R |
R.H. | — | — | — | —

Ṡᴿ Nˢ etc.
Nˢ Dᴺ etc.
Dᴺ Pᴰ etc.

L.H. 　2
Notes: Pᴰ Mᴾ Gᴹ Rᴳ Sᴿ Ṇˢ Ḍᴺ P |
R.H. | — | — | — | —

Exercise 3. (Chhoot Murchhana)

Arohana

L.H. 　　2
Notes: ᴰP̣ Ḍ Pᴰ Mᴾ Gᴹ Rᴳ Sᴿ Ṇ |
R.H. | — | — | — | —

L.H. 　　　2
Notes: ᴺḌ Ṇ Dᴺ Pᴰ Mᴾ Gᴹ Rᴳ S |
R.H. | — | — | — | —

ˢṆ S Nˢ etc.
ᴿS R Ṡᴿ etc.
ᴳR G Ṙᴳ etc.

L.H. 　　2
Notes: ᴹG M Ġᴹ Ṙᴳ Ṡᴿ Nˢ Dᴺ P |
R.H. | — | — | — | —

Avarohana

L.H. 2
Notes: Ġᴹ Ṙ ᴹG M P D N Ṡ |
R.H. | — | — | — | —

L.H. 2
Notes: Ṙᴳ Ṡ ᴳR G M P D N |
R.H. | — | — | — | —

Ṡᴿ N ᴿS etc.
Nˢ D ˢṆ etc.
Dᴺ P ᴺḌ etc.

L.H. 2
Notes: Pᴰ M ᴰP̣ Ḍ Ṇ S R G |
R.H. | — | — | — | —

112

EXERCISES FOR THE MIZRAB

Each of these exercises should be played on each note of the scale from P to Ġ and down again.

Eight Aksharas

1. Da Ra Da, Da Ra Da, Da Ra   (3-3-2)
2. Da Ra Da, Da Ra, Da Ra Da   (3-2-3)
3. Da Ra, Da Ra Da, Da Ra Da   (2-3-3)

Sixteen Aksharas

1. Da Ra Da, Da Ra Da, Da Ra Da, Da Ra Da, Da Ra Da Ra,   (3-3-3-3-4)
2. Da Ra, Da Ra Da, Da Ra, Da Ra Da, Da Ra Da, Da Ra Da,   (2-3-2-3-3-3)
3. Da Ra Da, Da Ra Da, Da Ra, Da Ra, Da Ra Da, Da Ra Da,   (3-3-2-2-3-3)
4. Da Ra Da, Da Ra Da, Da Ra Da, Da Ra, Da Ra, Da Ra Da,   (3-3-3-2-2-3)

COMBINATION FIGURES

Each of these patterns should be played on each note of the scale from P to Ġ.

1. Da Diri Diri Diri, Da Diri Da Ra, Da Ra Diri Diri, Da — rDa — r Da —
2. Diri Diri Da — rDa — r Da —, Diri Diri Da — rDa — r Diri, Da — rDa — r Da —

ADVANCED EXERCISES USING THE COMBINATION FIGURES

Exercise 1.

Arohana

(Exercise 1 continues overleaf)

exercise 1
(continued)

Avarohana

L.H. 2   2   2   2   2

Notes Ġ ṘR ṠṠ ṘR, Ġ ṘR Ṡ Ṙ, Ġ Ṙ ṠṠ ṘR, Ġ – ĠR – Ṙ Ṡ –|

R.H. | v v v | v | – | – v v | . –| . – |

L.H.

Notes Ṙ ṠṠ NN ṠṠ, Ṙ ṠṠ N Ṡ, Ṙ Ṡ NN ṠṠ, Ṙ – ṘṠ – Ṡ N –|

R.H. | v v v | v | – | – v v | . –| . – |

↓

L.H. 2   2   2   2   2

Notes G RR SS RR, G RR S R, G R SS RR, G – GR – R S –|

R.H. | v v v | v | – | – v v | . –| . – |

Exercise 2.   **Arohana**

L.H.   2 2   22   2   2

Notes SS RR G – GR – RS –, RR GG R – RS – SRR, G – GR – RS –|

R.H. v v | . –| . –| v v | . –| . –v | . –| . –|

L.H.   2 2   22   2   2

Notes RR GG M – MG – GR –, GG MM G – GR – RGG, M – MG – GR –|

R.H. v v | . –| . –| . v v | . –| . –v | . –| . –|

↓

L.H.   2 2   22   2   2

Notes ṠṠ ṘR Ġ – ĠR – ṘṠ –, ṘR ĠĠ Ṙ – ṘṠ – ṠṘR, Ġ – ĠR – ṘṠ –|

R.H. v v | . –| . –| v v | . –| . –v | . –| . –|

Avarohana

L.H. 2 2   2   2   2   2

Notes ĠĠ ṘR Ṡ – ṠR – ṘĠ –, ṘR ṠṠ Ṙ – ṘĠ – ĠRR, Ṡ – ṠR – ṘĠ –|

R.H. v v | . –| . –| v v | . –| . –v | . –| . –|

L.H. 22   2   2   2   2

Notes ṘR ṠṠ N – NṠ – ṠṘ –, ṠṠ NN Ṡ – ṠṘ – ṘṠṠ, N – NṠ – ṠṘ –|

R.H. v v | . –| . –| v v | . –| . –v | . –| . –|

↓

L.H. 22   2   2   2   2

Notes GG RR S – SR – RG –, RR SS R – RG – GRR, S – SR – RG –|

R.H. v v | . –| . –| v v | . –| . –v | . –| . –|

PALTAS (ALANKAR)

Paltas should be played in the same manner as the *murchhana* exercises — <u>with an embellishing note on the first note of every ascending figure and after each note except the last of every descending figure in both the *arohana* and *avarohana* passages.</u> The *chhoot murchhana* best illustrates this principle. As in the *sapat* and *murchhana* exercises, the student should know the exercise and be able to play it as written without difficulty before adding the embellishing notes, but it must be practiced with the embellishing notes before proceeding to the next exercise.

Two Aksharas

Exercise 1.　　**Arohana**

L.H.	2	2	2	2	2	2	2	2	2	2	2
Notes	Ḍ P	N̤ Ḍ	S N̤	R S	G R	M G	P M	D P	N D	Ṡ N	Ṙ Ṡ	Ġ Ṙ	
R.H.	I —	I —	I —	I —	I —	I —	I —	I —	I —	I —	I —	I —

Avarohana

L.H.	2	2	2	2	2	2	2	2	2	2	2
Notes	Ṙ Ġ	Ṡ Ṙ	N Ṡ	D N	P D	M P	G M	R G	S R	N̤ S	Ḍ N̤	Ḍ	
R.H.	I —	I —	I —	I —	I —	I —	I —	I —	I —	I —	I —	I —

Exercise 2.　　**Arohana**

L.H.	2	2	2	2	2	2	2	2	2	2
Notes	P̤ N̤	Ḍ S	N̤ R	S G	R M	G P	M D	P N	D Ṡ	N Ṙ	Ṡ Ġ	
R.H.	I —	I —	I —	I —	I —	I —	I —	I —	I —	I —

Avarohana

L.H.	2	2	2	2	2	2	2	2	2	2
Notes	Ġ Ṡ	Ṙ N	Ṡ D	N P	D M	P G	M R	G S	R N̤	S Ḍ	N̤ P̤	
R.H.	I —	I —	I —	I —	I —	I —	I —	I —	I —	I —

Three Aksharas

Exercise 1.　　**Arohana**

Continue this pattern on successive notes of the scale.

L.H.	2	2	2		2	2	2
Notes	P̤ Ḍ N̤	Ḍ N̤ S	N̤ S R	⟶	D N Ṡ	N Ṡ Ṙ	Ṡ Ṙ Ġ	
R.H.	I — I	I — I	I — I		I — I	I — I	I — I

Avarohana

L.H.	2	2	2		2	2	2
Notes	Ġ Ṙ Ṡ	Ṙ Ṡ N	Ṡ N D	⟶	R S N̤	S N̤ Ḍ	N̤ Ḍ P̤	
R.H.	I — I	I — I	I — I		I — I	I — I	I — I

115

Exercise 2.

Arohana

L.H.	2	2	2		2	2	2
Notes	P̣ Ḍ P̣	Ḍ Ṇ Ḍ	Ṇ S Ṇ	→	N Ṡ N	Ṡ Ṙ Ṡ	Ṙ Ġ Ṙ
R.H.	ı − ı	ı − ı	ı − ı		ı − ı	ı − ı	ı − ı

Avarohana

L.H.	2 2	2	2		2	2	2
Notes	Ġ Ṙ Ġ	Ṙ Ṡ Ṙ	Ṡ N Ṡ	→	S Ṇ S	Ṇ Ḍ Ṇ	Ḍ P̣ Ḍ
R.H.	ı − ı	ı − ı	ı − ı		ı − ı	ı − ı	ı − ı

Four Aksharas

Exercise 1.

Arohana

L.H.	2	2	2		2	2	2
Notes	P̣ Ḍ Ṇ S	Ḍ Ṇ S R	Ṇ S R G	→	P D N Ṡ	D N Ṡ Ṙ	N Ṡ Ṙ Ġ
R.H.	ı − ı −	ı − ı −	ı − ı −		ı − ı −	ı − ı −	ı − ı −

Avarohana

L.H.	2	2	2		2	2	2
Notes	Ġ Ṙ Ṡ N	Ṙ Ṡ N D	Ṡ N D P	→	G R S Ṇ	R S Ṇ Ḍ	S Ṇ Ḍ P
R.H.	ı − ı −	ı − ı −	ı − ı −		ı − ı −	ı − ı −	ı − ı −

Exercise 2.

Arohana

L.H.	2	2	2		2	2	2
Notes	P̣ Ḍ Ṅ P̣	Ḍ Ṇ S Ḍ	Ṇ S R Ṇ	→	D N Ṡ D	N Ṡ Ṙ N	Ṡ Ṙ Ġ Ṡ
R.H.	ı − ı −	ı − ı −	ı − ı −		ı − ı −	ı − ı −	ı − ı −

Avarohana

L.H.	2 2	2	2		2	2	2
Notes	Ġ Ṙ Ṡ Ġ	Ṙ Ṡ N Ṙ	Ṡ N D Ṡ	→	R S Ṇ R	S Ṇ Ḍ S	Ṇ Ḍ P̣ Ṇ
R.H.	ı − ı −	ı − ı −	ı − ı −		ı − ı −	ı − ı −	ı − ı −

Five Aksharas

Exercise 1.

Arohana

L.H.		2		2		2	
Notes	P Ḍ Ṇ S R |	Ḍ Ṇ S R G |	Ṇ S R G M |	⟶	P D N Ṡ Ṙ |	D N Ṡ Ṙ Ġ |
R.H.	I — I — I	I — I — I	I — I — I		I — I — I	I — I — I

Avarohana

L.H.	2		2		2		2		2
Notes	Ġ Ṙ Ṡ N D |	Ṙ Ṡ N D P |	Ṡ N D P M |	⟶	G R S Ṇ D |	R S N Ḍ P |
R.H.	I — I — I	I — I — I	I — I — I		I — I — I	I — I — I

Exercise 2. (Division: 2+3)

Arohana

L.H.	2 2	2 2	2 2		2 2	2 2
Notes	P Ḍ , P Ḍ Ṇ |	Ḍ Ṇ , Ḍ Ṇ S |	Ṇ S , Ṇ S R |	⟶	N Ṡ , N Ṡ Ṙ |	Ṡ Ṙ , Ṡ Ṙ Ġ |
R.H.	I — I — I	I — I — I	I — I — I		I — I — I	I — I — I

Avarohana

L.H.	2 2	2 2	2 2		2 2	2 2
Notes	Ġ Ṙ , Ġ Ṙ Ṡ |	Ṙ Ṡ , Ṙ Ṡ N |	Ṡ N , Ṡ N D |	⟶	S Ṇ , S Ṇ Ḍ |	Ṇ Ḍ , Ṇ Ḍ P |
R.H.	I — I — I	I — I — I	I — I — I		I — I — I	I — I — I

Six Aksharas

Exercise 1.

Arohana

L.H.		2		2		2		2
Notes	P Ḍ Ṇ S R G |	Ḍ Ṇ S R G M |	⟶	M P D N Ṡ Ṙ |	P D N Ṡ Ṙ Ġ |
R.H.	I — I — I —	I — I — I —		I — I — I —	I — I — I —

Avarohana

L.H.	2		2		2		2
Notes	Ġ Ṙ Ṡ N D P |	Ṙ Ṡ N D P M |	⟶	M G R S Ṇ Ḍ |	G R S Ṇ Ḍ P |
R.H.	I — I — I —	I — I — I —		I — I — I —	I — I — I —

117

Exercise 2.

Arohana

L.H.	2 2	2 2		2 2	2 2
Notes	P Ḍ P N Ḍ P	Ḍ N Ḍ S N Ḍ	⟶	N Ṡ N Ṙ Ṡ N	Ṡ Ṙ Ṡ Ġ Ṙ Ṡ
R.H.	ǀ – ǀ – ǀ –	ǀ – ǀ – ǀ –		ǀ – ǀ – ǀ –	ǀ – ǀ – ǀ –

Avarohana

L.H.	2 2 2	2 2		2 2	2 2
Notes	Ġ Ṙ Ġ Ṡ Ṙ Ġ	Ṙ Ṡ Ṙ N Ṡ Ṙ	⟶	S N S Ḍ N S	N Ḍ N P Ḍ N
R.H.	ǀ – ǀ – ǀ –	ǀ – ǀ – ǀ –		ǀ – ǀ – ǀ –	ǀ – ǀ – ǀ –

Seven Aksharas

Exercise 1.

Arohana

L.H.	2	2		2
Notes	P Ḍ N S R G M	Ḍ N S R G M P	⟶	M P D N Ṡ Ṙ Ġ
R.H.	ǀ – ǀ – ǀ – ǀ	ǀ – ǀ – ǀ – ǀ		ǀ – ǀ – ǀ – ǀ

Avarohana

L.H.	2	2		2
Notes	Ġ Ṙ Ṡ N D P M	Ṙ Ṡ N D P M G	⟶	M G R S N Ḍ P
R.H.	ǀ – ǀ – ǀ – ǀ	ǀ – ǀ – ǀ – ǀ		ǀ – ǀ – ǀ – ǀ

Exercise 2. (Division: 3 + 4)

Arohana

L.H.	2	2	2	2		2	2
Notes	P Ḍ N , P Ḍ N S	Ḍ N S , Ḍ N S R	⟶	N Ṡ Ṙ , N Ṡ Ṙ Ġ
R.H.	ǀ – ǀ ǀ – ǀ –	ǀ – ǀ ǀ – ǀ –		ǀ – ǀ ǀ – ǀ –

Avarohana

L.H.	2	2	2	2		2	2
Notes	Ġ Ṙ Ṡ , Ġ Ṙ Ṡ N	Ṙ Ṡ N , Ṙ Ṡ N D	⟶	S N Ḍ , S N Ḍ P
R.H.	ǀ – ǀ ǀ – ǀ –	ǀ – ǀ ǀ – ǀ –		ǀ – ǀ ǀ – ǀ –

Eight Aksharas

Exercise 1. (Division: 3+5)

Arohana

L.H.		2		2	2		2			2		2	

Notes: P Ḍ Ṇ , P Ḍ Ṇ S R | Ḍ Ṇ S , Ḍ Ṇ S R G | ⟶ D N Ṡ , D N Ṡ Ṙ Ġ |

R.H.: l — l l — l — l l — l l — l — l   l — l l — l — l

Avarohana

Notes: Ġ Ṙ Ṡ , Ġ Ṙ Ṡ N D | Ṙ Ṡ N , Ṙ Ṡ N D P | ⟶ R S N , R S N Ḍ P |

R.H.: l — l l — l — l l — l l — l — l   l — l l — l — l

Exercise 2. (Division: 2+6)

Arohana

Notes: P Ḍ , G R S Ṇ Ḍ P | Ḍ Ṇ , M G R S Ṇ Ḍ | ⟶ P D , Ġ Ṙ S N D P |

R.H.: l — l — l — l — l — l — l — l —   l — l — l — l —

Avarohana

Notes: Ġ Ṙ , P D N Ṡ Ṙ Ġ | Ṙ Ṡ , M P D N Ṡ Ṙ | ⟶ G R , P Ḍ Ṇ S R G |

R.H.: l — l — l — l — l — l — l — l —   l — l — l — l —

Exercise 3.

Arohana

Notes: P Ṇ Ḍ Ṇ S Ṇ Ḍ P | Ḍ S Ṇ S R S Ṇ Ḍ | ⟶ N Ṙ Ṡ Ṙ Ġ Ṙ Ṡ N |

R.H.: l — l — l — l — l — l — l — l —   l — l — l — l —

Avarohana

Notes: Ġ Ṡ Ṙ Ṡ N Ṡ Ṙ Ġ | Ṙ N Ṡ N D N Ṡ Ṙ | ⟶ S Ḍ Ṇ Ḍ P Ḍ Ṇ S |

R.H.: l — l — l — l — l — l — l — l —   l — l — l — l —

Nine Aksharas

Exercise 1. (Division: 3+3+3)

Arohana

L.H.	2	2		2	2			2	2

Notes   P̣ Ḍ Ṇ , Ḍ Ṇ S , Ṇ Ḍ P | Ḍ Ṇ S , Ṇ S R , S Ṇ Ḍ | ⟶ N Ṡ Ṙ , Ṡ Ṙ Ġ , Ṙ Ṡ N |

R.H. | — | | — | | — | | — | | — | | — | | — | | — | | — |

Avarohana

L.H.	2	2	2	2	2		2	2

Notes   Ġ Ṙ Ṡ , Ṙ Ṡ N , Ṡ Ṙ Ġ | Ṙ Ṡ N , Ṡ Ṇ Ḍ , N Ṡ Ṙ | ⟶ S Ṇ Ḍ , Ṇ Ḍ P , Ḍ Ṇ S |

R.H. | — | | — | | — | | — | | — | | — | | — | | — | | — |

Exercise 2. (Division: 2+3+4)

Arohana

L.H.	2	2	2	2	2	2		2	2	2

Notes   P̣ Ḍ , P̣ Ḍ Ṇ , P̣ Ḍ Ṇ S | Ḍ Ṇ , Ḍ Ṇ S , Ḍ Ṇ S R | ⟶ N Ṡ , N Ṡ Ṙ , N Ṡ Ṙ Ġ |

R.H. | — | — | | | — | — | — | | — | | | — | — | — | | — | | | — | —

Avarohana

L.H.	2	2	2		2	2	2		2	2	2

Notes   Ġ Ṙ , Ġ Ṙ Ṡ , Ġ Ṙ Ṡ N | Ṙ Ṡ , Ṙ Ṡ N , Ṙ Ṡ N Ḍ | ⟶ S Ṇ , S Ṇ Ḍ , S Ṇ Ḍ P̣ |

R.H. | — | — | | — | — | | | — | — | | | — | — | — | | — | — | | | — | —

Ten Aksharas

Exercise 1. (Division: 4+2+2+2)

Arohana

L.H.		2	2	2		2	2	2	

Notes   P̣ Ḍ Ṇ S , R Ṇ , S Ḍ , Ṇ P̣ | Ḍ Ṇ S R , G S , R Ṇ , S Ḍ | ⟶ D N Ṡ Ṙ , Ġ Ṡ , Ṙ N , Ṡ Ḍ |

R.H. | — | — | — | — | — | | — | — | — | — | — | — | — | — | — | —

Avarohana

L.H.	2		2	2	2		2	2	2

Notes   Ġ Ṙ Ṡ N , Ḍ Ṡ , N Ṙ , Ṡ Ġ | Ṙ Ṡ N D , P N , D Ṡ , N Ṙ | ⟶ R S N D , P N , D S , N R |

R.H. | — | — | — | — | — | | — | — | — | — | — | — | — | — | — | —

Exercise 2. (Division: 2+2+2+4)

Arohana

L.H.　　2　2　　2　　　2　2　　2　　　　　　　2　2　　2
Notes　P̣ Ḍ , P̣ Ṇ , Ḍ Ṇ , S Ṇ Ḍ P | Ḍ Ṇ , Ḍ S , Ṇ S , R S Ṇ Ḍ |　⟶　N Ṡ , N Ṙ , Ṡ Ṙ , Ġ Ṙ Ṡ N |
R.H.　　| − | − | − | − | − | − | − | − | − | −　　　　| − | − | − | − | −

Avarohana

L.H.　　2　2　2　　　2　　2　2　　　2　　　　　　2　2　　　2
Notes　Ġ Ṙ , Ġ Ṡ , Ṙ Ṡ , N Ṡ Ṙ Ġ | Ṙ Ṡ , Ṙ N , Ṡ N , D N Ṡ Ṙ |　⟶　S Ṇ , S Ḍ , Ṇ Ḍ , P̣ Ḍ Ṇ S |
R.H.　　| − | − | − | − | − | − | − | − | − | −　　　　| − | − | − | − | −

Eleven Aksharas

Exercise 1. (Division: 5+3+3)

Arohana

L.H.　　　　2　　　　2　　　　　2　　2　　　　　　　　　2　　　　2
Notes　P̣ Ḍ Ṇ S R , S Ṇ Ḍ , Ṇ Ḍ P | Ḍ Ṇ S R G , R S Ṇ , S Ṇ Ḍ |　⟶　D N Ṡ Ṙ Ġ , Ṙ Ṡ N , Ṡ N D |
R.H.　　| − | − | | − | | − | − | − | | − | | − |　　　　| − | − | | − | | − |

Avarohana

L.H.　　2　　　　　2　　2　　　　　　　2　　2　　　　　　　　　2　　2
Notes　Ġ Ṙ Ṡ N D , N Ṡ Ṙ , Ṡ Ṙ Ġ | Ṙ Ṡ N D P , D N Ṡ , N Ṡ Ṙ |　⟶　R S Ṇ Ḍ P , Ḍ Ṇ S , Ṇ S R |
R.H.　　| − | − | | − | | − | − | − | | − | | − |　　　　| − | − | | − | | − |

Exercise 2. (Division: 2+2+2+5)

Arohana

L.H.　　2　2　　2　　　　2　2　　2　　　　　　　2　2　　2
Notes　P̣ Ḍ , P̣ Ṇ , Ḍ S , R S Ṇ Ḍ P | Ḍ Ṇ , Ḍ S , Ṇ R , G R S Ṇ Ḍ |　⟶　D N , D Ṡ , N Ṙ , Ġ Ṙ Ṡ N D |
R.H.　　| − | − | − | − | − |　| − | − | − | − | −　　　| − | − | − | − | − |

Avarohana

L.H.　　2　2　2　　　　2　　2　2　　　　2　　　　　2　2　　　　2
Notes　Ġ Ṙ , Ġ Ṡ , Ṙ N , D N Ṡ Ṙ Ġ | Ṙ Ṡ , Ṙ N , Ṡ D , P D N Ṡ Ṙ |　⟶　R S , R Ṇ , S Ḍ , P̣ Ḍ Ṇ S R |
R.H.　　| − | − | − | − | − |　| − | − | − | − | −　　　| − | − | − | − | − |

121

Twelve Aksharas

Exercise 1. (Division: 2+2+2+3+3)

Arohana

L.H.	2 2	2		2 2	2		2 2	2	

Notes P Ḍ , Ḍ Ṇ , Ṇ S , S Ṇ Ḍ , Ṇ Ḍ P | Ḍ Ṇ , Ṇ S , S R , R S Ṇ , S Ṇ Ḍ | ⟶ N Ṡ , Ṡ Ṙ , Ṙ Ġ , Ġ Ṙ Ṡ , Ṙ Ṡ N |

R.H. | – | – | – | – | | – | – | – | – | – | | – | – | – | – | – |

Avarohana

L.H. 2   2   2   2   2   2   2

Notes Ġ Ṙ , Ṙ Ṡ , Ṡ N , N Ṡ Ṙ , Ṡ Ṙ Ġ | Ṙ Ṡ , Ṡ N , N Ḍ , Ḍ N Ṡ , N Ṡ Ṙ | ⟶ S Ṇ , Ṇ Ḍ , Ḍ P , P Ḍ Ṇ , Ḍ Ṇ S |

R.H. | – | – | – | – | | – | | – | – | – | – | | – | | – | – | – | – | – | | – |

Exercise 2. (Division: 2+2+2+3+3)

Arohana

L.H. 2 2 2   2 2   2 2 2   2 2   2 2 2   2 2

Notes P Ḍ , P Ṇ , Ḍ Ṇ , P Ḍ Ṇ , Ṇ Ḍ P | Ḍ Ṇ , Ḍ S , Ṇ S , Ḍ Ṇ S , S Ṇ Ḍ | ⟶ Ṡ Ṙ , Ṡ Ġ , Ṙ Ġ , Ṡ Ṙ Ġ , Ġ Ṙ Ṡ |

R.H. | – | – | – | – | | – | | – | – | – | – | | – | | – | – | – | – | | – |

Avarohana

L.H. 2 2 2 2   2   2 2 2   2   2 2 2   2

Notes Ġ Ṙ , Ġ Ṡ , Ṙ Ṡ , Ġ Ṙ Ṡ , Ṡ Ṙ Ġ | Ṙ Ṡ , Ṙ N , Ṡ N , Ṙ Ṡ N , N Ṡ Ṙ | ⟶ Ṇ Ḍ , Ṇ P , Ḍ P , Ṇ Ḍ P , P Ḍ Ṇ |

R.H. | – | – | – | – | | – | | – | – | – | – | | – | | – | – | – | – | | – |

Exercise 3. (Division: 2+3+3+4)

Arohana

L.H. 2   2 2   2   2   2 2   2   2   2   2   2

Notes P Ḍ , P Ḍ Ṇ , P Ṇ Ḍ , P Ḍ Ṇ S | Ḍ Ṇ , Ḍ Ṇ S , Ḍ S Ṇ , Ḍ Ṇ S R | ⟶ N Ṡ , N Ṡ Ṙ , N Ṙ Ṡ , N Ṡ Ṙ Ġ

R.H. | – | – | | – | | – | – | | – | – | | – | | – | – | | – | | – | – | | – | – |

Avarohana

L.H. 2 2   2   2   2 2   2   2   2   2   2   2

Notes Ġ Ṙ , Ġ Ṙ Ṡ , Ġ Ṡ Ṙ , Ġ Ṙ Ṡ N | Ṙ Ṡ , Ṙ Ṡ N , Ṙ N Ṡ , Ṙ Ṡ N Ḍ | ⟶ S Ṇ , S Ṇ Ḍ , S Ḍ Ṇ , S Ṇ Ḍ P |

R.H. | – | – | | – | | – | – | | – | – | | – | – | | – | | – | | – | – |

122

Thirteen Aksharas

Exercise 1. (Division: 3+3+3+4)

Arohana

L.H.		2		2		2				2		2		2					2		2		2	

L.H.   2   2   2   2   2   2   2   2   2

Notes P Ḍ Ṇ , Ḍ Ṇ S , Ṇ S R , S Ṇ Ḍ P | Ḍ Ṇ S , Ṇ S R , S R G , R S Ṇ Ḍ | ⟶ D N Ṡ , N Ṡ Ṙ , Ṡ Ṙ Ġ , Ṙ Ṡ N D |

R.H. I − I I − I I − I I − I −   I − I I − I I − I I − I −   I − I I − I I − I I − I −

Avarohana

L.H. 2   2   2   2   2   2   2   2   2   2

Notes Ġ Ṙ Ṡ , Ṙ Ṡ N , Ṡ N D , N Ṡ Ṙ Ġ | Ṙ Ṡ N , Ṡ N D , N D P , D N Ṡ Ṙ | ⟶ R S Ṇ , S Ṇ Ḍ , Ṇ Ḍ P , Ḍ Ṇ S R |

R.H. I − I I − I I − I I − I − I − I I − I I − I I − I −   I − I I − I I − I I − I −

Exercise 2. (Division: 2+2+2+2+5)

Arohana

L.H.   2   2 2   2   2 2   2   2 2

Notes P Ḍ , S Ṇ , Ḍ Ṇ , R S , R S Ṇ Ḍ P | Ḍ Ṇ , R S , Ṇ S , G R , G R S Ṇ Ḍ | ⟶ D N , Ṙ Ṡ , N Ṡ , Ġ Ṙ , Ġ Ṙ Ṡ N D |

R.H. I − I − I − I − I − I − I − I − I   I − I − I − I − I − I − I − I − I   I − I − I − I − I − I − I

Avarohana

L.H. 2   2   2   2   2   2   2   2   2   2

Notes Ġ Ṙ , N Ṡ , Ṙ Ṡ , D N , D N Ṡ Ṙ Ġ | Ṙ Ṡ , D N , Ṡ N , P D , P D N Ṡ Ṙ | ⟶ R S , Ḍ Ṇ , S Ṇ , P Ḍ , P Ḍ Ṇ S R |

R.H. I − I − I − I − I − I − I − I − I − I − I I − I − I − I − I − I − I − I − I   I − I − I − I − I − I − I

Fourteen Aksharas

Exercise 1. (Division: 3+2+2+2+5)

Arohana

L.H.   2 2 2 2 2 2 2
Notes P P P , R R , R R , R R , R S N D P |
R.H. | — | | — | — | — | — | — |

L.H.   2 2 2 2 2 2 2
Notes D D D , G G , G G , G G , G R S N D |
R.H. | — | | — | — | — | — | — |

↓

L.H.   2 2 2 2 2 2 2
Notes D D D , G G , G G , G G , G R S N D |
R.H. | — | | — | — | — | — | — |

Avarohana

L.H. 2 2 2   2
Notes G G G , D D , D D , D D , D N S R G |
R.H. | — | | — | — | — | — | — |

L.H.   2
Notes R R R , P P , P P , P P , P D N S R |
R.H. | — | | — | — | — | — | — |

↓

L.H.   2
Notes R R R , P P , P P , P P , P D N S R |
R.H. | — | | — | — | — | — | — |

Exercise 2. (Division: 3+3+4+4)

Arohana

L.H.   2   2   2 2
Notes P N D , P S N , P D N S , S N D P |
R.H. | — | | — | | — | — | — | —

L.H.   2   2   2 2
Notes D S N , D R S , D N S R , R S N D |
R.H. | — | | — | | — | — | — | —

↓

L.H.   2   2   2 2
Notes N R S , N G R , N S R G , G R S N |
R.H. | — | | — | | — | — | — | —

Avarohana

L.H. 2   2   2   2
Notes G S R , G N S , G R S N , N S R G |
R.H. | — | | — | | — | — | — | —

L.H.   2   2   2
Notes R N S , R D N , R S N D , D N S R |
R.H. | — | | — | | — | — | — | —

↓

L.H.   2   2   2
Notes S D N , S P D , S N D P , P D N S |
R.H. | — | | — | | — | — | — | —

Fifteen Aksharas

Exercise 1. (Division: 2+2+2+3+3+3)

Arohana

```
L.H.    2  2    2    2    2
Notes  P Ḍ , P Ṇ , Ḍ S , R S Ṇ , S Ṇ Ḍ , Ṇ Ḍ P |
R.H.   | — | — | — | — | | — | | — |
```

```
L.H.     2  2    2    2    2
Notes  Ḍ Ṇ , Ḍ S , Ṇ R , G R S , R S Ṇ , S Ṇ Ḍ |
R.H.   | — | — | — | — | | — | | — |
```

```
L.H.     2  2    2    2    2
Notes  D N , D Ṡ , N Ṙ , Ġ Ṙ Ṡ , Ṙ Ṡ N , Ṡ N D |
R.H.   | — | — | — | — | | — | | — |
```

Avarohana

```
L.H.   2 2  2    2    2    2
Notes  Ġ Ṙ , Ġ Ṡ , Ṙ N , D N Ṡ , N Ṡ Ṙ , Ṡ Ṙ Ġ |
R.H.   | — | — | — | — | | — | | — |
```

```
L.H.      2  2    2    2    2
Notes  Ṙ Ṡ , Ṙ N , Ṡ D , P D N , D N Ṡ , N Ṡ Ṙ |
R.H.   | — | — | — | — | | — | | — |
```

```
L.H.      2  2    2    2    2
Notes  R S , R Ṇ , S Ḍ , P Ḍ Ṇ , Ḍ Ṇ S , Ṇ S R |
R.H.   | — | — | — | — | | — | | — |
```

Exercise 2. (2+3+2+3+5)

Arohana

```
L.H.    2    2  2      2
Notes  P Ḍ , P Ḍ Ṇ , Ḍ Ṇ , Ḍ Ṇ S , R S Ṇ Ḍ P |
R.H.   | — | — | | — | — | | — | — |
```

```
L.H.    2    2  2      2
Notes  Ḍ Ṇ , Ḍ Ṇ S , Ṇ S , Ṇ S R , G R S Ṇ Ḍ |
R.H.   | — | — | | — | — | | — | — |
```

```
L.H.     2    2  2     2
Notes  D N , D N Ṡ , N Ṡ , N Ṡ Ṙ , Ġ Ṙ Ṡ N D |
R.H.   | — | — | | — | — | | — | — |
```

Avarohana

```
L.H.   2 2  2  2          2
Notes  Ġ Ṙ , Ġ Ṙ Ṡ , Ṙ Ṡ , Ṙ Ṡ N , D N Ṡ Ṙ Ġ |
R.H.   | — | — | | — | — | | — | — |
```

```
L.H.      2    2  2      2
Notes  Ṙ Ṡ , Ṙ Ṡ N , Ṡ N , Ṡ N D , P D N Ṡ Ṙ |
R.H.   | — | — | | — | — | | — | — |
```

```
L.H.      2    2  2        2
Notes  R S , R S Ṇ , S Ṇ , S Ṇ Ḍ , P Ḍ Ṇ S R |
R.H.   | — | — | | — | — | | — | — |
```

125

Sixteen Aksharas

Exercise 1. (Division: 3+3+3+3+4)

Arohana

L.H.	2	2	2	2	2 2	2	2	2	2
Notes	P D N ,	D N S ,	N S R ,	S R G ,	R G M P ,	P M G ,	M G R ,	G R S ,	R S N ,	S N D P	
R.H.	I — I	I — I	I — I	I — I	I — I —	I — I	I — I	I — I	I — I	I — I —

L.H.	2	2	2	2	2 2	2	2	2	2
Notes	D N S ,	N S R ,	S R G ,	R G M ,	G M P D ,	D P M ,	P M G ,	M G R ,	G R S ,	R S N D	
R.H.	I — I	I — I	I — I	I — I	I — I —	I — I	I — I	I — I	I — I	I — I —

L.H.	2	2	2	2	2 2	2	2	2	2
Notes	G M P ,	M P D ,	P D N ,	D N Ṡ ,	N Ṡ Ṙ Ġ ,	Ġ Ṙ Ṡ ,	Ṙ Ṡ N ,	Ṡ N D ,	N D P ,	D P M G	
R.H.	I — I	I — I	I — I	I — I	I — I —	I — I	I — I	I — I	I — I	I — I —

Avarohana

L.H.	2	2	2	2	2 2	2	2	2	2
Notes	R G M ,	G M P ,	M P D ,	P D N ,	D N Ṡ Ṙ ,	Ṙ Ṡ N ,	Ṡ N D ,	N D P ,	D P M ,	P M G R	
R.H.	I — I	I — I	I — I	I — I	I — I —	I — I	I — I	I — I	I — I	I — I —

L.H.	2	2	2	2	2 2	2	2	2	2
Notes	S R G ,	R G M ,	G M P ,	M P D ,	P D N Ṡ ,	Ṡ N D ,	N D P ,	D P M ,	P M G ,	M G R S	
R.H.	I — I	I — I	I — I	I — I	I — I —	I — I	I — I	I — I	I — I	I — I —

L.H.	2	2	2	2	2 2	2	2	2	2
Notes	P D N ,	D N S ,	N S R ,	S R G ,	R G M P ,	P M G ,	M G R ,	G R S ,	R S N ,	S N D P	
R.H.	I — I	I — I	I — I	I — I	I — I —	I — I	I — I	I — I	I — I	I — I —

Exercise 2. (Division: 5+5+6)

Arohana

L.H.		2		2		2 2		2		2	

L.H.   2   2   2 2   2   2

Notes P̣ Ḍ Ṇ S R, Ḍ Ṇ S R G, Ṇ S R G M P, P M G R S, M G R S Ṇ, G R S Ṇ Ḍ P̣ |

R.H. | — | — | | — | — | | — | — | — | — | — | | — | — | | — | — | —

L.H.   2   2   2 2   2   2

Notes Ḍ Ṇ S R G, Ṇ S R G M, S R G M P D, D P M G R, P M G R S, M G R S Ṇ Ḍ |

R.H. | — | — | | — | — | | — | — | — | — | — | | — | — | | — | — | —

↓

L.H.   2   2   2 2   2   2

Notes G M P D N, M P D N Ṡ, P D N Ṡ Ṙ Ġ, Ġ Ṙ Ṡ N D, Ṙ Ṡ N D P, Ṡ N D P M G |

R.H. | — | — | | — | — | | — | — | — | — | — | | — | — | | — | — | —

Avarohana

L.H.   2   2   2 2   2   2

Notes R G M P D, G M P D N, M P D N Ṡ Ṙ, Ṙ Ṡ N D P, Ṡ N D P M, N D P M G R |

R.H. | — | — | | — | — | | — | — | — | — | — | | — | — | | — | — | —

L.H.   2   2   2 2   2   2

Notes S R G M P, R G M P D, G M P D N Ṡ, Ṡ N D P M, N D P M G, D P M G R S |

R.H. | — | — | | — | — | | — | — | — | — | — | | — | — | | — | — | —

↓

L.H.   2   2   2 2   2   2

Notes P̣ Ḍ Ṇ S R, Ḍ Ṇ S R G, Ṇ S R G M P, P M G R S, M G R S Ṇ, G R S Ṇ Ḍ P̣ |

R.H. | — | — | | — | — | | — | — | — | — | — | | — | — | | — | — | —

Exercise 3. (Division: 4+4+4+4)

Arohana

L.H.	2	2	2		2
Notes	P̣ Ṇ Ḍ S,	Ṇ R S Ṇ,	Ḍ Ṇ S R,	S Ṇ Ḍ P̣	
R.H.	❘ — ❘ —	❘ — ❘ —	❘ — ❘ —	❘ — ❘ —	

L.H.	2	2	2		2
Notes	Ḍ S Ṇ R,	S G R S,	Ṇ S R G,	R S Ṇ Ḍ	
R.H.	❘ — ❘ —	❘ — ❘ —	❘ — ❘ —	❘ — ❘ —	

↓

L.H.	2	2	2		2
Notes	D Ṡ Ṅ Ṙ,	Ṡ Ġ Ṙ Ṡ,	N Ṡ Ṙ Ġ,	Ṙ Ṡ N D	
R.H.	❘ — ❘ —	❘ — ❘ —	❘ — ❘ —	❘ — ❘ —	

Avarohana

L.H.	2	2	2		2		2
Notes	Ġ Ṡ Ṙ N,	Ṡ D N Ṡ,	Ṙ Ṡ N D,	N Ṡ Ṙ Ġ			
R.H.	❘ — ❘ —	❘ — ❘ —	❘ — ❘ —	❘ — ❘ —			

L.H.	2	2		2		2
Notes	Ṙ N Ṡ D,	N P D N,	Ṡ N D P,	D N Ṡ Ṙ		
R.H.	❘ -- ❘ —	❘ — ❘ —	❘ — ❘ —	❘ — ❘ —		

↓

L.H.	2	2	2		2
Notes	R Ṇ S Ḍ,	Ṇ P D Ṇ,	S Ṇ Ḍ P,	Ḍ Ṇ S R	
R.H.	❘ — ❘ —	❘ — ❘ —	❘ — ❘ —	❘ — ❘ —	

Exercise 4. (Division: 6+3+3+4)

Arohana

L.H.	2		2		2
Notes	P̣ G R S Ṇ Ḍ,	P̣ Ḍ Ṇ,	Ḍ Ṇ S,	R S Ṇ Ḍ	
R.H.	❘ — ❘ — ❘ —	❘ — ❘	❘ — ❘	❘ — ❘ —	

L.H.	2		2		2
Notes	Ḍ M G R S Ṇ,	Ḍ Ṇ S,	Ṇ S R,	G R S Ṇ	
R.H.	❘ — ❘ — ❘ —	❘ — ❘	❘ — ❘	❘ — ❘ —	

↓

L.H.	2		2		2
Notes	P Ġ Ṙ Ṡ N D,	P D N,	D N Ṡ,	Ṙ Ṡ N D	
R.H.	❘ — ❘ — ❘ —	❘ — ❘	❘ — ❘	❘ — ❘ —	

Avarohana

L.H.	2		2	2		2
Notes	Ġ P D N Ṡ Ṙ,	Ġ Ṙ Ṡ,	Ṙ Ṡ N,	D N Ṡ Ṙ		
R.H.	❘ — ❘ — ❘ —	❘ — ❘ ❘	❘ — ❘	❘ — ❘ —		

L.H.	2		2	2		2
Notes	Ṙ M P D N Ṡ,	Ṙ Ṡ N,	Ṡ N D,	P D N Ṡ		
R.H.	❘ — ❘ — ❘ —	❘ — ❘ ❘	❘ — ❘ ❘	❘ — ❘ —		

↓

L.H.	2		2	2		2
Notes	G P Ḍ Ṇ S R,	G R S,	R S Ṇ,	Ḍ Ṇ S R		
R.H.	❘ — ❘ — ❘ —	❘ — ❘ ❘	❘ — ❘ ❘	❘ — ❘ —		

Exercise 5. (Division: 3+3+6+4)

Arohana

L.H.	2 2 2 2	2

Notes P̣ P̣ P̣ , G G G , G R S Ṇ Ḍ P , Ḍ Ṇ S R |
R.H. | – | | – | | – | – | – | | – | –

L.H.	2 2 2 2	2

Notes Ḍ Ḍ Ḍ , M M M , M G R S Ṇ Ḍ , Ṇ S R G |
R.H. | – | | – | | – | – | – | | – | –

↓

L.H.	2 2 2 2

Notes P P P , Ġ Ġ Ġ , Ġ Ṙ Ṡ N D P , D N Ṡ Ṙ |
R.H. | – | | – | | – | – | – | | – | –

Avarohana

L.H.	2 2 2	2

Notes Ġ Ġ Ġ , P P P , P D N Ṡ Ṙ Ġ , Ṙ Ṡ N D |
R.H. | – | | – | | – | – | – | – | – |

L.H.	2 2 2	2

Notes Ṙ Ṙ Ṙ , M M M , M P D N Ṡ Ṙ , Ṡ N D P |
R.H. | – | | – | | – | – | – | – | – |

↓

L.H.	2 2 2	2

Notes G G G , P̣ P̣ P̣ , P̣ Ḍ Ṇ S R G , R S Ṇ Ḍ |
R.H. | – | | – | | – | – | – | – | – |

Exercise 6. (Division: 2+2+2+3+3+4)

Arohana

L.H.	2 2	2	2

Notes P̣ Ḍ , Ḍ Ṇ , Ṇ S , S Ṇ Ḍ , Ṇ Ḍ P , Ḍ Ṇ S Ṇ |
R.H. | – | | – | | – | | – | | – | | – |

L.H.	2 2	2	2

Notes Ḍ Ṇ , Ṇ S , S R , R S Ṇ , S Ṇ Ḍ , Ṇ S R S |
R.H. | – | | – | | – | – | | – | | – |

↓

L.H.	2 2	2	2

Notes N Ṡ , Ṡ Ṙ , Ṙ Ġ , Ġ Ṙ Ṡ , Ṙ Ṡ N , Ṡ Ṙ Ġ Ṙ |
R.H. | – | – | – | | – | – | | – | –

Avarohana

L.H.	2	2	2

Notes Ġ Ṙ , Ṙ Ṡ , Ṡ N , N Ṡ Ṙ , Ṡ Ṙ Ġ , Ṙ Ṡ N Ṡ |
R.H. | – | | – | | – | | – | – | | – | | – |

L.H.	2	2	2

Notes Ṙ Ṡ , Ṡ N , N D , D N Ṡ , N Ṡ Ṙ , Ṡ N D N |
R.H. | – | | – | | – | | – | – | | – | | – |

↓

L.H.	2	2	2

Notes S N , N Ḍ , Ḍ P , P Ḍ Ṇ , Ḍ Ṇ S , Ṇ Ḍ P Ḍ |
R.H. | – | | – | | – | | – | – | | – | | – |

EXERCISES FOR IMPROVEMENT OF LAYA

Exercise 1. L.H.   2   2   2

Notes – S R G M P D N – Ṡ N D P M G R , S – R G M P D N Ṡ – N D P M G R , S R – G M P D N Ṡ N – D

R.H.   c l – l – l – l c l – l – l – l l c l – l – l – l c l – l – l – l – c l – l – l c l

L.H.   2   2

Notes P M G R , S R G – M P D N Ṡ N D – P M G R , S R G M – P D N Ṡ N D P – M G R , S R G M P – D N

R.H.   – l – l l – l c l – l – l – l c l – l – l – l c l – l – l – l c l – l l – l – l c l –

L.H.   2   2   2

Notes Ṡ N D P M – G R , S R G M P D – N Ṡ N D P M G – R , S R G M P D N – Ṡ N D P M G R –

R.H.   l – l – l c l – l – l – l – c l – l – l – l l c l l – l – l – l c l – l – l – l c

Exercise 2. **Arohana**

L.H.   2   2   2

Notes P D N , P – D – N – S – R – G – M , P M G P – M – G – R – S – N – D |

R.H.   l – l l c l c l c l c l c l l l – l l c l c l c l c l c l

L.H.   2   2   2

Notes D N S , D – N – S – R – G – M – P , D P M D – P – M – G – R – S – N |

R.H.   l – l l c l c l c l c l c l l l – l l c l c l c l c l c l

L.H.   2   2   2

Notes G M P , G – M – P – D – N – Ṡ – Ṙ , Ġ Ṙ Ṡ , Ġ – Ṙ – Ṡ – N – D – P – M |

R.H.   l – l l c l c l c l c l c l l c l l c l c l c l c l c l

Avarohana

L.H.   2   2   2

Notes G M P , G – M – P – D – N – Ṡ – Ṙ , Ġ Ṙ Ṡ , Ġ – Ṙ – Ṡ – N – D – P – M |

R.H.   l – l l c l c l c l c l c l l – l l c l c l c l c l c l

L.H.   2   2   2

Notes R G M , R – G – M – P – D – N – Ṡ Ṙ Ṡ N , Ṙ – Ṡ – N – D – P – M – G |

R.H.   l – l l c l c l c l c l c l l – l l c l c l c l c l c l

L.H.   2   2   2

Notes P D N , P – D – N – S – R – G – M , P M G P – M – G – R – S – N – D |

R.H.   l – l l c l c l c l c l c l l l – l l c l c l c l c l c l

130

Exercise 3. **Arohana**

L.H.   2   2

Notes P D N S R S N D P – – D – – N – – S – – R – – G – – M – – P – –

R.H. I – I – I – I – I   c I   c I   c I   c I   c I   c I   c

L.H. 2   2

Notes P M G R S R G M P – – M – – G – – R – – S – – N – – D – – P – – |

R.H. I – I – I – I – I   c I   c I   c I   c I   c I   c I   c

L.H.   2   2

Notes D N S R G R S N D – – N – – S – – R – – G – – M – – P – – D – –

R.H. I – I – I – I – I   c I   c I   c I   c I   c I   c I   c

L.H. 2   2

Notes D P M G R G M P D – – P – – M – – G – – R – – S – – N – – D – – |

R.H. I – I – I – I – I   c I   c I   c I   c I   c I   c I   c

L.H. 2   2

Notes G M P D N D P M G – – M – – P – – D – – N – – S – – R – – G – –

R.H. I – I – I – I – I   c I   c I   c I   c I   c I   c I   c

L.H. 2   2

Notes G R S N D N S R G – – R – – S – – N – – D – – P – – M – – G – – |

R.H. I – I – I – I – I   c I   c I   c I   c I   c I   c I   c

Avarohana

L.H.   2   2

Notes G M P D N D P M G – – M – – P – – D – – N – – S – – R – – G – –

R.H. I – I – I – I – I   c I   c I   c I   c I   c I   c I   c

L.H. 2   2

Notes G R S N D N S R G – – R – – S – – N – – D – – P – – M – – G – – |

R.H. I – I – I – I – I   c I   c I   c I   c I   c I   c I   c

L.H.   2   2

Notes R G M P D P M G R – – G – – M – – P – – D – – N – – S – – R – –

R.H. I – I – I – I – I   c I   c I   c I   c I   c I   c I   c

(Exercise 3 continues overleaf)

exercise 3
(continued)

L.H.   2   2
Notes R̊ S N D P D N S̊ R̊ — — S̊ — — N — — D — — P — M — — G — — R — — |
R.H.   I — I — I — I — I   c I   c I   c I   c I   c I   c I   c I   c

L.H.   2   ↓   2
Notes P D N S R S N D P — — D — — N — — S — — R — — G — — M — — P — —
R.H.   I — I — I — I — I   c I   c I   c I   c I   c I   c I   c I   c

L.H.   2   2
Notes P M G R S R G M P — — M — — G — — R — — S — — N — — D — — P — — |
R.H.   I — I — I — I — I   c I   c I   c I   c I   c I   c I   c I   c

KRINTAN, ZAMZAMA, MEEND, AND GAMAK

These four types of figures are all ways of embellishing notes. They should be practiced with careful attention to accurate timing and distinct note production.

Krintan

Exercise 1.   **Arohana**

L.H.   2   2   2   2   2   2   2   2   2   2   2   2
Notes D P | N D | S N | R S | G R | M G | P M | D P | N D | S̊ N | R̊ S̊ | G̊ R̊ |
R.H.   I   I   I   I   I   I   I   I   I   I   I   I

Avarohana

L.H.   2   2   2   2   2   2   2   2   2   2   2   2
Notes G̊ R̊ | R̊ S̊ | S̊ N | N D | D P | P M | M G | G R | R S | S N | N D | D P |
R.H.   I   I   I   I   I   I   I   I   I   I   I   I

Performance:

1. Place the second finger of the left hand (2) on the note D and the first finger (1) on the note P
2. Pluck the string with the *mizrab* stroke da, producing the note D
3. Lift the second finger from the string with a slight plucking motion, producing the note P
   Note: This action will hereafter be referred to as a cut (that is, we just performed a cut from D to P)
4. Repeat this same process with N and D, then S and N, and so on as indicated

132

Exercise 2.

Arohana

L.H.	2	2	2		2	2	2
Notes	N D P	S N D	R S N	⟶	S N D	R Ṡ N	G Ṙ Ṡ
R.H.	ǀ	ǀ	ǀ				

Avarohana

L.H.	2	2	2		2	2	2
Notes	Ġ Ṙ Ṡ	Ṙ Ṡ N	S N D	⟶	R Ṡ N	S N D	N D P
R.H.	ǀ	ǀ	ǀ		ǀ	ǀ	ǀ

Performance:
1. Place (2) on N and (1) on D
2. Pluck the string with the *mizrab* stroke da, producing the note N
3. Cut from N to D (see exercise 1)
4. Slide (1) from D to P just before the note P is to be heard. Maintain pressure on the string so that when P is reached it will be heard as a distinct note, even though the string is not plucked with the *mizrab* at this time
   Note: This action will hereafter be referred to as a slip (that is, we just performed a slip from D to P)
5. Repeat this same process with S N D, then R S N, and so on as indicated

Exercise 3.

Arohana

L.H.	2	2	2	2	2	2		2	2	2	2	2	2
Notes	N D P D	S N D N	R S N S	⟶	S N D N	R Ṡ N Ṡ	G Ṙ Ṡ Ṙ
R.H.	ǀ	ǀ	ǀ		ǀ	ǀ	ǀ

Avarohana

L.H.	2	2	2	2	2	2		2	2	2	2	2	2
Notes	Ġ Ṙ Ṡ Ṙ	Ṙ Ṡ N Ṡ	S N D N	⟶	R Ṡ N Ṡ	S N D N	N D P D
R.H.	ǀ	ǀ	ǀ		ǀ	ǀ	ǀ

Performance:
1. Place (2) on N and (1) on D
2. Pluck the string with the *mizrab* stroke da, producing the note N
3. Cut from N to D
4. Slip from D to P
5. Bring (2) down firmly on the note D just at the moment the note should be heard
   Note: This action will hereafter be referred to as a hammer (that is, we just performed a hammer on D)
6. Repeat this same process with S N D N, then R S N S, and so on as indicated

133

Exercise 4.   **Arohana**

L.H.   2 2   2 2 2   2   2 2   2 2 2   2
Notes Ḍ P Ṇ D P D | Ṇ Ḍ S Ṇ Ḍ Ṇ | ⟶   Ṡ N R̄ Ṡ N Ṡ | R̄ Ṡ Ḡ R̄ Ṡ R̄ |
R.H. | | | |

          Avarohana

L.H.   2 2   2 2 2   2   2 2   2 2 2   2
Notes R̄ Ṡ Ḡ R̄ Ṡ R̄ | Ṡ N R̄ Ṡ N Ṡ | ⟶   Ṇ Ḍ S Ṇ Ḍ Ṇ | Ḍ P Ṇ D P D |
R.H. | | | |

Performance: 1. Place (2) on Ḍ and (1) on P
                   2. Pluck the string with the *mizrab* stroke da, producing the note Ḍ
                   3. Cut from Ḍ to P
                   4. Hammer on Ṇ
                   5. Cut from Ṇ to Ḍ
                   6. Slip from Ḍ to P
                   7. Hammer on Ḍ
                   8. Repeat this same process with Ṇ Ḍ S Ṇ Ḍ Ṇ, then
                      S Ṇ R S Ṇ S, and so on as indicated

Zamzama

Exercise 1.   **Arohana**

L.H.   2 2   2   2   2   2   2   2   2   2   2   2
Notes Ḍ P | Ṇ D | S Ṇ | R S | Ḡ R | M G | P M | Ḍ P | Ṇ D | Ṡ N | R̄ Ṡ | Ḡ R̄ |
R.H. | | | | | | | | | | | |

          Avarohana

L.H.   2   2   2   2   2   2   2   2   2   2   2   2
Notes Ḡ R̄ | R̄ Ṡ | Ṡ N | Ṇ D | Ḍ P | P M | M G | Ḡ R̄ | R Ṡ | Ṡ N | Ṇ D | Ḍ P |
R.H. | | | | | | | | | | | |

Performance: 1. Place (2) on Ḍ and (1) on P
                   2. Pluck the string with *mizrab* stroke da, producing the note Ḍ
                   3. Cut from Ḍ to P
                   4. Hammer on Ḍ
                   5. Cut from Ḍ to P
                   6. Repeat this same process with Ṇ and D, then S and Ṇ, and so on as indicated

Exercise 2. **Arohana**

L.H.
Notes D P | N D | S N | R S | G R | M G | P M | D P | N D | S N | R S | G R |
R.H.

Avarohana

L.H.
Notes G R | R S | S N | N D | D P | P M | M G | G R | R S | S N | N D | D P |
R.H.

Performance:
1. Place (2) on Ḍ and (1) on P
2. Pluck the string with *mizrab* stroke da, producing the note Ḍ
3. Cut from Ḍ to P
4. Hammer on Ḍ
5. Cut from Ḍ to P
6. Hammer on Ḍ
7. Cut from Ḍ to P
8. Repeat this same process with Ṇ and Ḍ, then S and Ṇ, and so on as indicated

Combination Figures

Exercise 1. **Arohana**

L.H.
Notes N Ḍ P P Ḍ – | S N Ḍ Ḍ N – | ⟶ R S N N S – | G R S S R – |
R.H. | • – | | • – | | • – | | • – |

Avarohana

L.H.
Notes G R S S R – | R S N N S – | ⟶ S N Ḍ Ḍ N – | N Ḍ P P Ḍ – |
R.H. | • – | | • – | | • – | | • – |

Performance:
1. Place (2) on Ṇ and (1) on Ḍ
2. Pluck the string with *mizrab* stroke da, producing the note Ṇ
3. Cut from Ṇ to Ḍ
4. Slip from Ḍ to P
5. Play the note P with a weak ra stroke
6. Place (2) on Ḍ and play the note with a strong da stroke
7. Rest half a *matra*
8. Repeat this same process beginning on S then R, and so on as indicated
   Note: When this figure is mastered add a *zamzama* on the first two notes, that is,

N Ḍ P P Ḍ –   would be played: N Ḍ N Ḍ P P Ḍ –
| • – | | • – |

Exercise 2.

Arohana

L.H.

Notes P – N D P P D – | D – S N D D N – | ⟶ Ṡ – Ġ Ṙ Ṡ Ṡ Ṙ – |

R.H.

Avarohana

L.H.

Notes Ṡ – Ġ Ṙ Ṡ Ṡ Ṙ – | N – Ṙ Ṡ N N Ṡ – | ⟶ P – N D P P D – |

R.H.

Performance: 1. Play P with a *mizrab* stroke da
2. Rest half a *matra*
3. Play N D P P D – as described in the previous exercise

4. Repeat this same process beginning on D, then N, and so on as indicated
   Note: When this figure is mastered add a *zamzama* in the manner described in the previous exercise, that is,

   P – N D P P D –   is played   P – NDND P P D –

Exercise 3.

Arohana

L.H.

Notes P P D D P – N D P P D – | D D N N D – S N D D N – | ⟶ Ṡ Ṡ Ṙ Ṙ Ṡ – Ġ Ṙ Ṡ Ṡ Ṙ – |

R.H.

Avarohana

L.H.

Notes Ṡ Ṡ Ṙ Ṙ Ṡ – Ġ Ṙ Ṡ Ṡ Ṙ – | N N Ṡ Ṡ N – Ṙ Ṡ N N Ṡ – | ⟶ P P D D P – N D P P D – |

R.H.

Performance: 1. Play P P D D with *mizrab* strokes diri diri
2. Play P – N D P P D – in the manner described in the previous exercise

3. Repeat this same process beginning on D then N, and so on as indicated
   Note: When this is mastered add a *zamzama* as in previous exercises

136

Exercise 4.

Arohana

L.H.   2 2   2 2   2   2
Notes P – Ḍ Ḍ P P Ḍ Ḍ P – N Ḍ P P Ḍ – |
R.H.   I   v   v   v   I   I   · – I

Avarohana

L.H.   2 2   2 2   2   2
Notes Ṡ – Ṙ Ṙ Ṡ Ṡ Ṙ Ṙ Ṡ – Ġ Ṙ Ṡ Ṡ Ṙ – |
R.H.   I   v   v   v   I   I   · – I

L.H.   2 2   2 2   2   2
Notes Ḍ – N N Ḍ Ḍ N N Ḍ – S N Ḍ Ḍ N – |
R.H.   I   v   v   v   I   I   · – I

L.H.   2 2   2 2   2   2
Notes N – Ṡ Ṡ N N Ṡ Ṡ N – Ṙ Ṡ N N Ṡ – |
R.H.   I   v   v   v   I   I   · – I

L.H.   2 2   2 2   2   2
Notes Ṡ – Ṙ Ṙ Ṡ Ṙ Ṙ Ṡ – Ġ Ṙ Ṡ Ṡ Ṙ – |
R.H.   I   v   v   v   I   I   · – I

L.H.   2 2   2 2   2   2
Notes P – Ḍ Ḍ P P Ḍ Ḍ P – N Ḍ P P Ḍ – |
R.H.   I   v   v   v   I   I   · – I

Performance: 1. Play P – Ḍ Ḍ with *mizrab* strokes da diri

2. Play P P Ḍ Ḍ P – N Ḍ P P Ḍ – in the manner described in the previous exercise
          v   v   I   I   · – I

3. Repeat this same process beginning on Ḍ then N, and so on as indicated
    Note: When this is mastered add a *zamzama* as in previous exercises

Meend

Exercise 1.

Arohana

L.H.   2   2   2   2   2   2
Notes P Ḍ , Ḍ P | Ḍ N , N Ḍ | N Ṡ , Ṡ N | ⟶ N Ṡ , Ṡ N | Ṡ Ṙ , Ṙ Ṡ | Ṙ Ġ , Ġ Ṙ |
R.H.   I   I   I   I   I   I   I   I   I   I   I   I

Avarohana

L.H.   2   2   2   2   2   2
Notes Ṙ Ġ , Ġ Ṙ | Ṡ Ṙ , Ṙ Ṡ | N Ṡ , Ṡ N | ⟶ N Ṡ , Ṡ N | Ḍ N , N Ḍ | P Ḍ , Ḍ P |
R.H.   I   I   I   I   I   I   I   I   I   I   I   I

Performance: 1. Place (2) on P and play with *mizrab* stroke da

2. Pull the string sideways (away from the other playing strings) at such a rate that Ḍ is reached in half a *matra*
    Note: When pulling the string the student should maintain pressure on the string and the finger should follow the contour of the fret as it moves

3. Pluck the string with *mizrab* stroke da, producing the note Ḍ

4. Bring the string back up to its original position at such a rate that P is reached in half a *matra*

5. Repeat this same process beginning on Ḍ then N, and so on as indicated
    Note: Strict rhythm must be maintained in all *meend* exercises. Great care should be taken to pull the string at the proper rate so that the note or notes pulled-to will be reached at the correct moment. *Meend* exercises should be practiced very slowly at first and the student should be extremely careful to make sure that the notes pulled-to are of the correct pitch

Exercise 2. Three Matras

Arohana

L.H.   2   2   2   2

Notes   P Ḍ N , N Ḍ P | Ḍ N S , S N Ḍ | ⟶ N Ṡ Ṙ , Ṙ Ṡ N | Ṡ Ṙ Ġ , Ġ Ṙ Ṡ |

R.H. | | | | | | | |

Avarohana

L.H.   2   2   2   2

Notes   Ṡ Ṙ Ġ , Ġ Ṙ Ṡ | N Ṡ Ṙ , Ṙ Ṡ N | ⟶ Ḍ N S , S N Ḍ | P Ḍ N , N Ḍ P |

R.H. | | | | | | | |

Performance:

1. Place (2) on P and play with *mizrab* stroke da
2. Pull the string to produce Ḍ as in the previous exercise
3. After Ḍ has been reached and distinctly heard pull the string farther until N is reached
4. Pluck the string with *mizrab* stroke da, producing the note N
5. Bring the string back up until Ḍ is heard
6. After Ḍ has been reached and distinctly heard, bring the string back up to its original position so that P is heard
7. Repeat this same process beginning on Ḍ then N, and so on as indicated

Exercise 3. Four Matras

Arohana

L.H.   2   2   2

Notes   P Ḍ N S , S N Ḍ P | Ḍ N S Ṙ , Ṙ S N Ḍ | ⟶ N Ṡ Ṙ Ġ , Ġ Ṙ Ṡ N |

R.H. | | | | | |

Avarohana

L.H.   2   2   2

Notes   N Ṡ Ṙ Ġ , Ġ Ṙ Ṡ N | Ḍ N Ṡ Ṙ , Ṙ Ṡ N Ḍ | ⟶ P Ḍ N S , S N Ḍ P |

R.H. | | | | | |

Performance:

1. Place (2) on P and play with *mizrab* stroke da
2. Pull the string to produce Ḍ then N and then S in the manner of the previous exercises
3. Play S with a da stroke and then bring the string back up to produce N, then Ḍ, then P in the manner of the previous exercises
4. Repeat this same process beginning on Ḍ, then N, and so on as indicated

Exercise 4. Six Matras

Arohana

L.H. 2   2   2

Notes P̣ Ḍ , P̣ Ṇ , Ḍ Ṇ , P̣ Ḍ Ṇ , Ṇ Ḍ P̣ | Ḍ Ṇ , Ḍ S , Ṇ S , Ḍ Ṇ S , S Ṇ Ḍ | ⟶ Ṡ R , Ṡ G , R G , Ṡ R G , G R Ṡ |

R.H. | | | | | | | | | | | | | | | | | |

Avarohana

L.H. 2   2   2

Notes Ṡ R , Ṡ G , R G , Ṡ R G , G R Ṡ | N Ṡ , N R , Ṡ R , N Ṡ R , R Ṡ N | ⟶ P̣ Ḍ , P̣ Ṇ , Ḍ Ṇ , P̣ Ḍ Ṇ , Ṇ Ḍ P̣ |

R.H. | | | | | |

Performance:

1. Place (2) on P̣ and play with *mizrab* stroke da
2. Pull to Ḍ
3. Bring the string back to P̣ and play P̣ with a da stroke
4. Pull to Ṇ without stopping on Ḍ
5. Bring the string back to Ḍ and play Ḍ with a da stroke
6. Pull to Ṇ
7. Bring the string back to P̣ and play P̣ Ḍ Ṇ , Ṇ Ḍ P̣ in the manner described in exercise 2
8. Repeat this same process beginning on Ḍ, then Ṇ, and so on as indicated

Exercise 5. Eight Matras

Arohana

L.H. 2

Notes P̣ Ḍ Ṇ , P̣ Ḍ Ṇ , P̣ Ḍ , P̣ Ḍ Ṇ S , S Ṇ Ḍ P̣ |

R.H. | | | | |

L.H. 2

Notes Ḍ Ṇ S , Ḍ Ṇ S , Ḍ Ṇ , Ḍ Ṇ S R , R S Ṇ Ḍ |

R.H. | | | | |

↓

L.H. 2

Notes N Ṡ R , N Ṡ R , N Ṡ , N Ṡ R G , G R Ṡ N |

R.H. | | | | |

Avarohana

L.H. 2

Notes N Ṡ R , N Ṡ R , N Ṡ , N Ṡ R G , G R Ṡ N |

R.H. | | | | |

L.H. 2

Notes Ḍ Ṇ Ṡ , Ḍ Ṇ Ṡ , Ḍ Ṇ , Ḍ Ṇ Ṡ R , R Ṡ Ṇ Ḍ |

R.H. | | | | |

↓

L.H. 2

Notes P̣ Ḍ Ṇ , P̣ Ḍ Ṇ , P̣ Ḍ , P̣ Ḍ Ṇ S , S Ṇ Ḍ P̣ |

R.H. | | | | |

Performance:

1. Place (2) on P̣ and play P̣ Ḍ Ṇ in the manner described in exercise 2
2. Bring the string back to P̣ and repeat P̣ Ḍ Ṇ as before
3. Bring the string back to P̣ and play P̣ Ḍ in the manner described in exercise 1
4. Bring the string back to P̣ and play

P̣ Ḍ Ṇ S , S Ṇ Ḍ P̣

in the manner described in exercise 3
5. Repeat this same process beginning on Ḍ, then Ṇ, and so on as indicated

Gamak

Exercise 1. Three Matras

Arohana

L.H.	2 2 2	2 2 2	2 2 2		2 2 2	2 2 2	2 2 2			
Notes	PDPDP–	DNDND–	NSNSN–	⟶	NSNSN–	SRSRS–	RGRGR–			
R.H.	⏐ ⏐ –	⏐ ⏐ –	⏐ ⏐ –		⏐ ⏐ –	⏐ ⏐ –	⏐ ⏐ –			

Avarohana

L.H.	2 2 2	2 2 2	2 2 2		2 2 2	2 2 2	2 2 2			
Notes	RGRGR–	SRSRS–	NSNSN–	⟶	NSNSN–	DNDND–	PDPDP–			
R.H.	⏐ ⏐ –	⏐ ⏐ –	⏐ ⏐ –		⏐ ⏐ –	⏐ ⏐ –	⏐ ⏐ –			

Performance:

1. Place (2) on P and play with a da stroke
2. Pull to D
3. Bring the string back to P and play with a da stroke
4. Pull to D
5. Bring the string back to P and play with a ra stroke
6. Rest half a *matra*
7. Repeat this same process beginning on D, then N, and so on as indicated

Exercise 2. Six Matras

Arohana

L.H.	2 2 2 2	2 2 2 2		2 2 2 2	2 2 2 2	
Notes	P–D–DNDND–P–	D–N–NSNSN–D–	⟶	N–S–SRSRS–N–	S–R–RGRGR–S–	
R.H.	⏐ – ⏐ ⏐ ⏐ –	⏐ – ⏐ ⏐ ⏐ –		⏐ – ⏐ ⏐ ⏐ –	⏐ – ⏐ ⏐ ⏐ –	

Avarohana

L.H.	2 2 2 2	2 2 2 2		2 2 2 2	2 2 2 2	
Notes	S–R–RGRGR–S–	N–S–SRSRS–N–	⟶	D–N–NSNSN–D–	P–D–DNDND–P–	
R.H.	⏐ – ⏐ ⏐ ⏐ –	⏐ – ⏐ ⏐ ⏐ –		⏐ – ⏐ ⏐ ⏐ –	⏐ – ⏐ ⏐ ⏐ –	

Performance:

1. Play P with a da stroke
2. Play D with a ra stroke
3. Play the *gamak* DNDN in the manner described in the previous exercise
4. Play D with a da stroke
5. Play P with a ra stroke
6. Repeat this same process beginning on D, then N, and so on as indicated

140

Exercise 3. Eight Matras

Arohana

L.H.   2 2 2 2 2 2   2 2 2 2 2 2   2 2 2 2 2 2

Notes P̣–Ḍ–ḌNḌNḌNḌNḌ–P̣– | Ḍ–N̦–N̦SN̦SN̦SN̦SN̦–Ḍ– | ⟶ Ṣ–Ṛ–ṚGṚGṚGṚGṚ–Ṣ–

R.H.   I – I I I I I – I – I I I I I –   I – I I I I I –

Avarohana

L.H.   2 2 2 2 2 2   2 2 2 2 2 2   2 2 2 2 2 2

Notes Ṣ–Ṛ–ṚGṚGṚGṚGṚ–Ṣ– | N̦–Ṣ–ṢRṢRṢRṢRṢ–N̦– | ⟶ P̣–Ḍ–ḌNḌNḌNḌNḌ–P̣–

R.H.   I – I I I I I – I – I I I I I –   I – I I I I I –

Performance:

1. Play P̣ with a da stroke
2. Play Ḍ with a ra stroke
3. Play the *gamak* ḌNḌNḌNḌN in the manner described in exercise 1

4. Play Ḍ with a da stroke
5. Play P̣ with a ra stroke

SARGAMS

Sargams are exercises in a given *raga*. They are in *tala* and are the first introduction that a student receives to *raga* forms. Merely student exercises, they are not to be confused with *gats* (fixed compositions played with *tabla* in the performance of a *raga*).

The vertical lines are to indicate the divisions of the *tala*, i.e. 4-4-4-4, 4-4-2-2, 3-2-2 etc.

The two parts, *asthai* and *antara*, should each be repeated. When one or two notes appear in brackets at the end of the *asthai* section, they should be played at the beginning of that section when it is repeated. These notes should also be played at the beginning of *asthai* if the entire *sargam* is immediately repeated.

The tuning of the *taraf* (sympathetic strings) should be closely observed. The tunings given correspond to the strings in the order of the longest to the shortest string.

The *matra* symbol, the L.H., Notes, and R.H. indications have been omitted from these exercises. It is assumed that the student is by now familiar enough with the notation that these indications are no longer needed.

The same principle of playing applied to the *paltas* should be applied to the *sargams*, namely, an embellishing note on the first note of every ascending figure and an embellishing note on all the notes, except the last, of every descending figure. Practice each *sargam* very slowly at first. Once it is memorized and absolutely clear, increase the speed step by step.

Exercise 1.

Evening Raga: YAMAN KALYAN   Tala: TEEN-TAL 4-4-4-4

Notes used: S R G M M̓ P D N Ṡ

Taraf strings: Ș Ṉ S R G M M̓ P D N Ṡ

Asthai

```
  o 2          x 2        2          o 2        2
| G R S N | S R G M | P – R – | G R S N | S – G R | G R S N |
  I – I –   I – I –   I C I C   I – I –   I C I –   I – I –

  x              2        o 2        2          x        2
| Ḍ – D – | N D P M̓ | P – G R | G D P – | G R G M | G R S – |
  I C I C   I – I –   I C I –   I – I C   I – I –   I – I C
```

Antara

```
  o 2          x 2        2          o 2        2
| N D P M̓ | P D N Ṡ | Ṙ – D – | Ġ Ṙ Ṡ N | Ṡ – N D | N D P M̓ |
  I – I –   I – I –   I C I C   I – I –   I C I –   I – I –

  x 2          2        o          2        2          x        2
| D – R – | G R S N | S – M P | M D P – | G R G M | G R S – |
  I C I C   I – I –   I C I –   I – I C   I – I –   I – I C
```

141

Exercise 2.   Evening raga: YAMAN KALYAN   Tala: TEEN — TAL 4-4-4-4

Notes used: S R G M M᷑ P D N Ṡ   Taraf strings: S Ṇ S R G M M᷑ P D N Ṡ

(An old composition)

Asthai

```
o 2           x 2        2        o 2
|N D P M | G R G M | N D M᷑ — | P M᷑ G R | G M P M᷑ | G R S Ṇ |
 | — | —   | — | —   | — |  c   | — | —   | — | —   | — | —


x 2         o 2         2          x 2
|Ḍ Ṇ — M᷑ | — Ḍ , Ṇ R | G R , G M᷑ | P D , N D | P M᷑ , G M | G R S — |
 | —  |  c |  | —  | —   | — | —    | — | —    | — | —    | — | c
```

Antara

```
o 2          x 2         o            2             x           2         o 2          2        2
|N D P M | G R G M | S R G , S | — R G M᷑ | P D N Ṡ | N D P M | G R G M | P D N Ṙ | D — Ġ Ṙ | — D — Ṙ |
 | — | —   | — | —   | — | |  c   | | — | —   | — | —   | — | —   | — | —   | — | —   | c | —    | — |


x            2          o 2        2         x 2        o 2         2          x           2
|Ṡ N D P | M᷑ P N D | P M᷑ G M | G R S Ṇ | Ḍ Ṇ — M᷑ | — Ḍ , Ṇ R | G R , G M᷑ | P D , N D | P M᷑ , G M | G R S —
 | — | —   | — | —   | — | —    | — | —    | — |  c   | | —  | —   | — | —    | — | —    | — | —    | — | c
```

Exercise 3.   Evening raga: YAMAN   Tala: TEEN — TAL 4-4-4-4

Notes used: S R G M᷑ P D N Ṡ   Taraf strings: S Ṇ S R G G M᷑ P D N Ṡ

Asthai

```
o 2  2        x 2        2        o
| — G R G | Ṇ R G M᷑ | N D — M᷑ | — D P M᷑ | G R Ṇ Ḍ | M᷑ — Ḍ Ṇ |
  | — |  | — | —   | — |  c    | | —  | — | —    |  | c | —


x 2  2        o 2          x           2
|R , Ṇ R G , | R G M᷑ D | N Ṙ Ġ Ṙ , | Ṡ N D P | M᷑ P , N D | P M᷑ G R | [S]
 |  | — |   | — | —    | — | —    | — | —   | — | —    | — | —    |
```

Antara

```
o 2  2        x 2        2        o          2        2  2
|S , G R G | Ṇ R G M᷑ | D N D M᷑ | G R , G M᷑ | D N Ṙ — | N Ġ Ṙ Ġ |
 |  | | —   | — | —    | — | —    | — | | —    | — | c   | — | —


x            2          o 2          2         x           2
|Ṙ N , D Ṙ | N D M᷑ G , | R M᷑ G R , | Ṇ G R Ṇ , | G M᷑ N D | P M᷑ G R |
 | — | —    | — | —    | — | —    | — | —    | — | —   | — | —
```

142

Exercise 4. Evening raga: KHAMAJ   Tala: TEEN—TAL 4-4-4-4

Notes used: S R G M P D N̲ N Ṡ   Taraf strings: S Ṇ S R G M P D N̲ N Ṡ

(An old composition)

Asthai

```
 x 2 2       2   o 2       2       x           2   o 2
 | G G S G | M P G M | N̲ D – M | P D – M | G – – ᴺḊ | – N Ṡ – | Ṡ N̲ D P | M G R S |
   | – | –   | – | –   | | c |   – | c |   | c c |   c | | c   | – | –   | – | –
```

Antara

```
 x 2 2       2 2 o           2       2 x       2
 | G G S G | M P G M | G M D N | S , D N S , | D N Ṡ Ṙ | Ṡ N̲ D – |
   | – | –   | – | –   | – | –   | | – |     | – | –   | – | c
```

```
 o     2*      x       2       o 2     2
 | – Ġ – Ṁ | Ġ Ṙ Ṡ N̲ | D – M , G | – Ṡ , D N | Ṡ , G – M , | G R S – |
   c | c |   | – | –   | c | |   c | |       c | | – |   | – | c
```

*If the student has a sitar with only nineteen frets, the high Ṁ must be produced by pulling from Ġ.

Exercise 5. Morning raga: BHAIRAV   Tala: TEEN—TAL 4-4-4-4

Notes used: S R̲ G M P D̲ N Ṡ   Taraf strings: S Ṇ S R̲ G G M P D̲ N Ṡ

Asthai

```
 o   2     2   x 2       o         2       2
 | – M G R̲ , | G R̲ S Ṇ | R̲ S Ṇ , Ḍ | – S Ṇ R̲ | – G M R̲ | – G M P , |
   c | – |   | – | –   | – | |     c | – |   c | – |   c | – |
```

```
 x   2 2 2 2   o             2 x     2               2
 | G M P D̲ | DNDND P | M G R̲ S | – D̲ N Ṡ , | P D̲ N , M | P D̲ , G M | [ P , ]
   | – | –   | | | –   | – | –   c | – |   | – | |   | – | |   | –
```

Antara

```
 o       2 x       2   o     2     2
 | P , M G R̲ | G M P G | M – D̲ N | Ṡ Ṙ Ṡ – | D̲ N , D̲ Ġ | Ṙ , D̲ Ṙ Ṡ , |
   | | – |   | – | –   | c | –   | – | c   | – | –   | | – |
```

```
 x       2 2 2   o           2 x     2
 | N D̲ M P | DNDND P | M G R̲ S | – D̲ N Ṡ , | P D̲ N , M | P D̲ , G M |
   | – | –   | | | –   | – | –   c | – |   | – | |   | – | |
```

143

Exercise 6. Morning raga: GUNKALI   Tala: JHAPTAL 2-3-2-3

Notes used: S R̲ G M P D̲ N S   Taraf strings: S Ṇ S R G G M P D N S

Asthai

```
     o 2        2      2       o 2
x           x
| S R̲ | M – P | D̲ – | P – D̲ | M P | D̲ – P | M P | M R̲ S |
  | –  |  C |   C |   C |  | – |   C |  | – |  – |
```

```
     o 2        2 x     2      o 2
x
| D̲ D̲ | S – S | R̲ – | S – R̲ | M P | D̲ – P | M D̲ | P M R̲ |
  | –  |  C |   C |   C |  | – |   C |  | – |  – |
```

Antara

```
     o 2      2 x    2*       o 2
x
| S R̲ | M – P | D̲ Ṙ | Ṡ – Ṙ | Ṡ R̲ | Ṁ Ṙ Ṡ | Ṙ Ṡ | D̲ – P |
  | –  |  C |  | – |   C |  | – |  – |  | – |   C |
```

```
       2  o 2          2       o 2
x           x
| M P | D̲ Ṙ Ṡ | Ṙ Ṡ | D̲ – P | M P | D̲ – P | M D̲ | P M R̲ |
  | –  | | – |  | – |   C |  | – |   C |  | – |  – |
```

*If there is no high Ṁ fret, pull to Ṁ from Ṙ.

Exercise 7. Morning raga: BHAIRAVI   Tala: TEEN – TAL 4-4-4-4

Notes used: S R̲ G̲ M P D̲ N Ṡ   Taraf strings: S Ṇ S R̲ G̲ M M P D̲ N Ṡ

Asthai

```
o 2            x 2  2    2     o 2 2   2            x     2      2
| R̲ Ṇ – S | R̲ G M – | P M P , G̲ | M G̲ R S | D̲ D̲ P , N | D P M – | G M P , G̲ | M G̲ R S |
  | – C |   – |  – C |  | – | |   – | – |  | – | |   – | – C |  | – | |   – | – |
```

Antara

```
o 2 2        2 x   2      2 2  o 2              x 2        2
| D̲ M P , G̲ | M D̲ N Ṡ | N Ṡ Ṙ Ṡ | N Ṡ N̄D̲P | G̲ Ṙ Ṡ N | D P , M G̲ | P – M , G̲ | M G̲ R S |
  | – | |   – | – |  – | – |  – | |     | – | – |  – | – |   C |  | – | – |
```

144

Exercise 8.   Evening raga: KEDARA   Tala: TEEN — TAL 4-4-4-4

Notes used: S R G M M̊ P D N Ṡ   Taraf strings: S Ṉ S R G M M̊ P D N Ṡ

Asthai

```
   o   2    2   2    x              2   2      o  2 2        2   x   2            2
  |Ṉ S M G | P M̊ D P | M — — G , | P M̊ D P | M P Ṡ Ṡ | D P M̊ P | M G P — | M͞ GMR S |
   | — | —   | — | —    | C C |     | — | —    | — | —    | — | —    | — | C    | — | | —
```


Antara

```
   o   2    2   2    x               2   2     o  2
  |Ṉ S M G | P M̊ D P | M — M G | P M̊ D P | M P Ṡ — | — Ṡ — — |
   | — | —   | — | —    |   | —    | — | —    | — | C   C | C C
```

```
   x 2 2*     2        o      2     2   x 2         2
  |M̊ M̊ Ṙ Ṡ | N Ṙ , Ṡ N | Ḍ P M̊ P , | M G P M̊ | D P M G | M R S — |
   | — | —    | — | —      | — | —     | — | —    | — | | —    | — | C
```

*If the student's sitar has only nineteen frets rather than twenty, the M̊ should be produced by placing the second finger on Ṙ and pulling the string in order to produce the M̊.

Exercise 9.   Evening raga: KAMOD   Tala: TEEN — TAL 4-4-4-4

Notes used: S R G M P D N Ṡ   Taraf strings: S Ṉ S R G G M P D N Ṡ

Asthai

```
   x 2   2         2     o   2    2        x              2    2    o  2      2
  |M R P — | M P D P | G M P , G | M R S — | Ḍ Ḍ P — | S Ṉ R S | G M P , G | M R S — |
   | — | C   | — | —    | — | |      | — | — C   | — | C   | — | —    | — | |    | — | — C
```


Antara

```
   x    2      2      o 2    * 2       x   2          2      o   2    2
  |P — Ṡ — | N Ṙ Ṡ — | Ġ M̊ Ṗ , Ġ | M̊ Ṙ Ṡ — | N Ṙ Ṡ — | D P M̊ P | G M P , G | M R S — |
   | C | C   | — | C    | — | |   | — | — C    | — | C   | — | —    | — | |      | — | — C
```

*If there is no high M̊ fret, the entire passage Ġ M̊ Ṗ , Ġ M̊ should be played by pulling from the Ġ fret. If there is an M̊ fret only the Ṗ will have to be pulled to as indicated.

Exercise 10. Evening raga: HAMSA DHWANI   Tala: EKTAL 4-4-2-2

Notes used: S R G P N Ṡ   Taraf strings: S Ṇ S S R G G P P N Ṡ

Asthai

```
x      2            2        x        2    2
|G P N Ṙ|N P G S|R G|R – |Ṇ P Ṇ S|R,P G,P|G,R|S – |
 | – | –   | – | –   | –   | C   | – | –   | | – |   – |   – |   – c
```

Antara

```
x 2  2            2   2      x      2            2
|P G P,G|R G,P N|Ṡ N|Ṡ – |P N Ṙ Ġ|Ṙ N,P G|P G|R S|
 | – |  | – |  | – | –    | C   | – | –   | – | –   | – | – 
```

Exercise 11. Evening raga: TILAK KAMOD   Tala: TEEN – TAL 4-4-4-4

Notes used: S R G M P D N Ṡ   Taraf strings: S Ṇ S R G G M P D N Ṡ

Asthai

```
x        2    2 o      2        x        2    2 o        2
|Ṇ S R|G S,R P|M G,S R|G,S – Ṇ|S R M P|Ṡ – P D|M G,S R|G S – Ṇ|
 | – | –   | – | –     | – | –     | | C |   | – | –     | C | –     | – | –     | – C |
```

Antara

```
x        2    2 o      2        x 2*    2      2
|R M P N|Ṡ – Ṡ – |P N Ṡ Ṙ|Ġ – Ṡ – |Ṙ Ṁ Ġ Ṙ|Ġ,Ṡ Ṙ Ġ|
 | – | –   | C | C   | – | –   | C | C     | – | –   | | – |
```

```
o        2        2    x      2    2 o        2
|Ṡ N,P D|M G R G|S R M P|Ṡ – P D|M G,S R|G S – Ṇ|
 – | | –   | – | –   | – | –     | C | –     | – | –     | – C |
```

*If there is no high Ṁ fret, pull to Ṁ from the Ġ fret.

146

Exercise 12. Evening raga: TILANG   Tala: TEEN—TAL 4-4-4-4

Notes used: S G M P N̲ N Ṡ   Taraf strings: S N̤ S S G M P P N̲ N Ṡ

Asthai

```
            2*        o  2              x  2          2     o  2
x
| S G M P | N – (Ṡ) – | P N̲ P M | G – G – | P Ṡ N – | P N̲ P – | G P M G | (S) – N̤ – |
  | – | –   | c | c    | – | –    | c | c    | – | c    | – | c    | – | –    | c | c
```

Antara

```
  2           2     o     2†        x  2     2          2  o  2
x
| M G M P | N – (Ṡ) – | P N Ṡ Ṁ | Ġ – Ṡ – | Ġ Ṡ N , Ṡ | N̲ P , M P | G P M G | (S) – N̤ – |
  | – | –   | c | c    | – | –    | c | c    | – | |    – |    | –    | – | –    | c | c
```

*(Ṡ) is an abbreviated way of notating the krintan Ṙ Ṡ N Ṡ. Whenever parentheses appear, this same type of krintan should be played around the note. The brackets that appear around notes at the end of certain asthai passages have a different meaning as explained in the introduction to the sargams on page 141.

†If there is no high Ṁ fret, pull to Ṁ from the Ġ fret.

Exercise 13. Evening raga: DESH   Tala: TEEN—TAL 4-4-4-4

Notes used: S R G M P D N̲ N S   Taraf strings: S N̤ S R G M P D N̲ N Ṡ

Asthai

```
        2      o  2           2  x     2     2     o  2           2
x
| N̤ S R M | P D ,ᴾM G | R G , S R | M P N Ṡ | N – – Ṡ | N Ṙ , ˢN D | P D ,ᴾM G | R G R – |
  | – | –   | – | –    | – | –    | c c |   – |    | – | –    | – | –    | – | c
```

```
    2   2         2  o        2        2    x    2        o  2   2          2
x
| – ˢN D N̲ | – ᴺD P D | – ᴾM G M | G R G S | R Ṙ SṘ̇S | Ṡ N̲ D P | D P D ,ᴾM | G , R G S |
  c | – |    c | – |    c | – |    | – | –   | – | –    | – | –    | – |    | – | – |
```

Antara

```
    2   2              2        x  2        2    2    o        2
x
| M M M , P | M (P) , – R | R R , M – | P , N – Ṡ | N – N – | Ṡ N Ṡ – | P N Ṡ Ṙ | ˢN D P – |
  | – | |     | | c |      – | c       | | c |     c | c     | – | c    | – | –     | – | c
```

```
    2 2 2*         2        2    x     2  2 2     o  2          2
x
| Ṙ P̂ Ṗ Ṁ | Ġ Ṙ Ṡ N | Ṡ Ṙ N̲ D | P D M G | R R R , Ṙ | Ṙ Ṙ , ˢN D | P D M G | R G S – |
  | – | –    | – | –    | – | –    | – | –    | – | |       – |    | –    | – | –    | – | c
```

*If there is no high Ṁ fret, the Ṗ should be played by pulling the string from Ġ to Ṗ, otherwise pull from the Ṁ fret.

Exercise 14.   Evening raga: DURGA   Tala: RUPAK 3-2-2

Notes used: S R M P D Ṡ   Taraf strings: S Ḍ S S R M M P P D Ṡ

Asthai

```
 o 2    2 2        2            2        2
 |PMP|Ṡ Ṡ|D –|MPD|MR|SR|P – –|DP|M –|PMR|SḌ|SR|
  |–| |–  |C |–| |–|–| |C C |– |C |–| |–|–|–
```

Antara

```
 o      2        o    2   2   o   2*       o   2
 |PMP|DM|PD|Ṡ – Ṡ|ṘD|Ṡ –|DṠṘ|ṀṘ|ṠD|MPD|MR|SR|
  |–| |–| |–| |C| |–| |C |–| |–| |–|–| |–| |–|–
```

*If there is no Ṁ fret, pull from Ṙ to Ṁ.

Exercise 15.   Morning raga: ALIHIYA BILAVAL   Tala: TEEN – TAL 4-4-4-4

Notes used: S R G M P D N̠ N Ṡ   Taraf strings: S Ṇ S R G M P D N̠ N Ṡ

Asthai

```
 x 2        o 2 2         x      2        o   2
 |GM ᴳṘ–|GP ᴺD̠N|Ṡ–ṠN|D̠N̠DP|ᴺD̠NṠṘ|ṠNDP|GMPM|GRS–|
  |–| C |–| |–| |C|– |C|–   |–|– |–|– |–|– |–|C
```

Antara

```
 x         2 2  o    2      x 2        o    2
 |GP ᴺD̠N|Ṡ–Ṡ–|D̠NṠṘ|ṠNDP|ĠṘṠN|D̠N̠DP|GMPM|GRS–|
  |–| |– |C|C |–|– |–|– |–|– |C|– |–|–| |–|C
```

Exercise 16. Afternoon raga: KAFI   Tala: TEEN – TAL 4-4-4-4

Notes used: S R G̲ M P D N̲ Ṡ   Taraf strings: S Ṇ S R G̲ G̲ M P D N̲ Ṡ

Asthai

```
        2  2    2       2    x   2          o  2        2
x                 o
| – – R M | P D M P | G̲ R G̲ , S | R M P M | P – D P | M G̲ R – | M N̲ D P | M P G̲ R | [N̲ S]
   | –   | – | –   | – | |  | – | – |  – c | –   | – | c  | – | –   | – | –    | –
```

Antara

```
        2  2         2  2    x   2          o     2
x            o
| Ṇ S D – | N̲ D P D | M P D N̲ | Ṙ N̲ Ṡ – | D N̲ Ġṙ | Ṡ N̲ D P | M P D P | M G̲ R S |
    | –  | c  | – | –   | – | –   | – | c  | – | –   | – | –   | – | –   | – | –
```

Exercise 17. Evening raga: BHUPALI   Tala: RUPAK 3-2-2

Notes used: S R G P D Ṡ   Taraf strings: S Ḍ S S R G G P P D Ṡ

Asthai

```
o   2        o   2        o   2        o   2
| S Ṛ G | S Ḍ | S R | G – P | G R | S – | Ḍ S | Ḍ S | R G | P D P | G S | R – |
   | – |    | – | –   | c |   | – |  | c  | – |  | – |  | – |  | – | |  | – | c
```

Antara

```
o 2    2      o   2   2    o   2      2      o   2
| G R G | P G | P D | Ṡ – Ṙ | D Ṙ | Ṡ – | D Ġṙ | Ṡ Ṙ | Ṡ D | P D P | G S | R – |
   | – |   | – |  | – | c |   | – | c  | – |  | – |  | – |  | – | |  | – | c
```

149

Exercise 18. Afternoon raga: SARANG   Tala: TEEN – TAL 4-4-4-4

Notes used: S R M P N̲ N Ṡ   Taraf strings: S Ṇ S S R M P P N̲ N Ṡ

Asthai

```
        o 2        2          x 2             o 2              2  x 2
|– – R M|P M , R S|R , Ṇ – S|R – P M|R S , R M|P N̲ P , M|P N – S|P N̲ P M|[R S]
 |  –  |  –  |  –  |  |  C  |  C  |  –  |  –  |  –  |  –  |  |  –  |  C  |  – |  –  |  –
```

Antara

```
   2   o        2        x 2   2        o 2*       2   x 2
|R S P N̲|P M , R M|P , M P N|Ṡ – N Ṙ|Ṡ – N Ṡ|Ṙ M̊ Ṙ Ṡ|N Ṙ Ṡ N̲ ,|P N̲ P M|
 |  –  |  –  |  –  |  –  |  |  –  |  C  |  –  |  –  |  –  |  –  |  –  |  –  |  –
```

*If there is no high Ṁ fret, pull from Ṙ to Ṁ.

Exercise 19. Evening raga: PURIYA KALYAN   Tala: EKTAL 4-4-2-2

Notes used: S R̲ G M̊ P D N Ṡ   Taraf strings: S Ṇ S R̲ G G M̊ P D N Ṡ

Asthai

```
x    2        2        2    x          2        2
|M D N –|D , P M P|M G|M R̲|G – – M|P M G M|G R̲|S –|
 |  –  |  C  |  |  –  |  –  |  –  |  C  C  |  –  |  –  |  –  |  C
```

```
x      2          2   2    x      2        2        2
|N R̲ G , M|R̲ G , M P|M D|(P) – |G M̊ G , D|P M , G M|G R̲|S –|
 |  –  |  |  –  |  |  –  |  –  |  C  |  –  |  |  –  |  |  –  |  –  |  C
```

Antara

```
x       2             2      x           2*
|G M̊ D N|(P) – M̊ D|N Ṙ|Ṡ –|N – Ṙ G|– M̊ G̊ R̲|Ṡ N|D P|
 |  –  |  –  |  C  |  –  |  –  |  C  |  C  |  |  C  |  |  –  |  –  |  –
```

```
x         2        2          2  x  2   2          2
|M D N Ṙ|N D , N –|D P|M P|G M G D|P M G M|G R̲|S –|
 |  –  |  –  |  –  |  C  |  –  |  –  |  –  |  –  |  –  |  –  |  –  |  C
```

*If there is no high Ṁ fret, pull to Ṁ from the G̊ fret.

150

Exercise 20. Morning raga: JAUNPURI   Tala: JHAPTAL 2-3-2-3

Notes used: S R G̲ M P D̲ N̲ Ṡ   Taraf strings: S Ṉ S R G̲ M P D̲ D̲ N̲ Ṡ

Asthai

```
       2   2 2      2   x 2     2    o 2
x                 o              2
|R M|P Ṡ, N̲|Ṡ ᴺD̲|P, D̲ M|P –|– ᴹG̲ R|M G̲|R S –|
 | – | – | – | – | – | c  c | – | – | – c
```

```
x 2        o      2    x 2     2 o 2
|N̲ S|R, S R|M, P|D̲ M P|N̲ D̲|P M P|(G̲) –|R S –|
 | – | | | – | | | – | – | – | – | | | c  | – c
```

Antara

```
 x 2  2      o      x  2      o  2 2
|D̲ P|D̲ M P|D̲ N̲|Ṡ – Ṡ|Ṙ G̲|R S R|N̲ Ṡ|ᴺD̲ – P|
 | – | – | | – | C | | – | – | | – | C |
```

```
  2*        o 2 2    x    2      o
x
|Ṙ Ṁ|G̲ Ṙ Ṡ|N̲ Ṡ|ᴺD̲ – P|M P|N̲ D̲ P|M G̲|R – S|
 | – | – | | – | C | | – | – | | – | C |
```

*If there is no Ṁ fret, pull to Ṁ from the G̲ fret.

Exercise 21. Evening raga: PURIYA DHANASHRI   Tala: TEEN – TAL 4-4-4-4

Notes used: S R̲ G Ṁ P D̲ N Ṡ   Taraf strings: S Ṉ S R̲ G G Ṁ P D̲ N Ṡ

Asthai

```
o        2      2    x         2      o    2      2
|– Ṁ D̲ Ṙ|N D̲ N D̲|P – Ṁ G|M G R̲ S|– Ṁ D̲ Ṙ|N D̲ N D̲|
 | – | – | – | | C | – | | – | C | – | | – | – |
```

```
x      2      o        2    x   2      2
|P.– Ṁ G|M G R̲ S|– Ṉ.– R̲|G – Ṁ R̲|G Ṁ P D̲|P Ṁ G Ṁ|[P]
 | C | – | – | – | C | C | | C | – | – | – | – | – | – |  |
```

Antara

```
o      2      x 2      2      o   2*      2    x     2
|P, Ṁ G Ṁ|D̲ Ṁ D̲ N|Ṡ – N R̲|Ġ R̲ Ṡ –|N Ṙ Ṁ Ġ|Ṙ Ṡ N Ṙ|N D̲ P Ṁ|G Ṁ G R̲|
 | | – | | – | – | C | – | – | C | – | – | – | – | – | – | – | –
```

*If there is no Ṁ fret, pull to Ṁ from Ġ.

151

Exercise 22.   Morning raga: TODI   Tala: RUPAK 3-2-2

Notes used: S R̲ G̲ Ṁ P D̲ N Ṡ   Taraf strings: S Ṇ S R̲ G̲ G̲ Ṁ P D̲ N Ṡ

Asthai

```
   o 2           2 o            o  2         2 o        2
  |G̲ – R̲ | S N | S R̲ | S N D̲ | – Ṇ | S R̲ | G̲ – Ṁ | R̲ G | M D̲ | P – Ṁ | D̲ Ṁ | G̲ R̲ |
   | c |   | – |   | – |   | – |   c |   | – |   | c |   | – |   | – |   | c |   | – |   | – |
```

Antara

```
   o         2         o       2          o       2        o        2
  |G̲ – Ṁ | D̲ Ṁ | D̲ N | Ṡ – Ṙ | Ġ Ṙ | Ṡ – | D̲ – N | Ṡ Ṙ, | Ṡ N | D̲ P Ṁ, | D̲ Ṁ | G̲ R̲ |
   | c |   | – |   | – |   | c |   | – |   | c |   | c |   | – |   | – |   | – |   | – |   | – |
```

GLOSSARY

ada chautal — *tala* consisting of fourteen beats grouped 2-4-4-4, is usually played on the *tabla* with *khyal* compositions.

adbhuta — eighth of the nine *rasas*, or sentiments, it expresses wonderment, amazement, surprise, exhilaration, and also the mixed feelings of anticipation.

adi — original.

ahata nad — physical aspect of sound, perceived through the ears.

alankar — designation of a type of musical exercise. Dealt with in Sharangadeva's *Sangeeta Ratnakara* (thirteenth century) and in other musical treatises. See also PALTA.

alap, or **rag alapana** — in certain styles, the beginning of a musical composition. It is given the highest place in Indian music. The *alap* expresses and then unfolds the characteristics of a *raga* in respect to melody (phrases, important notes, tone range, etc.). The inherent *rasas* are usually *karuna* and *shanta*, serene and spiritual sentiments such as might be associated with invocations. The *alap* has no measured rhythm and is very slow in tempo.

anahata nad — metaphysical, unmanifested sound, said to be experienced by yogis or more highly developed beings.

andola, or **andolita** — free, swinging note that also allows the sounding of a higher note. One of the many *gamakas*, or graces.

anga — literally, "limb," or "body"; in music, a part. A scale consists of two *angas: purvanga* (SA, RI, GA, MA); and *uttaranga* (PA, DHA, NI, and the next higher SA).

anudatta — "unraised" tone. Refers to the singing-reciting of the *Rig Veda* on three tones.

anuvadi — in a *raga*, any of the notes other than the *vadi* and the *samvadi*.

ardha — half.

ardha jai — *tala* with six and a half beats.

ardha matta — *tala* with four and a half beats.

ardha sawari — *tala* with five and a half beats.

arohana — ascending motion — usually applied to scales.

ashram — small center, often in a forest, where a *guru* and his *shishyas* live austere lives, the *guru* guiding the disciples in yoga and other studies.

ati — very.

ati drut — very fast (referring to tempo).

ati vilambit — very slow (referring to tempo).

audava — group of five notes that may constitute a *raga*. One of the three *jatis*, or genuses.

avarohana — descending motion — usually applied to scales.

Baba — literally, "Father"; affectionate appellation bestowed on revered teachers by disciples, friends, and relatives.

bandish — fixed vocal or instrumental composition bound by a rhythmic cycle.

beenkar — one who plays the *been*. Also the name of the *gharana* descended from Tan Sen's family.

bhajan — Hindu religious song.

bhakti — sometimes mentioned as a tenth *rasa*, it is of a devotional, spiritual, and religious character, and it combines the feelings of *shanta*, *karuna*, and *adbhuta rasas*.

bhayanaka — sixth of the nine *rasas*, it conveys the sensation of fear, fright, and awe. It is difficult to express this in music on a solo instrument.

bilaval — scale consisting only of *shuddha* or natural notes; one of the ten *thats*, or categories, into which *ragas* are distributed in the classification system devised by V. N. Bhatkhande. The scale has the same interval relationship as the Western major mode. Also, a group of morning *ragas*.

Brahma — Creator of the Universe and the first aspect of the Hindu trinity.

chakra — inner spinal energy centers that yogis are believed to be able to activate.

chalan — description of the characteristic features of a *raga*, connected not only with melody but also with the rhythmic aspect of the tones. It should be as concise and economical as possible.

chanchar — *tala* of fourteen beats grouped 3-4-3-4, played on the *tabla* with light *thumri* compositions.

chartal ki sawari — *tala* with eleven beats.

cheeza, or **chiza** — fixed song composition, like *bandish*.

chhanda — structural arrangement of *matras*, the guiding principles of *talas*.

chhanda prabandha — *prabandha* with a text of praise, or *prabandha* with a definite *tala*.

dadra — (1) *tala* with six beats grouped 3-3, commonly played on the *tabla* and other drums, and employed as accompaniment for *dadra* compositions, *bhajans*, *qawali* songs, and certain types of light classical music; (2) light classical composition characterized by simple melodies with syncopation, resembling the *thumri* style.

deshi — regional music that is nonclassical, as folk songs, light popular music and theatrical music.

deshi sangeeta — regional art music, comprising vocal and instrumental music, and music for the dance.

dhaivata — sixth scale step of the seven-tone scale in ascending order, abbreviated as DHA.

dhamar — (1) cycle with fourteen beats grouped 5-5-4 and played on the *pakhawaj* to accompany voice or instrument; (2) form of composition also called *Hori-dhamar* that often follows *dhrupad*, but is also performed by itself. Its origin is to be found in folk songs from Vrindavan and Mathura (in Uttar Pradesh). The text in Braja Bhasha is in praise of Lord Krishna and describes his pranks, playing with the *gopis* and sprinkling color during the Holi festival. It is romantic and sensuous.

dhrupad, or **dhruvapada** (from *dhruva*, "definite, fixed," and *pada*, "word") — composition type evolved from the *prabandha* and popular from the fifteenth to nineteenth centuries. It is a noble and grand style. The texts of the *dhrupad(s)* are in a dialect of Hindi and are in praise of gods, kings, noblemen, and nature.

drut — fast.

dhruvā — religious song or hymn used for operalike stage performances only.

dhruva — literally, fixed, determined, definite; a song with a set pattern, in existence in the third century A.D.

dhruvapada — see DHRUPAD.

ektal — cycle with twelve beats grouped 4-4-2-2 and played on the *tabla* for *khyal* compositions only. It can be in any tempo.

gamaka — particular ornament or embellishments used in Indian music. It is an essential part of the melodic structure.

ganda or **nara** (from *ganda*, "thread"), designating the formal ceremony held when a pupil is accepted by a *guru* for the study of music. It is performed in the presence of a few musicians and their students. The *guru* or *ustad* ties a yellow-red thread around the wrist of the pupil three times and recites a benediction. A little candy is put into the pupil's mouth and a rudimentary lesson is given. The pupil touches the *guru*'s feet with his head and offers a gift according to his means. The ceremony is considered sacred and creates a formal relationship between the *guru* and his *shishya* for life.

gandhara — name of the third scale step of the seven-tone scale in ascending order, and abbreviated as GA.

gandharva — one who belongs to a semidivine class of beings who are musicians and dancers; a "heavenly" or "celestial" singer.

gandharva music — "celestial" music, also called *marga* music. It was said to please the gods and the *gandharvas*. Vedic music represents *gandharva* music. It lost its wide popularity and was replaced by *deshi* music in about the third and fourth centuries A.D.

gat — fixed instrumental composition in any tempo accompanied by *tabla*. A *gat* can be in any *tala* and can be from two to sixteen rhythmic cycles in length.

geeti, or **giti** — song of ancient origin.

gharana — literally, "family tradition"; a school or center of musical culture created by instruction from teacher to pupil, sometimes by members of one family through succeeding generations. The different *gharanas* have distinctive characteristics in musical presentation.

ghazal — romantic song composition in Urdu of a light classical nature.

gopi — milkmaid. The word is often used in association with Lord Krishna.

grama — obsolete name for the three ancient scales: SA, MA, and GA *gramas*. GA *grama* fell out of use by the second century A.D.

guru — spiritual guide, competent teacher, master and preceptor.

hasya — second of the nine *rasas* or sentiments. It is humorous and comic, happy and joyful and provokes laughter.

hatha yoga — yoga practice which aims to prepare for spiritual experience by perfecting the body.

Holi festival — spring festival in which Lord Krishna plays an important role. It is attended by much merrymaking, and boys and girls throw powdered colors and colored water on everyone.

Holi songs — songs basically of a folk nature that describe the Color Festival associated with Krishna to the accompaniment of the pakhawaj in *dhamar tala*. The songs in the classical style are known as *Hori-dhamar*.

jati — (1) scale or melody type. The term, which antedates "*mela*," "*that*," and "*raga*," is no longer used, and the form evolved to a higher musical form. According to Bharata, seven *shuddha jatis* and eleven mixed *jatis* were used in ancient days; (2) any of three classes of *raga* differentiated according to the number of notes used — the seven-note *raga* (*sampurna*), the six-note *raga* (*shadava*), and the five-note *raga* (*audava*). There are also "mixed" *jatis* that use any two *jatis* together.

jawabi sangat — imitation by the *tabla* of the rhythm pattern played by the main instrument. It can be in any *tala* and tempo.

jawab sawal — interplay between the main instrument and the *tabla*; a kind of question-and-answer dialogue between the main instrument and the drum.

jhala — third part of a *raga*, following the *jor*. It was evolved by the Beenkar and Rababiya *gharanas* and is characterized by increasing speed and excitement, ending with a climax. It is now also played at the end of a *gat* as a climax.

jhaptal — *tala* of ten beats grouped 2-3-2-3. It can be played on the *tabla* to accompany *khyal* singing or an instrumental *gat*, though it used to be played on the *pakhawaj* to accompany *sadra* songs.

jhumra — *tala* of fourteen beats grouped 3-4-3-4 and played on the *tabla* to accompany very slow *khyal* compositions.

jor — second part of the solo exposition of a *raga*, the part into which an instrumental *alap* leads. It differs from the *alap* in having some rhythmic elements and usually an increase in tempo.

kaharva — *tala* with eight beats grouped 4-4, played on the *tabla* to accompany compositions in light classical styles.

kampita — large shake; note inserted between adjacent notes. One of the many *gamakas*.

karuna — third of the nine *rasas*. It is sad, pathetic, tragic, and expresses loneliness, longing and yearning for the absent lover or god.

kathak — style of dancing performed by both men and women in the North of India. The *kathika*, the storyteller, mimes, dances, and sings the stories. Fast footwork and interplay of rhythms are the highlights of this style.

kathakali — style of dancing performed by men only in the South of India. *Kathakali* combines dance and drama and enacts stories from the great epics.

khali — one of the important beats in a *tala*. Usually precedes the *sam*. It is unstressed and referred to as an "empty beat." For time-beating, it is shown by a wave of the hand.

khyal — literally, "imagination," "fancy." Some of the elements of *khyal* can be found in *qawali* songs, though some scholars give Amir Khusru of the thirteenth century credit for inventing the style. The rich, delicately ornamented phrases have more importance than the lyrics of the text. It is currently the predominant vocal style of Indian classical music.

komal — literally "tender." *Shuddha* notes made flat. Notes can be made *komal*, or flat, to varying degrees.

Krishna — Lord Krishna is the eighth incarnation of Vishnu, the second aspect of the Hindu trinity. He destroyed Kamsa, the evil king of Mathura, and grew up among the *gopis*, or milkmaids, in Vrindavan. Their love for him symbolizes the yearning of human beings for the union with God. In the great war between the Kauravas and the Pandavas described in the *Mahabharata*, Lord Krishna, as the charioteer of Arjuna, a Pandava, gives advice to this prince. This episode, containing Krishna's teachings to Arjuna, is known as the *Bhagavad Gita*. Krishna is often represented as a handsome youth, sky-blue in color, playing the flute.

kriti — most highly developed and at present the most used vocal forms in Karnatic music. The music is considered to be as important as the text.

kundalini — fiery power that lies in its *chakra* at the root of the spine. According to yoga doctrine, at a late stage in spiritual development, this power is awakened and moves up the spine to the other *chakras* to open up the "thousand-petalled" lotus in the brain that gives the yogi complete control of the body and enlightenment.

larant sangat — interplay between the main instrument and the *tabla*. A kind of dialogue of rhythm patterns, containing an element of challenge for the two artists.

Lasya — the female counterpart of the male cosmic dance of Shiva. It is a soft and feminine dance, originally attributed to Parvati, Shiva's wife.

laukika — post-Vedic music.

madhya — medium.

madhya drut — medium fast.

madhyama — name of the fourth scale step of the seven-tone scale in ascending order, abbreviated as MA.

madhya vilambit — medium slow.

Mahabharata — one of the two great Indian epics, containing 90,000 stanzas. Many hundreds of years are thought to have elapsed before the epic was completed. The basis of the story is the battle of Kurukshetra (north of Delhi), the war between the Pandavas and the Kauravas, or a fight between good and evil forces. The most popular part of the *Mahabharata* is the *Bhagavad Gita*.

marga — literally, "path," "way"; designating music that is classical.

matra — metrical unit or beat.

matta tala — *tala* with nine beats.

meend — slide from one note to another, connecting their sounds, using *shrutis*, or microtones. One of the embellishments.

mela — classification of *ragas* in Karnatic music.

melakarta — designation for the ragas based on the 72 scales of the South. These ragas correspond exactly to the 72 scales in their ascending and descending structures, unlike the Hindustani system, in which the ragas do not have the same structure as the primary *thats* on which they are based.

Mian Tan Sen — *Mian* is a term of address for an eminent person. Our musicians explain that Tan Sen means "one who brings a peaceful, relaxed feeling (*chaien* or *saien*, later contracted to *sen*) by his musical phrases (*tan*).

murchhana — scale-wise progressions in descending motion from the fundamental notes.

nada — sound, including its unmanifested, metaphysical aspect (*anahata*) and its manifested, physical aspect (*ahata*).

nada Brahma — "Sound is God."

nad-siddha — one who has attained mastery of musical sound.

namaskar, or **namaste** — Indian greeting, expressing respect. Hands are placed palm to palm in front of the forehead and the head is bowed.

nava rasa — literally, "nine juices"; the nine sentiments. The concept of *rasa* is connected with drama, poetry, dance, music, and even with painting and sculpture. In music it implies a strong connection between musical ideas and emotional impact on the listener. There are nine sentiments expressed in the arts. In Indian music every composition is usually dominated by one or a few related sentiments.

nayaka — title for expert musicians.

nibaddha prabandha — *prabandha* with time measures that strictly follow certain musical rules.

nishada — name of the seventh scale step of the seven-tone scale in ascending order, abbreviated as NI.

num tum — syllables that are used for singing, especially for the part into which the *alap* leads. It differs from the *alap* in that it contains some rhythmic elements.

pakad — literally, "catch"; a short section of a particular *raga* that embodies its characteristic, recognizable features that distinguish one *raga* from another.

palta — melodic figures performed in different scales in sequential order, executed in any *tala* and in different tempi. *Paltas* help the student to gain technical facility. See also ALANKAR.

panchama — name of the fifth scale step of the seven-tone scale in ascending order, abbreviated as PA.

parampara — tradition as the assumption for knowledge and cultural progress.

Parvati — consort of Lord Shiva, the Mother goddess, also known as Durga, and Kali.

prabandha — literally, "bound up," "knit together"; a vocal composition form, a systematic and organ-ized type of *giti* (song) with Sanskrit text. This style influenced the *dhrupad* that became popular in the fifteenth century and then replaced the *prabandha*.

prana — vital energy that can be drawn in by man from the surrounding universe and by which man lives. All powers of the body, functions of the mind and senses are vitalized by *prana*. It is sometimes translated as "breath" or "soul." In music, it is the spirit the musician brings to the notes that make them come alive.

pranam — obeisance; a respectful greeting consisting of touching the greeted person's feet, then one's own eyes and forehead with the hands held palm to palm. It is a symbolic act of surrender, indicating the sense of one's own smallness in the presence of a superior.

purab — east. Used to describe the style of *thumri* singing of the Lucknow and Benares *gharanas*.

purvanga — lower tetrachord of a scale consisting of the notes SA, RI, GA, and MA.

qawali — Muslim devotional song.

rababiya — one who plays the *rabab*, a stringed instrument, or belongs to the *gharana* of the same name, descended from the family of Tan Sen.

Radha — Lord Krishna's most beloved and the loveliest of the *gopis* (milkmaids) of Vrindavan. Her beautiful body is depicted and described as golden, with movements delicate and quick as a flash. She sometimes expresses her jealousy over **Krishna's** playfulness with other *gopis* and then feels regret and renewed longing and love when Krishna repents. The love of Krishna and Radha is eternal.

raga — the melodic basis of Indian classical music on which the musicians improvise. Each *raga* has definite melodic qualities that distinguish it from all other *ragas*. It is assumed that *ragas* create an emotional impact on the listener.

rag alapana — see ALAP.

raga sangeet — Indian classical music.

Ramayana — one of the two great Indian epics said to have been written by the sage Valmiki. These are stories centering around Prince Rama and his wife Sita. Rama is one of the incarnations of Vishnu.

rasa — sentiment or feeling dominating an artistic creation or composition. The concept of *rasa* is connected with drama, poetry, dance, music, painting and sculpture. In music, it implies that there is a strong connection between musical ideas and emotional impact on the listener. See also NAYA RASA.

rasa leela — religious dance symbolizing the union of the individual with the Supreme. This is interpreted in terms of the divine love of Lord Krishna for the milkmaids of Vrindavan, and Radha in particular. *Rasa leela* is a kind of operatic dance, and the dancers often participate in the singing. The accompanying music calls for flutes, cymbals, and drums. It is performed in the spring, and was originally supposed to have been danced by Krishna with the milkmaids under the full moon. Now the story is presented more or less as a passion play in various parts of the cities throughout northern India.

raudra — fourth of the nine *rasas*, depicting anger or excited fury.

rishaba — name of the second scale step of the seven-tone scale in ascending order, abbreviated as RI.

rishi — seer. The great savants of legendary times who originated and developed theories in all branches of the arts and sciences and passed them on to their disciples. The *rishis* are said to form a class of saintly beings distinct from gods, men, or demons.

rupak — cycle with seven beats grouped 3-2-2, quite popular and played generally on the *tabla* to accompany instrumental music or vocal music in the *khyal* style.

sadhana — practice performed for musical training or for the purpose of preparing oneself for self-realization through any medium.

sadra — medium-fast song in *dhrupad* style accompanied by the *pakhawaj* in *jhaptal*.

sam — literally, "together, equal"; in a *tala*, the most important beat, on which the melodic phrase of the singer or the main instrument and the rhythmic phrase of the accompanist come together. When beating time, the *sam* is indicated by a hand clap.

samagana — method of singing the Vedic music, especially the *Sama Veda*. Dealt with in the *Naradishiksha* (first century) and other treatises.

saman — music used for singing the hymns of the *Sama Veda*.

sampurna — group of seven notes that may constitute a *raga*. One of the three *jatis* (genuses).

samvadi, or **samavadi** — second most important note after the *vadi*, or sonant, in a *raga*, sometimes compared to a "minister." Its position is in a different *anga* than the *vadi*, at an interval of a fourth or fifth from the *vadi*.

sandhiprakasha — times of very early morning and evening twilight, approximately between 4 A.M. and 7 A.M., and 4 P.M. and 7 P.M. The time of day in which certain *ragas* are played.

sangat — accompaniment of the *tabla* or *pakhawaj*.

saptaka — seven notes (*shuddha svaras*) of the octave: *shadja, rishaba, gandhara, madhya, panchama, dhaivata, nishada*, abbreviated SA, RI, GA, MA, PA, DHA, NI.

sargam — word made up from the first four notes of the seven notes of the octave — (SA, RI, GA, MA) fixed compositions, sung to the names of the seven notes within a *raga* and *tala* framework and executed in any tempo in any *tala*. Solfa passages within a song are also called *sargams*.

sath sangat — interplay between the main instrument or the singer, and the *tabla*. Within the shortest possible time interval, the rhythm pattern of the main instrument is imitated by the *tabla* almost simultaneously.

shadava — six notes that may constitute a *raga*. One of the three *jatis* (genuses).

shadja — name of the first scale step of the seven-tone scale in ascending order, abbreviated as SA.

shanta — last of the nine *rasas*, or sentiments, describing peaceful, tranquil, and relaxed states of mind and feelings.

shikhar tal — *tala* with seventeen beats.

shiksha — training. This term is used in the treatise on music by Narada, the *Naradishiksha*.

shishya — disciple. One who has to surrender himself completely to the *guru* in the pursuit of music, a spiritual life, or any discipline of higher learning.

Shiva — Maheshvara, the great god; the third aspect of the Hindu trinity; the one who changes the universe, the ruler of Nature. Lord Shiva is believed to have created music, dance, and drama. He is often represented as the Cosmic Dancer, Nataraja.

shringara (also known as **Adi**) — the first *rasa*, or sentiment, representing the universal creative force and embodying romantic and erotic feelings, love between men and women, the longing for the absent lover, and sensitivity to the beauty of nature.

shooltal — rhythm with ten beats grouped 4-2-4 and played on the *pakhawaj* for *dhrupad* or *dhamar* compositions.

shruti — microtones; the twenty-two intervals used within an octave.

shuddha — literally, "pure." The seven natural notes of the octave.

Sufi mysticism — philosophy of Islam that arose in the tenth century and was most popular in Persia. Sufis aspire to the union of the soul with God; it also has some affinities with Hindu philosophy.

svara — tone of definite pitch. There are seven basic *shuddha* tones in the octave, and chromatic tones formed by altering the basic tones are the *vikrit svaras*. The basic tones can be raised (*tivra* and *ati tivra*) or lowered (*komal* and *ati komal*).

svarita — "sounded" tone. Refers to the singing of the *Rig Veda* to three tones. It may originally have been between the pitches of the *udatta* and *anudatta*, but in the *Rig Veda* was above the *udatta*.

swaroop — short section of a particular *raga* that embodies its characteristic recognizable features (forms) distinguishing it from all other *ragas*.

tala — rhythmic cycles, the essential element of time and rhythm in Indian music. *Talas* having the same number of beats may have the stress on different beats, e.g. a bar of ten beats may be divided 2-3-2-3 or 3-3-4 or 3-4-3.

tala vadya katcheri — percussion ensembles consisting of different kinds of drums, mainly heard in the Karnatic system.

taleem — training, in Urdu.

tali — the main beats within a rhythmic cycle. Apart from the *sam*, *talis* are also given the main stress. For instance, in *teental* grouped 4-4-4-4, *sam* is on the first, *khali* on the ninth, *tali* on the fifth and thirteenth beats. When counting time, *talis* are indicated by hand claps.

tamasha — fair, usually with musical performances and short comedies.

tan — musical phrase sung on vowels, syllables, or words drawn out or stretched by expressive passages. *Tans* can be sung or played in any tempo. *Tan* varieties are determined by an added word, such as *bol tan*, *jabra tan*, and so on.

tandava — cosmic dance of Shiva symbolizing energy and dynamism.

Tantra — writings, dating from about the sixth century A.D., that deal with the basic quality of duality in manifestation; the active male, using the female power and wisdom.

tapasya — meditation undertaken with the definite object of attaining spirituality.

tappa — vocal style whose origin is found in folk melodies sung by Punjabi Muslim camel drivers. *Tappas* have a continuous melody with much ornamentation. Their rhythm is strong, and the tempo fast. The texts are love lyrics.

taraf, or **tarab** — on a stringed instrument, sympathetic strings that are not actually touched by the fingers in playing.

tarana — song style using as text meaningless words or nonsense syllables, or even mnemonic syllables used for drumming, and sometimes Persian words.

teental — *tala* with sixteen beats grouped 4-4-4-4. The most popular *tala*.

tempered system, also **equal temperament** — in Western music, the current tuning system wherein the octave is divided in twelve equal half steps.

teora — see *tivra* 2.

that — classification of Hindustani *ragas* devised by Pandit Vishnu Narayam Bhatkhande (1860–1936) of Bombay. He distinguished ten *thats*. This classification is accepted by a large number of musicians and musicologists of North India.

theka — the basic mnemonic sound syllables (*bol*) combined to form rhythmic phrases used by the drummer to play a *tala*.

thumri — vocal as well as instrumental form, freer than any other classical style. Though already long in existence, it has been developed and much performed since the middle of the nineteenth century. The melodies are of a lyric and romantic nature. The tonic (SA) may be shifted, different *ragas* can be used, and folk and popular songs can be included in one composition. The texts express desire, longing, and sadness for Lord Krishna or an absent lover.

tiripa — stressing one note of a phrase. One of the many *gamakas* or embellishments.

tivra — (1) *shuddha* notes made sharp. MA is the only note that is sharped and it can have three degrees of sharpness; (2) *teora:* a *tala* with seven beats grouped 3-2-2 that was played on the *pakhawaj* to accompany a song type in *tivra tala,* usually with a fast tempo.

tonic — fundamental note in Western music, the main note of a key, or its tonal center.

udatta — "raised" tone, referring to the singing-reciting of the *Rig Veda* to three tones.

ustad — counterpart of *guru* in Urdu, used mostly by Muslims. A title of respect for any notable, highly learned man.

uttaranga — upper tetrachord of a scale consisting of the notes PA, DHA, NI and the next higher SA.

vadi — most important note in a *raga,* sometimes compared to a "king." The *vadi* is used more often than any other note in a *raga.* It expresses the *rasa* of a *raga,* and its position in either the *purvanga* or *uttaranga* is one of the factors that determine the performance time.

vaidika — Vedic music.

Vasanta Utsav — spring festival associated with the beauty of nature during the spring season, the flowers and birds, the reawakening of nature.

Veda — book of the sacred scriptures of the Hindus. According to orthodox faith, the Vedas are not human compositions, but are supposed to have been revealed by the Godhead; the hymns of the Vedas are ascribed to several *rishis.* The four Vedas are the Rig Veda, Sama Veda, Yajur Veda, and Atharva Veda.

veera, or **vira** — fifth of the nine *rasas,* expressing dignity, majesty and glory, courage and heroism.

vibhatsa — *rasa,* or sentiment, of hate, hostility, and disgust, usually made explicit in dramas.

vikrit — note that is sharp (*tivra*), very sharp (*ati tivra*), flat (*komal*) or very flat (*ati komal*). Opposite of *shuddha,* or unaltered note.

vilambit — slow.

vinaya — humility. The attitude of the student toward the *guru.*

Vishnu — Preserver and Sustainer of the Universe. The second aspect of the Hindu trinity. Lord Vishnu has had nine incarnations on earth and was successively reborn as a fish, tortoise, boar, man-lion, dwarf, Balram of the Ax, Rama, the hero of the epic *Ramayana,* Krishna, the hero of the *Bhagavad Gita,* and as Lord Buddha. One more incarnation is expected in the future, the Kalki.

vistar — extension, elaboration, and gradual unfolding of a *raga,* usually in a slow, free-flowing unmeasured rhythm.

vivadi — any dissonant note usually not used in a *raga,* only rarely for special dissonant effects. *Vivadi* are figuratively designated as "enemy" notes.